Rent Review, Arbitration and Third Party Determination

A Surveyor's Handbook

Mark Loveday, Andy Guest and Philip Rainey

RICS BOOKS

Acknowledgments

Crown copyright material is reproduced with the permission of the Controller of HMSO and the Queen's Printer for Scotland.

Please note: References to the masculine include the feminine, where appropriate.

Published by the Royal Institution of Chartered Surveyors (RICS)

Surveyor Court

Westwood Business Park

Coventry CV4 8JE

UK

www.ricsbooks.com

No responsibility for loss or damage caused to any person acting or refraining from action as a result of the material included in this publication can be accepted by the authors or RICS.

ISBN 978 1 84219 410 2

Typeset by Columns Design Ltd, Reading, Berks

Printed by Page Bros, Norwich

Mixed Sources
Product group from well-managed forests, and other controlled sources
www.fsc.org Cert no. TT-COC-002706
© 1996 Forest Stewardship Council
FSC

Contents

Foreword

Any professional regularly working in the area of commercial rent reviews, whether for the landlord or the tenant, knows how important it is for the client that the numerous technical issues involved in such rent reviews are dealt with correctly. Large sums may be involved, both in terms of rent and capitalised values. Any error can be commercially harmful for the client and equally harmful for the professional's insurers. This Handbook recognises that a surveyor will usually be conducting a rent review for a client who has not engaged a solicitor to undertake the legal aspects of the review. I have no doubt that surveyors involved in this area of work will therefore warmly welcome a Handbook which provides an accurate and concise guide to the several steps that need to be followed. The authors, Mark Loveday, Andy Guest and Philip Rainey, bring to bear a combined depth of experience and knowledge on this subject. What they have produced is a Handbook in a superbly structured, clearly laid out manner which is designed for practical day-to-day use.

The authors' practical approach guides the reader through the several stages of a typical rent review whilst pointing out the necessary practical tasks to be performed at each stage. It provides an *aide memoire* for the essential features, both evidential and legal, to be considered and taken into account at each stage. They also identify possible pitfalls awaiting the unwary practitioner, thus allowing them to be safely circumvented.

There can be little doubt that such a useful work will be widely welcomed by all practitioners in this important and technical area of work.

Geraint Jones QC, Tanfield Chambers,

London WC1R 5DJ

August 2008

Introduction

Commercial rent reviews are a staple of the work of the general practice surveyor. Nearly 400 firms in the UK are currently registered with RICS as specialists in the field, and many thousands of other practitioners are involved in this area of work on a regular basis.

Despite the long-term trend towards shorter commercial lease terms without any rent review machinery (British Property Federation/Investment Property Databank, *Annual Lease Review 2007*[1]), there is no evidence of an accompanying decrease in the number of disputes in this often contentious area. The RICS Disputes Panel alone made over 7,000 third party appointments in each of the years between 2000 and 2006. Reported decisions of the higher courts on points of law arising from reviews are currently running at the rate of over 15 a year.

There are already other books on rent review, the majority of which analyse the legal aspects of the subject. Although such books are of assistance to the surveyor, the authors of this book prefer a workflow methodology.

This book intends to provide the surveyor with practical guidance on how to deal with the rent review process. The process starts on the day of instruction, but it may not finish until an arbitration or expert determination has been concluded and the new rent noted on the lease. There are many steps that need to be taken along the way. This book leads the surveyor through those steps in a logical way.

The first step is to consider what the surveyor is instructed to do. Part A of this book looks at what should be considered under the title '**Accepting the instruction**'.

The second step is to gather the evidence. The evidence will come from three principal sources. There will be physical evidence, which will primarily be gathered at the time that the subject property is inspected. There will be legal evidence that will derive from the lease. Finally, there will be market evidence, which will be indicative of market rents and trends. The surveyor must gather evidence from these three sources and then consider each element before arriving at a rental value. These steps in the process are considered in Part B of this book under the title 'Gathering the evidence'.

Once the surveyor has arrived at an opinion of value he must next implement the review. Part C of the book considers how this is done under the title 'Implementing the review'.

Most rent reviews are settled by negotiation. However, in some situations negotiated settlement is not possible and reference to a third party is necessary. Part D of the book looks at 'Concluding the review', whether by agreement or by an arbitrator or independent expert. This is dealt with in some detail, since many surveyors only infrequently encounter a fully contested third party determination in practice.

We end with a short chapter on what to do after the review is concluded.

The book deals with the law as it applies in England and Wales as at 1 July 2008. Chapter 10 anticipates the RICS practice statements and guidance notes *Surveyors acting as expert witnesses* (3rd edition) and *Surveyors acting as advocates* (1st edition practice statement, 2nd edition guidance note); both of which come into force on 1 January 2009.

Mark Loveday BA (Hons) MCIArb

Andy Guest BSc (Hons) DipArb FRICS FCIArb

Philip Rainey LLB MCIArb

August 2008

Legislation

The following Acts and Statutory Instruments are referred to in this publication.

Arbitration Act 1950

Arbitration Act 1979

Arbitration Act 1996

Civil Evidence Act 1995

Companies Act 1985

Disability Discrimination Act 1995

Landlord and Tenant Act 1927

Landlord and Tenant Act 1954

Landlord and Tenant (Covenants) Act 1995

Law of Property Act 1925

Law of Property Act 1969

Civil Procedure Rules 1998, SI 1998/3132

Regulatory Reform (Business Tenancies) (England and Wales) Order 2003, SI 2003/3096

Town and Country Planning (Use Classes) Order 1987, SI 1987/764

UK legislation passed after 1988 is published in its original form by the Office of Public Sector Information on www.opsi.gov.uk and UK legislation prior to 1988 can be purchased through the Stationery Office Limited on www.tso.co.uk.

An online database of revised UK primary legislation can be found at www.statutelaw.gov.uk, the Statute Law Database. The database is the official revised version of the statute book (primary legislation) for the UK in electronic form and contains primary legislation that was in force at 1 February 1991 and primary and secondary legislation that has been produced since that date.

RICS material

RICS *Bye-Laws*

RICS *Code of Measuring Practice* (6th edition)

RICS *Code of Practice for Commercial Leases* (2007)

RICS *Code of Practice for Commercial Leases in England and Wales* (2002)

RICS *Rules of Conduct* 2007

RICS *Supplemental Charter* 1973

RICS guidance note: *Protecting against money laundering: A guide for members*

RICS practice statement and guidance note: *Surveyors acting as advocates*

RICS practice statement and guidance note: *Surveyors acting as expert witnesses*

Table of cases

Part A

Accepting the instruction

1

Accepting the instruction

1.1 Introduction

Before the valuer accepts a rent review instruction, he should consider whether he is suitably qualified to undertake the task and whether he has any conflicts of interest that may prevent him from acting. He will need to undertake an initial check through the lease documentation and confirm his terms of engagement with his client.

1.2 Qualification of the valuer

The first question that the valuer should consider is whether he has sufficient knowledge, experience, qualification and training to undertake the instruction. He should also consider whether he has sufficient resources to complete the task within the required timescales and to the required standard.

Not all markets are alike. Commercial property comprises a variety of market sectors, each of which operates in a different way and which may require a different valuation technique. For example, office property, industrial property and retail property will form distinct sectors. Within these sectors there may be subsectors that are particularly specialist. For example, distribution centres form a distinct subsector in the industrial market, as does out of town retailing in the retail sector. No valuer can be expected to be expert in all sectors but if the valuer is to retain credibility then he must confine himself to the market in which he has sufficient knowledge, experience and qualification.

The valuer must also consider geographical issues. For example, a valuer who can justifiably claim to be an expert in the London office market may not have much knowledge of the office market in Carlisle.

As the valuer progresses through a rent review instruction he undertakes several different roles. The first is to advise the client on value. The second is to negotiate with the other side. It may be the case that at this point agreement is reached. On the other hand, if agreement cannot be reached it may be necessary to refer the matter to a third party for determination. It is at this point that the issue of credibility becomes particularly important; the valuer may well have to convince an arbitrator or independent expert that his expert evidence carries weight. If the valuer lacks credibility then the third party will attach little weight to that valuer's evidence. It is advisable to consider this at the outset. If there is any doubt that the valuer does have the required knowledge and skill then he should either decline the instruction or consider whether he can improve or supplement his knowledge with additional research or assistance from other professionals.

1.3 Conflicts of interest

With effect from 4 June 2007 RICS introduced new principles-based *Rules of Conduct* for members. The were made by the regulatory board of RICS under Article 18 of the *Supplemental Charter* 1973 and Section V of the RICS *Bye-Laws*. Failure to follow them is a disciplinary matter for members of RICS.

Part two of the rules refers to personal and professional standards. Amongst other things these standards require that a member shall avoid conflicts of interest.

Conflicts of interest are also dealt with in other RICS guidance (see Chapter 10). The rules do not define a conflict of interest and indeed it would be impossible to provide a definitive list of situations where the threat to the valuer's independence or objectivity may arise when deal with a rent review.

In situations where the valuer considers that a conflict may exist, it will usually be necessary for him to take one of two courses. Either he should make an appropriate written disclosure or (where it is considered that any conflict which might arise could not be resolved or managed in a satisfactory way) decline to act.

1.4 Terms of engagement

At the time of receiving the initial instruction it is all too easy to focus on the subject property and to ignore more mundane matters such as the identity of the client and the terms of engagement. This is an error for a number of reasons.

First, it is important to identify the client. It is common for a business to be carried on in commercial premises by entities other than the tenant – and equally common for buildings to be owned by companies or individuals who do not undertake the day-to-day management. Take care to ensure that any instructions are confirmed by the actual landlord or tenant. When acting for businesses and organisations, the valuer should establish that the person instructing him has authority to do so. Local managers may not necessarily have the authority to bind the companies for whom they work.

It is worth mentioning that the identity of the client is also important from the point of view of money laundering. RICS has produced guidance on this subject in the form of a guidance note, *Protecting against money laundering: A guide for members*, which is available to download from the RICS website (www.rics.org).

Secondly, recognise the client's needs. Clients come in all shapes and sizes. These range from the well-informed property company or institutional fund, on the one hand, through to the private individual who has no experience of rent review, on the other. Clearly, it would unreasonable to provide advice in the same form to both. The valuer therefore needs to gauge the knowledge of the client and the advice needs to be tailored accordingly. If the valuer does not think carefully enough about the type of client, he may find that one of his best defences to a negligence claim – the caveats, disclaimers and exclusion clauses in his terms and conditions of business – prove completely useless.

Thirdly, it should be remembered that it is the client who will in the end pay the valuer's fees. It is therefore important to agree the exact nature of fees in writing. This avoids disagreement later. If the prospective client objects to paying a reasonable fee then it is better to find this out at the start before undertaking any work rather than at the end when the work has all been done. For a new company client, check whether they are insolvent or have been struck off the Companies Register. This can be achieved by carrying out an online check on the Companies House website (www.companieshouse.gov.uk).

1.5 Initial lease check

On receiving a rent review instruction the valuer should immediately review the lease documentation. More detailed consideration of the impact of the various clauses within the lease is given in Chapter 3.

The pertinent points to clarify initially, however, are what is to be valued and the dates for serving notices. It is particularly important to identify any provision making 'time of the essence'. Missing such a provision may ultimately lead to a negligence claim.

The overwhelming majority of rent review provisions involve a valuation of the market rent for a property on the valuation date adopting the various disregards and assumptions set out in the lease. However, there are a variety of other forms of review provision and hybrids which incorporate some features of a conventional review and these alternative forms. The valuer should at the outset identify the general form of review clause to enable him to pursue the more appropriate course. No amount of market evidence will be relevant if the rent is index-linked, and the valuer would simply be wasting the client's money. These alternative forms of review are covered in Chapter 6.

Part B
Gathering the evidence

2
The physical evidence – the property

2.1 Introduction

As mentioned above, the evidence for a rent review will come from three principal sources. There will be physical evidence, there will be legal evidence, and finally there will be market evidence. These factors will all impact upon value.

The majority of the physical evidence for a rent review will be gathered at the time of the initial inspection. It is therefore important that the initial inspection is sufficient to enable the valuer to produce the valuation that is required for the purpose of the rent review. Clearly, the degree of investigation will vary from property to property depending upon the nature of the property, the valuer's knowledge of the particular location and property and the terms of engagement that have been agreed with the client. It is suggested that the following matters should be considered as a minimum.

2.2 Location and situation

Sufficient information should be gathered at the time of inspection to enable the valuer to give a commentary upon the location and situation of the subject property from both a 'macro' and 'micro' perspective. Having done this the valuer will be able to consider how these factors impact upon rental value.

It is envisaged that the 'macro' level means the town, region or national area where the property is located. The 'micro' level would consider the particular local situation.

The sort of issues that might be of relevance on a macro level would be the as follows:

- the physical location of the town;
- the position of the town in the particular market hierarchy;
- the key economic drivers in the town;
- transport links to the town; and
- the town's population and demographic profile.

This is not exhaustive list but it is indicative of the sort of issues that the valuer needs to consider. The particular considerations will need to be tailored to suit each individual rent review.

These issues will be particularly important if comparable evidence is drawn from a wide geographical area. The reason for this is that the valuer must ensure that the market evidence is drawn from comparable locations. Normally the best evidence will come from within the immediate vicinity of the subject property but in some cases no comparable evidence will be available close by. In these situations the valuer is left with no option but to look further afield. This can be true of properties such as food stores, large retail warehouses, department stores and distribution centres. Comparable evidence for these types of properties is generally drawn from a regional or even national area.

The valuer should consider whether there are going to be, or have been, any fundamental changes in the subject location that might impact upon value. For example, the building of a new road might open up a particular area and make it much more valuable for distribution than had previously been the case, or the construction of a new shopping centre nearby may depress rental values in a lower order retail centre. These are just two examples and again the particular consideration will very much depend upon the nature of the specific job.

At a micro level the valuer should consider the intricacies of local markets. For example, a particular prestigious office address may command considerably higher values than similar office accommodation close by. Similarly, retail rents in secondary locations can be a fraction of the price of retail rent in prime retail locations – despite the fact that often the two are only a short distance apart. For this reason, the valuer must ensure that he gains a full understanding of the particular market at a micro level.

At the time of inspection, the valuer should note the nature of nearby properties and whether they are in a similar use to the subject property. If they are then details should be gathered of occupiers (and if possible landlords, managing agents and letting agents). This enables investigations to be made at a later stage into the rental value and specification of those properties. Details should also be taken of any other properties in the area that are to let.

It is helpful to record as much photographic evidence as possible at the time of inspection. This should include not only photographs of the subject property but also photographs of nearby properties, key comparables and the general environment around the subject property. In the age of the digital camera this is easily and cheaply achieved.

In the case of retail property, a Goad Plan should be updated.

2.3 The nature of the subject property

At the time of inspection, detailed notes should be taken of the exact nature of the subject property. The details that need to be recorded will vary between different types of property. There are some details that will be common to all such as the age of the building, details of its construction and details of its use. Other details will be specific to the particular type of property, for example, the trunking provision in offices. Some suggestions are made below of the minimum degree of detail that would be necessary in the case of office, industrial and retail property.

Office property	Industrial property	Retail property
Date built	Date built	Date built
Date of refurbishment	Date of refurbishment	Date of refurbishment
Construction	Construction	Construction
Open plan/partitioned	Roof lights	Air conditioning
Heating type	Heating	Heating
Lighting type	Lighting type	Lighting type
Air con type	Passenger lifts	Ceiling type
Floors	Goods lifts	Ceiling height
Full access/under	Eaves height	Sprinkler system
floor/perimeter	Shell	Passenger
trunking	Loading door	lifts/escalators
Carpets	Loading bays/canopies	Goods lifts
Windows (type)	Floor loading	Loading

Ceiling type	Sprinkler system	Shell
Ceiling height	Mezzanine	Mezzanine
Passenger lifts	Site area	Condition
Floor loading	Yard area	Other
Goods lifts	Car parking	Car parking
Sprinkler system	Condition	Update Goad Plan
Toilets	Other	Photographs
Car parking		
Condition		
Other		

It is suggested that valuers should develop their own detailed checklist for the specific type of property that they are involved with in order that details of the specification can quickly and easily be recorded. This will eliminate the chance of any crucial details being missed. There is nothing more infuriating than having to return to a property to undertake a second inspection because something as simple as the height of the eaves has not been recorded.

At the time of inspection, the valuer should consider whether the property complies with relevant legislation. Two examples illustrate the impact that legislation can have upon the value of the demise.

Checking for compliance with relevant legislation

Fire regulations. The lack of alternative means of escape from upper floors and/or basement areas may mean that the fire officer will either restrict the number of people who can be accommodated in the property or not allow these areas to be occupied at all. This may have the effect of depressing value. For example, the authors have found this to be an issue when dealing with the rent review of basement nightclubs. In this situation, the restriction imposed on the capacity of the nightclub impacts upon the rental bid of the tenant. Two clubs of the same size may not therefore be directly comparable because the capacity of the two clubs may be very different as a result of fire regulations.

Disability Discrimination Act 1995. Recently, this has become an increasingly important issue. The need to adapt premises in order to make them accessible to the disabled will have an impact on the useable retail floor area of some shops due to the need to install ramps, lifts and other access features.

From the above, the basic point to be aware of is that a valuer armed with detailed information as to the nature of the subject property and its specification will be able to compare it with other properties and determine the extent of the comparability from a physical point of view.

2.4 Floor areas

One of the main tasks that will usually be undertaken at the time of inspection is to measure the subject property accurately. We say 'usually', because sometimes a lease might specifically say what floor area is to be adopted or indeed instruct the valuer to assume a hypothetical situation. This is why the valuer should establish what is to be valued when carrying out the initial lease check. If the lease specifically states the floor area to be valued then the calculation of the actual size of the demise will not be necessary – although ceilings heights may be relevant. However, on the assumption that the lease does not state the floor area to be used, the valuer will need to calculate this for himself.

The basis of measurement that should be adopted will be dependent upon the type of property. The *RICS Code of Measuring Practice (6th edition)* provides a succinct, precise definition of each basis of measurement. Whilst it is not mandatory, the Code is of quality practice and is almost universally adopted. Failure to comply with the Code could leave the valuer open to a negligence claim.

The Code is a code of measurement and not a code of valuation. It does not therefore deal with issues such as the zoning of retail property, which is a valuation technique that aids comparison rather than a basis of measurement.

RICS Code of Measuring Practice: **Core definitions of measurement**
- **GEA (Gross External Area).** GEA is used primarily in town planning, rating and building cost estimates. As such it rarely concerns the rent review surveyor.
- **GIA (Gross Internal Area).** GIA is the basis that the Code identifies as being appropriate for the valuation of industrial buildings, warehouses, retail warehouses, department stores, variety stores and food supermarkets.
- **NIA (Net Internal Area).** NIA is the basis that the Code identifies as being appropriate for the valuation of shops, supermarkets and offices.

Both GIA and NIA, however, are bases that the rent review surveyor must be fully conversant with.

It is outside of the scope of this book to define in detail each of the three bases of measurement set out in the Code. If the valuer is at all unsure then he is advised to consult a copy of the Code, which can be downloaded as a 'pdf' file from the RICS website.

It can be seen there is some crossover between the way each basis of measurement is applied. For the avoidance of doubt, it is therefore advisable always to state the basis of measurement used.

The Code identifies a number of special use definitions for shops, residential and leisure properties. For example, in the case of retail property these include 'Gross Frontage', 'Net Frontage', 'Shop Depth', 'Built Depth' and 'Shop Width'. Again the valuer is advised to consult the Code if unsure of these special use definitions.

2.5 Zoning

Retail premises are commonly valued on a zoning basis. Essentially, zoning is used to provide a means of comparing shops of differing shapes and sizes. The theory goes that from a retailer's point of view, the most valuable part of a shop is the first 20-foot depth measured back from the shop front. This is the area which generates most profit, in that it contains the window displays and products visible to shoppers in the street. This is known as Zone A. The next 20-foot depth, known as Zone B is of less value because it is less visible to casual potential customers. It is therefore reduced to half of the value of Zone A. The next 20-foot depth, Zone C, is then taken at half the rate of Zone B and so on. Thus a shop with a width of 20 feet and a depth of 60 feet with no interruptions will have the following area in Terms of Zone A (ITZA).

When measuring a shop, the valuer is advised to ensure that measurements are always taken in sufficient detailed to allow for the calculation of the areas of a retail unit on a zone-by-zone basis. In order to achieve this it is important to record the exact position of any obstructions, such as, for example, columns or staircases. The valuer must be able to net out these items from the correct zone. If the valuer has simply measured the dimensions of a staircase but not its position relative to the shop front then he will not know, for example, whether to deduct it from Zone A, Zone B or perhaps part from each.

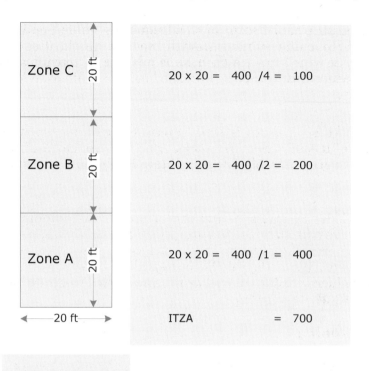

Zone C	20 ft	20 x 20 = 400 /4 = 100
Zone B	20 ft	20 x 20 = 400 /2 = 200
Zone A	20 ft	20 x 20 = 400 /1 = 400
20 ft		ITZA = 700

Shop frontage

The final point to mention in relation to measurement is that it is unwise simply to measure what is there at the time of inspection without first considering whether that is what was demised to the tenant. For example, it could be that the property has been altered since it was originally let. If alterations have been undertaken at the expense of the tenant then it is likely that the rent review clause will instruct the valuer to disregard those alterations when calculating the value of the property at the review date. Again therefore, it is stressed that it is important to establish what is to be valued. Sometimes there will be a detailed lease plan that will assist. On other occasions there will be a licence for alterations that will identify what improvements the tenant, with the landlord's consent, has carried out. In these situations it will be necessary for the valuer to use a combination of measurements taken on site and measurements scaled from the plans to establish the size of the demise to be assumed for the purpose of the rent review clause.

Non-retail premises are only infrequently valued on a zoning basis. Difficult issues arise with modern hybrid uses such as coffee or wine bars which have a mixture of traditional retail and restaurant use.

3

The legal evidence – the lease

3.1 Introduction

The legal framework for the rent review is provided by the terms of the lease itself. It is impossible to form a judgment about the level of rent at the review date without considering the rent review provisions of the lease. At a very early stage, the surveyor should therefore carefully read the whole of the lease and take a note of the terms which may affect the valuation.

Rent review surveyors often adopt their own checklists of provisions which may be important and adapt them in the light of experience. An example appears below.

Example of lease checklist

LEASE CHECKLIST	
Address	*1 Shopping Street, RT1 1AA*
Town	*Retailtown*
Lessor	*Retail and Freehold Properties Ltd*
Lessee	*Sainsrose plc*
Lease date	*21 May 1998*
Commencement date	*25 March 1998*
Term	*15 yrs*
Current rent	*£32,000 p.a.*
Current rent effective from	*25.03.03*
Review pattern	*5 yearly*
Previous rent	*£28,000 p.a.*

Previous rent effective from	25.03.98		
Rent review date	25.03.08	Page	23
		Clause	sch. 2 para. 3
Lease covenants			
Insurance	L insures	Page	18
		Clause	5.2
Repairs	T keeps in good and substantial repair and condition	Page	7
		Clause	3.3
Decorations	T	Page	9
		Clause	3.5
Alterations	Structural w/consent NTBUW.* Internal non-structural permitted	Page	11
		Clause	3.7
User	A1	Page	13
		Clause	3.9
Alienation	No alienation part. No underlet whole. Assignment w/consent NTBUW	Page	15
		Clause	3.12
Service charge	Insurance rent. Otherwise no	Page	5
		Clause	2.3
Other covenants		Page	
		Clause	
Breaks	L only 25.03.02	Page	20
		Clause	9
VAT on rent?	Yes	Page	5
		Clause	2.1
Outside *Landlord and Tenant Act* 1954?	No	Page	
		Clause	
Rent review assumptions			
Upwards-only	Yes/no		
Vacant possession	Yes/no		
Willing parties	Yes/no		
Assumed term	10 yrs		
All covenants complied with	Yes/no		
Fit for immediate use and occupation	Yes/no		

Other terms as per lease	Yes/~~no~~
Other	
Rent review disregards	
Tenant's occupation	Yes/~~no~~
Tenant's goodwill	Yes/~~no~~
Tenant's improvements	Yes/~~no~~
Other	
Rent review notices	
Trigger notice date	*25.12.07*
Time of essence?	Yes/no
Counter-notice	*4 weeks*
Time of essence?	Yes/no
Agreement by date	
Time of essence?	Yes/no
Application to 3rd party by	~~L/T~~/either
Third party	Arbitrator/~~expert~~
Interest on late settlement	*4% above Barclays base*
Lease comments	

* Not to be unreasonably withheld

Rent review clauses in leases take many different forms. They range from the simpler forms of review clause adopted in older leases to the elaborate forms found in many modern business leases. The provisions may be set out in the body of the lease itself, in schedules attached to the lease or in both. For the purpose of rent review, there are broadly three types of relevant provision. These are:

- the terms of the existing lease;
- the terms of the hypothetical lease and any assumptions and disregards to be applied at rent review; and
- the rent review machinery.

The machinery of rent review is dealt with separately in Chapter 6.

3.2 Interpreting the lease terms

There is a great deal of case law on the meaning of particular forms of rent review covenant. A surveyor will be expected to have some understanding of how the courts interpret these provisions – although plainly legal advice should be sought if the issue is likely to make a significant difference to rental values.

The words of a lease are interpreted in accordance with legal principles that apply to contracts generally. To many surveyors, the rules followed by lawyers to interpret contract terms may seem a mystery. However, there is a logic to it all. The underlying principle is that the courts will strive in every case to find the intention of the parties when they made the lease and then give effect to that intention.

The starting point – the words of the lease

The intention of the parties is primarily ascertained by looking at what the parties say in the lease itself. Where the meaning of the words used is clear, it does not matter if the outcome is a commercial nonsense.

Example

In *Cadogan v Escada*, the lease of two shops (each with its own staircase) required the tenant to convert them into one unit with a single new staircase. The lease stated that the rent review was to disregard all the value of the alterations except for the new staircases. The landlord argued it was nonsense to value two separate shops with only one staircase. The judge accepted that the wording of the lease might not be 'commercially realistic' but nevertheless 'that does not mean however that the court can rewrite the words that the parties have used in order to make the contract conform to business common-sense'.

Ambiguity

If the rent review provision is not clear, the intention of the parties is gathered from the words of the lease read in the light of any admissible external evidence. That external evidence is sometimes known as 'the factual matrix'. The courts may adopt the most commercially realistic meaning and avoid a plainly absurd outcome. However, the courts will not generally take into account the parties' respective negotiating positions at the time of the lease or have regard to events which have occurred since that date. There are also a number of technical rules of legal construction outside the scope of this work. (For the principles of construction of contracts, see *Chitty on Contracts*[2]. They were succinctly summarised by Lord Bingham in *BCCI v Ali*.)

Extrinsic evidence of the terms of the lease

If the term is ambiguous, the surveyor will want to look into evidence of the 'factual matrix' at the date of the lease:

- The nature and layout of the premises.
- The prevailing economic conditions. Was the lease granted in a rising or a falling market?
- The common forms of rent review clauses in use at the time.

The nature of the business carried on at the premises at the date of the lease.

Some caution ought to be taken with previous decisions by the courts in relation to particular rent review provisions. A later court is not bound to follow the conclusion of an earlier court about the meaning of a similar (or even an identically worded) rent review provision since the parties may have intended a different result in different circumstances. However, in practice the decisions of earlier courts are useful guidance about the meaning of particular clauses and are referred to throughout in this book.

The presumption of reality

Apart from the general rules which apply to all contracts, the courts have applied a special rule of construction to rent review clauses. The so-called 'presumption of reality' emphasises the commercial purpose of the review procedure as opposed to the literal wording of the lease (*British Gas v Universities Superannuation Scheme*; *Basingstoke and Deane BC v The Host Group*; *Lynnthorpe Enterprises v Sidney Smith (Chelsea)*; *Chancebutton v Compass Services UK & Ireland*). The commercial purpose is said to be that the landlord will obtain the market rent for which the premises would be let in the open market at the rent review date. This rule has been applied in the context of the terms of a hypothetical lease, which is presumed to follow as closely as possible the terms of the existing lease. The courts have been reluctant to extend the presumption of reality to other situations. For example,

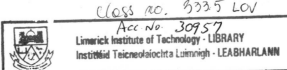

there is no presumption in a declining rental market that a rent review must be triggered at each review date (*Hemingway Realty v Clothworkers' Co*).

Implied terms

It frequently occurs that the rent review provisions omit terms which ought to be included. This is particularly the case with older leases where the rent review machinery is rudimentary. In such cases the courts may be prepared to imply a term into the lease.

Again, the courts follow the general legal rules which apply to implication of terms into all contracts. A reasonable and obvious term will be implied into the agreement if it is necessary to give 'business efficacy' to the agreement between the parties. The touchstone is whether the term to be implied is necessary to enable the agreement to work, and it is not enough that it would be convenient for either or both parties to include the term. The courts are reluctant to imply a term into an agreement which has been carefully drafted and negotiated between lawyers and they will not imply any term which contradicts another express term. (For the principles of implication of terms, see *Chitty on Contracts*[2].)

Examples where courts have refused to imply a term
- A term for interest to be paid if the rent is determined late.
- A term that the landlord should serve a trigger notice expeditiously.
- A term that the landlord's trigger notice should specify a reasonable rent.

Examples where courts have implied a term
- A disregard of goodwill.
- A term that in a third party determination of the rent, both parties should do everything necessary to procure a nomination by the President of RICS.
- A term that where there is an automatic review, the machinery for appointment of a third party to determine the new rent should be operated expeditiously.

Drafting errors: rectification

The above rules apply where the terms are ambiguous. However, the lease may clearly say something which is merely a drafting error. If the terms do not reflect the terms of the agreement made by the parties, the courts may be prepared to rectify the lease to accord with that mutual intention. Historically, the remedy of rectification was only granted in rare circumstances. However, there are signs that in recent years the courts are more prepared to rectify rent review provisions in leases.

The party seeking to rectify must show that prior to the lease, the parties had a common intention, that this common intention continued unchanged to the date of execution of the lease, that the lease mistakenly did not reflect that common intention and that that the court should exercise its equitable discretion to rectify. (For the principles of rectification, see *Chitty on Contracts*[2].)

Examples of rectification

- Changing an upwards-only rent review to an upwards/downwards one where there was persuasive evidence that this was what the parties intended.
- Inclusion of a rent review in a lease which did not include one at all to bring it into line with the terms of a headlease (*Hussain v Bahadir*).

Typically, rectification claims turn on evidence of the negotiations between the parties before the lease was entered into. A surveyor who wishes to run a rectification argument will need to obtain any files from solicitors or agents involved in negotiating the original lease terms.

Ordinarily, rectification claims are brought in the court. An arbitrator has the power to rectify a lease under s. 48(5)(c) of the *Arbitration Act* 1996, but this power is seldom invoked.

3.3 Terms of the existing lease

Many terms of the existing lease can have an effect on valuation. As stated above, the valuer should take a careful note of the important terms at the earliest possible stage.

> **Terms of existing lease that commonly affect valuation**
> - length of lease;
> - whether excluded from *Landlord and Tenant Act* 1954;
> - break clause;
> - rent review pattern;
> - repairing obligation;
> - narrow or open user covenant;
> - statutory restrictions on user;
> - narrow or open alienation covenant;
> - covenant against alterations or improvements;
> - obligation to pay a service charge; and
> - insurance.

3.4   The hypothetical lease

Most rent review provisions require the parties to value the open market rent payable to a willing landlord by a willing tenant at the review date under the terms of a new lease on hypothetical terms. The valuation is then to be conducted on certain specified assumptions and disregards.

In most instances it is irrelevant whether the clause uses words such as 'yearly rent', 'fair rent', 'market rent', 'reasonable rent', 'full market rent', 'rack rent', 'highest rent' or 'best rent'. These add nothing to the words 'open market rent'.

The terms of the hypothetical lease and the assumptions and disregards require the valuer to value something different from the rent payable under the existing lease at the review date. These differences can have a significant effect on valuation. The valuer will also have to note the provisions of the hypothetical lease and these assumptions and disregards in the checklist referred to above.

The terms of the hypothetical lease

The terms of the hypothetical lease may differ to a greater or lesser extent from the lease itself. Sometimes the hypothetical lease is identical in all respects to the actual lease. More commonly, the rent review provisions specify that the hypothetical lease will be on terms which differ from the existing lease.

When dealing with old leases, it is not unusual for the terms to have been varied by a deed made at some point before the rent review. Unless the lease (or the deed of variation) specifically says that at rent review the valuer must value the lease with the new terms, the parties will have to value on the basis of the lease in its original form. (Per Millet LJ in *Metropolitan Properties v Bartholomew*.)

Equally, one ignores personal concessions or restrictions made to the tenant in the original lease as opposed to terms which apply to all possible lessees. Thus, the courts are prepared to ignore the effect of a personal user clause in the original lease. The same applies to a break clause exercisable by the original tenant only (*Law Land Co v Consumers Association*; *St Martins Property Investments v CIB Properties*).

Instead of setting out disregards and assumptions separately, the hypothetical lease may simply incorporate specified provisions of the *Landlord and Tenant Act* 1954. One difficulty is that the 1954 Act has been substantially amended by the *Law of Property Act* 1969 and by the *Regulatory Reform (Business Tenancies) (England and Wales) Order* 2003. If the original lease was entered into before the coming into force of either of these statutory provisions, the amendments to the legislation will have to be ignored when making the appropriate disregard or assumption.

The hypothetical parties

The willing landlord is an abstraction. In the real world the landlord may not want to let the premises on the terms offered. By contrast, in the hypothetical world the parties always reach agreement. Whatever his actual plans may be for the premises, the landlord is assumed to be willing to let the premises to a tenant on the terms of the hypothetical lease. Furthermore, the valuer must ignore the landlord's personal characteristics. It has been said that the hypothetical willing landlord is not affected by 'personal ills such as a cash flow crisis or importunate mortgagees. Nor is he in the happy position of someone to whom it is largely a matter of indifference whether he lets in October 1976 or waits for the market to improve' (*FR Evans (Leeds) v English Electric Co*).

The willing tenant is also an abstraction. Even if the lease does not require there to be one, a hypothetical willing tenant must be assumed for the rent review to work (*Dennis & Robinson v Kiossos Establishment*).

In the usual case where there is an assumption that the hypothetical letting is with vacant possession, one assumes the tenant has vacated. Any effect of the property's previous occupation is disregarded and one ignores any premium to the market rent that it may be prepared to pay to remain in situ (*Cornwall Coast Country Club v Cardgrange*). However, the valuer should not ignore the demands of 'special' potential bidders for the property, even if that special bidder is the existing tenant. Thus, it is a question of fact whether the demand by a neighbouring occupier for extra space would mean it could outbid other potential lessees and pay a higher rent than would otherwise be the case.

Difficulties may arise where there is really only one potential tenant for the premises, such as where the review involves a large industrial unit or a property constructed for the unique requirements of the tenant. In such situations the valuer must try to decide how the parties would in fact behave if there was an open market letting. In *FR Evans (Leeds) v English Electric Co*, Donaldsdon J stated that the hypothetical tenant would be prepared to take the premises at the right price but would not be negotiating in a vacuum. The hypothetical tenant would take account of the alternative of leasing other premises, even thought this would not be its preferred option. The negotiations are assumed to be conducted in the light of all the bargaining advantages and disadvantages which each party had on the review date.

If there is no market for the premises, the valuer can find that a tenant would only take the premises at a low rent.

3.5 Terms which affect valuation

Length of term

The notional length of the term of the hypothetical lease may well have a significant effect on rent.

Length of term: four options

- A notional term equal to the unexpired term of the original lease at the rent review date. This is the most usual express provision, and the courts have given effect to it as part of the presumption of reality. If there is any ambiguity, it is assumed the parties intended the hypothetical lease to be granted for the unexpired residue of the term.* Indeed, the courts have strained the meaning of certain provisions to reach this conclusion. A notional term 'equal in duration to the original term' and a term 'equivalent' to the original lease have both been held to fall within this category.
- A notional term which is the same as the whole term of the original lease, but starting on the review date. This ensures that the value of the lease at each rent review is not diminished by the shortening term as the end of the lease approaches. Thus where a 25-year lease provided that the hypothetical lease was of 25 years, this meant a notional term of 25 years from the review date (*Canary Wharf Investments v Telegraph Group*).
- A fixed term of years. The parties can provide that at review, the hypothetical lease will be for a specified notional term of years from the review date.
- The prevailing length of lease in the market at review. If the rent is to be reviewed to a rack rent, the length of the notional term will generally be the length of lease typically granted by landlords to tenants at the review date. (See e.g. *Westside Nominees v Bolton MBC*.)

* There are numerous cases where the notional term has been held to run from the commencement of the original lease. See, for example, *Lynnthorpe Enterprises v Sidney Smith (Chelsea)* and *Norwich Union Life Insurance Society v Trustee Savings Bank Central Board*.

Landlord and Tenant Act 1954

The question frequently arises whether one takes into account any right that the lessee may have to renew the original tenancy under Part II of the *Landlord and Tenant Act* 1954. A well-drafted modern form of review clause will specifically deal with this, but many leases make no such provision. Absent such a provision, the valuer should (at least with shorter leases) include an element of hope value to reflect the possibility of the tenant being granted a new lease (*Pivot Properties v Secretary of State for the Environment*). In effect, this means the notional term may be longer than that expressly provided for in the lease. If a business tenant has no security of tenure under the 1954 Act, there is no hope value (*Plinth Property Investments v Mott Hay & Anderson*). However, if there is security of tenure, the valuer will have to assess the chance that the landlord will successfully resist the grant of a new tenancy on one of the grounds in s. 30(1) of the 1954 Act. Where the remaining period of the lease is short, it is therefore important for the valuer to gather evidence about the chances of a lease renewal, such as plans by the landlord to demolish the premises. (See *Business Tenancy Renewals: A Surveyor's Handbook*[3], Chapter 8.)

Break clause

Particular difficulties arise with break clauses. If the lease includes a break clause, and the hypothetical lease is to be on the same terms as the original, should a break clause be included in the hypothetical lease as well? The answer depends on the nature of the break clause itself. Typically, a break clause may be exercised on either:

1   one or more anniversaries of the start of the term; or
2   on a specified date or dates.

If the break clause is exercisable on an anniversary of the start of the term, the hypothetical lease should also include breaks on those anniversaries. If the break clause is exercisable on a fixed date or dates, the courts will not include any additional breaks into the hypothetical lease other than those specified in the original lease (*Millett (R & A) Shops v Legal & General Assurance Society*).

Rent review

A typical rent review period is now three to five years. However, in some older leases, the interval between rent reviews may well be over 20 years. The problem is that there is unlikely to be any market evidence of leases granted for such periods without a review.

In such circumstances, a third party determining the review is not permitted to insert a rent review provision unless the lease specifically allows it (*National Westminster Bank v BSC Footwear*).

Generally speaking, the parties cannot overcome this by adopting a differential rent. However, if the wording of the lease closely follows s. 34 of the *Landlord and Tenant Act* 1954, a differential rent may be permissible.

Repairing obligations

With a new letting on the open market, the state of repair of the premises may have a major impact on the value of the letting. An incoming tenant who is to be bound by repairing covenants would typically require any disrepair to be reflected in a rent-free period or a discounted initial rent. At review, the valuer plainly does not have the option of offering a rent-free period. Any allowance for the state of repair is therefore solely reflected in a discounted rent.

Repairing obligations in leases are many and varied. The lease may provide for either landlord or tenant to repair, or it may share these obligations. Furthermore, the scope of repairing obligations differs according to the specific words used. The valuer should first check the wording of the relevant covenant in the existing lease and make an assessment of the burden imposed. (For the authoritative treatment of the law of repairs, see *Dilapidations the Modern Law and Practice*[4].)

It is common for rent review provisions to assume the repairing obligations have been complied with at the date of the review. If the lease does not include such a provision, whether the rent should be discounted depends on which party is in breach. If the tenant is in breach, the rent should not generally be discounted to reflect the state of repair since a tenant cannot rely on its own default. It is irrelevant that the landlord may have a right to sue the tenant for damages. However, if the landlord is in breach, the rent payable under the hypothetical lease should be discounted to reflect the landlord's default.

User restrictions

The lease may include an absolute or a qualified covenant against the tenant using the premises for a specified purpose.

Forms of user covenant
- '**To use for X.**' This is the narrowest user covenant. The landlord may refuse consent for change of use on any grounds, no matter how unreasonable. At review the hypothetical lease should be valued without including any possibility that the landlord might permit a different user. It may have a significant effect on values.
- '**Not to use except for X.**' As above.
- '**Not to use for X without the consent of the landlord, such consent not to be unreasonably withheld.**' The valuer adopts the most profitable use that the landlord might reasonably permit.

- **'Not to use for X without the consent of the landlord.'** Under s. 19 of the *Landlord and Tenant Act 1927* this is taken to mean the same as a covenant not to use for X without the consent of the landlord, such consent not to be unreasonably withheld.
- **'Any use within *Class X of the Town and Country Planning (Use Classes) Order 1987*.'** The valuer must adopt the most profitable user within the relevant class. Note that the use classes were significantly amended with effect from 21 April 2005. If the lease was made before that date the valuer will generally have regard to the pre-2005 use classes.
- **Open user.** Where there is no restriction on user, the valuer must adopt the most profitable possible use.

If the lease is silent about the user basis of the hypothetical lease, the presumption of reality suggests that the hypothetical lease should adopt the same provisions as the lease. Commonly, the lease directs the parties to include or 'have regard to' the user clause in the lease. These mean the same thing (*Plinth Property Investments v Mott Hay & Alderson*).

It is not uncommon for the permitted user to be unique to the tenant or to a narrow class of tenants. Here, there is a tension between the narrow user covenant and provisions in the lease which envisage competition at rent review (e.g. a requirement to find a 'market' rent). The courts tend to adopt a different approach depending on how narrow the user is. If it is restricted to the business of the named tenant the courts will import the user covenant into the hypothetical lease but allow use by any hypothetical tenant (*Law Land Co v Consumers Association*). If the user covenant is restricted to a narrow class, it is probable that such a covenant will be imported into the hypothetical lease without amendment (*Post Office Counters v Harlow DC*).

On review, it is not permissible to take into account the fact that the landlord has or might waive the benefit of a narrow user covenant. If the landlord does purport unilaterally to waive a user restriction this is ignored unless the waiver was made at the request of the tenant (*Forte & Co v General Accident Life Assurance*).

Statutory restrictions on use

Many contemplated uses for a property are not feasible because they are restricted on planning or other grounds. In such a situation, the valuer must ignore the potential uses which are unlawful (*Compton Group v Estates Gazette*). This applies even if the unlawful use is that of the existing tenant. However, the valuer is entitled to reflect in the rent an element of hope value to reflect the prospect of potential tenants gaining planning consent. The hope value will be assessed in the light of any evidence that one potential occupier has already obtained a personal planning permission (*Wolff v Enfield LBC*).

It is open to the parties specifically to provide that the hypothetical lease should adopt a different user to that in the existing lease, and in practice such provisions are common. The clause will displace the presumption of reality. If there is such a provision, it is irrelevant that the hypothetical use is not permitted on planning or other grounds. The valuer assumes the premises can be used for the purpose lawfully (*Little Hayes Nursing Home v Marshall*). An exception is made in the case of gaming and other licences, which are not deemed to be granted for a hypothetical assumed user (*Daejan Investments v Cornwall Coast Country Club*).

Alienation

The lease will generally include some control over alienation, although there is a wide range of such restrictions. Typically, there will be an absolute bar on assigning or parting with possession of part, but a qualified covenant against assigning the whole without the consent of the landlord.

The valuer must consider the effect of the alienation clause in conjunction with the user covenant and any other linked provisions of the lease. Thus, a wide alienation covenant combined with a user so narrow that the tenant cannot assign except to a very limited range of businesses may have a similar effect to a narrow alienation restriction.

Service charge

Where a property forms part of a larger unit, there may be an express provision for payment of a service charge. The valuer will have to consider the service charge provision to understand whether the tenant faces potential liability to contribute to expensive items such as lifts, roof repairs or air conditioning plant. In some circumstances, the court will imply a term that the service charge must be fair and reasonable (*Finchbourne v Rodrigues*).

Insurance

The lease may impose an obligation on either landlord or tenant for insuring the premises. If the landlord is to insure, there will almost invariably be an obligation on the tenant to pay or contribute to the costs of insurance. The courts are reluctant to imply any limitation on the recoverable costs of insurance. (See e.g. *Havenridge v Boston Dyers*.)

3.6 Disregards and assumptions

Vacant possession

The vast majority of hypothetical leases are valued on the basis of vacant possession. Rent review provisions commonly require this assumption. However, if the lease does not expressly provide for an assumption of vacant possession, it is a question of construction whether this will be the case. The normal presumption is that the tenant has moved out or has never occupied. However, if the lease was originally subject to an existing tenancy (*Forte & Co v General Accident Life Assurance*), or where it contemplated the existence of subtenancies at the time of the review, the position may be different.

Examples
- Lease originally granted subject to existing tenancy which continued to the review date. To be valued with subtenant (*Forte & Co v General Accident Life Assurance*).
- Lease granted in contemplation of subleases being granted and head tenant to receive a rack rent for each sublet part. Headlease to be valued with subtenants (*Scottish & Newcastle Breweries v Sir Richard Sutton's Settled Estates*).

If the subletting is in breach of a covenant in the lease, the subletting should be ignored. Otherwise the tenant could benefit from its own wrong.

Fitting-out

For many years, it was common for landlords to offer their incoming tenants a rent-free period to allow for fitting out or to reflect disrepair. Inducements to tenants present real problems when valuing a lease at rent review. The difficulty arises because the parties are generally directed to value the hypothetical lease of the premises with vacant possession. Since an incoming tenant might ordinarily expect a rent-free period for fitting-out, tenants have long argued that at each review date the rent should be discounted to reflect the usual rent-free period. By contrast, landlords contended that such a discount was unfair, since the rent was discounted at each review to reflect a cost which the tenant only incurred once at the start of the lease. This argument was resolved by the Court of Appeal in favour of the tenants in the leading case of *99 Bishopsgate v Prudential Assurance*. The advantage which accrued to the tenant consequently became known as the '99 Bishopsgate effect'.

Landlords developed various forms of rent review disregards designed to overcome the 99 Bishopsgate effect. These clauses were subjected to a great deal of scrutiny by the courts. Few were held to be effective.

Disregards for fitting out		
Wording of assumption	**Effective to displace 99 Bishopsgate effect?**	**Case**
Premises 'fit for use and occupation'	No	*Orchid Lodge UK v Extel Computing*
Premises 'ready for immediate occupation and use'	No	*Iceland Frozen Foods v Starlight Investments*
Premises 'vacant but fit for immediate occupation and use'	No	*Pontsarn Investments v Kansallis-Osake-Pankki*
Premises 'suitable and available for immediate occupation and use and are fully carpeted'	Yes	*City Offices v Bryanston Insurance*
Premises 'fit for immediate occupation and use … and that all fitting out and other tenant's works required by such willing tenant have already been completed'	Yes	*London and Leeds Estates v Paribas*

Disregard 'any rent free period or any concessionary rent or any other inducement whether of a capital or revenue nature ... shall have expired or been given immediately before the relevant date of review'	Yes	*Cooperative Wholesale Society v National Westminster Bank*
Premises 'fully fitted out and equipped so as to be ready for immediate use and occupation by such willing tenant for such use'	Yes	*Ocean Accident & Guarantee Corporation v Next*

Other inducements

In the difficult market conditions which prevailed in the 1980s and 1990s, rent-free periods were adopted as a convenient inducement for tenants to enter into a lease. They enabled the landlord to maintain the value of their reversions by setting artificial headline rents which exceeded the market rent.

As stated above, some disregards were drawn in very wide terms to avoid the 99 Bishopsgate effect. One (perhaps) unintended consequence was that the disregards (originally designed to deal with only fitting-out periods) were also applied to the inducements which maintained the headline rents. Tenants faced arguments that the rent should be reviewed to an above-market headline rent because the lease directed the parties to ignore the value of all rent-free periods.

The effect of these provisions on headline rents was considered in four cases joined in the Court of Appeal in *Cooperative Wholesale Society v National Westminster Bank*. The court applied the presumption in favour of reality. A clause calculated to deal with the 99 Bishopsgate effect made commercial common sense. A provision which deemed the market rent to be the headline rent was not so preposterous so as to be rejected out of hand, but it did require that the words of the lease admitted no other construction.

Provision	Effect	Case
Disregard 'any rent free period or any concessionary rent or any other inducement whether of a capital or revenue nature ... shall have expired or been given immediately before the relevant date of review'	Market rent (but effective to negate 99 Bishopsgate effect)	*Cooperative Wholesale Society v National Westminster Bank*
Disregard 'any effect on rent of any initial rent free period or periods at concessionary rents or other inducements which might be offered in the open market'	Market rent	*Scottish Amicable Life Assurance v Middleton Potts & Co*
New rent is 'best yearly rent which would reasonably be expected to become payable ... after expiry of a rent-free period of such length as would be negotiated in the open market'	Headline rent	*Broadgate Square v Lehman Brothers*
'no reduction or allowance is to be made on account of any rent free period or other rent concession'	Market rent	*Prudential Nominees v Greenham Trading*

Chattels, fixtures and fittings

A requirement to assume vacant possession usually carries with it a presumption that the tenant has removed all removable fixtures at the review date.

The distinction between improvements and tenant's chattels and fixtures can sometimes be a fine one. Broadly speaking, a chattel is something which has been brought onto the land and which is easily removable. Although it is common to find references to fixtures and fittings, the label favoured by the courts is a tenant's 'removable fixture' (*Elitestone v Morris*). The test for a 'removable fixture' is complex, and depends on the degree to which the item is attached to the land and the purpose for which it is there.

Removable fixture?	
Yes	No
Fitted carpets attached to the floor with grippers	Fitted carpets/carpet tiles stuck to the floor
Partitions attached to floor with pins	
Free standing air conditioning unit	Part of air conditioning plant

Disregard of tenant's occupation and goodwill

These disregards derive from s. 34(1)(a) and (b) of the *Landlord and Tenant Act* 1954. It is common for the lease to require valuers to ignore the goodwill of the lessee. Goodwill means 'the expectation that an existing customer clientele of a business will continue' (*IRC v Muller & Co Margarine*). However, it will often be a matter of opinion whether the attractiveness to potential tenants of a particular location relates to the occupier or to the property itself. The fact that the property is a retail 'destination' may be taken into account even if the actual identity of the occupier is disregarded (*My Kinda Town v Castlebrook Properties*).

Closely linked is the disregard of the tenant's own occupation. This disregard requires the valuer to ignore the effect of the tenant as a special purchaser in the market.

Disregard of improvements and alterations

If there is no specific disregard of improvements in the lease, the court will not imply such a term (*Ponsford v HM Aerosols*).

However, it is usual for a lease expressly to disregard the effect on a reviewed rent of any tenant's improvements. It is considered unfair for the tenant to pay a rent for works he has paid for (*Sheerness Steel v Medway Ports Authority*). For the same reason, s. 34 of the *Landlord and Tenant Act* 1954 disregards certain tenant's improvements when determining the rent payable at lease renewal. An improvement will be construed as a physical rather than an economic concept. An improvement (such as internal partitioning erected by the tenant) which reduces the letting value of the property remains nevertheless an improvement. The concept extends to any alteration or addition to the structure carried out by the tenant or its contractors.

A common form of disregard is to ignore only those improvements carried out pursuant to an obligation to the landlord. However, the obligation need not be in the lease itself. Provided any licence to carry out alterations requires the tenant to carry out the works, this is will suffice (*Godbold v Martin (The Newsagents)*).

Care should be taken with leases entered into before 1969 which import the disregard by incorporating s. 34 of the 1954 Act. Section 34 was significantly amended by the *Law of Property Act* 1969 and the valuer will have to have regard to the original wording of the 1954 Act when assessing the scope of the disregard in a pre-1969 lease.

If the lessee is permitted by the lease to carry out improvements, but has not as yet done them, the improvements obviously cannot be rentalised. However, the right to carry them out may be (*Lewisham Investment Partnership v Morgan*).

If the improvements were carried out prior to the date of the lease, it may be that the disregard is sufficiently widely worded to cover these as well.

Improvements pre-dating the lease. Are they to be disregarded?			
Term of lease	When works carried out	Are they disregarded?	Authority
Section 34 incorporated (pre-1969 form)	Under previous tenancy	No	*Brett v Brett Essex Golf Club*
Section 34 incorporated (post-1969 form)	By tenant or predecessor in title	Yes, if carried out less than 21 years before	Section 34(c)
Disregard of improvements by named tenant	In anticipation of grant of lease	Yes	*Hambros Bank Executor & Trustee Co v Superdrug Stores*
Disregard of improvements by tenant	Under agreement for lease	Yes	*Scottish & Newcastle Breweries v Sir Richard Sutton's Settled Estates*
Disregard of improvements by tenant	Under agreement for lease (unenforceable)	No	*Euston Centre Properties v H&J Wilson*

Works carried out by an agent or contractor will be treated as an improvement by the tenant unless the lease expressly states otherwise. However, works carried out by licensees and subtenants will generally not qualify as tenant's improvements.

Assumption of compliance with terms of the lease

There are a number of examples above which show that the parties will generally be assumed to have complied with the terms of the lease. If the rent review provisions do not include an express term to this effect, one will be implied (*Harmsworth Pension Fund Trustees v Charringtons Industrial Holdings*).

4

The market evidence – comparables

4.1 Introduction

The final string of evidence that the valuer will need to gather, and then evaluate, is the evidence of transactions which bear upon the level of rent. This is largely, but not exclusively, market evidence of rental transaction relating to comparable properties. It is this rental evidence which is generally the key factor to successful negotiations and third party referrals in rent review. However, certain other types of evidence may be relevant – such as detailed records of trading accounts where the rent is calculated all or partly by reference to turnover or net profits.

4.2 Sources of information

As the rental evidence is the key to the negotiations, this is one area where the valuer really earns his fee. A valuer who is active in a particular market place will of course hold a database of rental transactions already but he will also be able to supplement this by drawing upon information from the network of contacts that he has developed over the years. This will include relationships with other agents as well as occupiers and landlords of comparable property. A valuer who is not so active in a particular market place will have much more work to do, as he will need to develop these contacts before he is able to source the information.

Other sources of useful information include the following websites:

Website	Web address	Comment
EGI (*Estates Gazette Interactive*)	www.egi.co.uk	Commercial website giving a substantial database of transactions. Details are basic and usually require further research but do provide a good lead.
Focus	www.focusnet.co.uk	Commercial website giving a substantial database of transactions. Details are basic and usually require further research but do provide a good lead.
Land Registry Online	www.landregisteronline.gov.uk	Details of the ownership of properties can be retrieved for a small fee. There are also details of some leasehold titles.
The Valuation Office	www.voa.gov.uk	Gives details of the rating assessments, which often include detailed valuations with floor areas.

4.3 Confidential documents in the hands of a party

Not infrequently, one party wishes to obtain evidence from the other party which is relevant to the dispute and the response is that this material is *prima facie* confidential. For example, a landlord in a rent review may not wish to reveal an incentive offered to the tenant of an adjacent property. It may also arise where there is a turnover rent, and the evidence is contained in commercially sensitive trading accounts.

The basic rule is that, unless covered by legal professional privilege or by public interest immunity, the fact that a document is confidential is itself no answer to a request for disclosure (*Alfred Crompton Amusement Machines v Commrs of Customs and Excise (No. 2)*).

Relevance

That is not to say that a court or arbitrator always order such documents to be disclosed. Absent some indication that the material is likely to advance the case, it may be hard to convince a court or arbitrator to order disclosure of such documents. Disclosure will only be ordered of **relevant** material. Many confidential pieces of information will not be relevant to a review where they would not been known to a hypothetical willing landlord or tenant at the review date.

Confidential trading accounts: *Cornwall Coast Country Club v Cardgrange Ltd*

In *Cardgrange*, disclosure was sought by the landlord of the tenant's trading accounts. It was accepted that with this type of property (a country club) turnover or profitability was relevant to the rent at the review date. Disclosure was nevertheless refused because the accounts were not publicly available and therefore they would not be available to the hypothetical willing lessee.

Legal professional privilege

Documents containing legal advice by a solicitor or barrister attract privilege in rent reviews to the same degree that they do in litigation before the court. They need never be disclosed. This privilege extends to documents sent from the client to his legal advisers (whether directly or via his surveyor) which conveys information for the purposes of seeking advice. On the other hand, the fact that a document which would not otherwise be privileged has been sent to the legal adviser for comment or advice does not render that document itself privileged.

There is no privilege attaching to a surveyor's general advice, even if it is effectively legal advice which would be privileged if given by a solicitor or barrister. This can be a serious problem in rent review arbitrations because very often there will be no input from a lawyer in the early stages. So, advice as to the meaning of the clause and the initial valuation advice to the client are potentially discloseable. However, once the lawyers become involved, subsequent material becomes privileged. Draft reports being worked up by a surveyor with legal input are usually legally privileged. (See in the context of litigation disclosure, *Jackson v Marley Davenport Ltd*.)

Previous arbitration awards and court judgments

An arbitration itself is confidential (*Dolling-Baker v Merrett*). This confidence extends to all documents disclosed in the process to all persons involved in the arbitration. There are certain narrow exceptions:

- where the other party consents;
- where there is an order of the court (e.g. a disclosure order);
- with the permission of the court;
- in order to protect the legitimate interests of the arbitrating party; and
- where it is in the 'public interest' (e.g. exposing inconsistency in evidence) (*Ali Shipping Corp v Shipyard Trogir*).

Where there is a common landlord of neighbouring properties, there are often co-terminous leases with coincident rent reviews. Understandably, there is intense interest in the outcome of arbitrations involving such leases. For the purposes of negotiation, this is perhaps understandable. However, disclosure of these awards in a subsequent arbitration will not be ordered because the awards are treated as confidential. In any event, although technically arbitration awards may not be inadmissible, they are treated as having little or no evidential weight (*Land Securities v Westminster City Council*). The matter is dealt with at section 4.6 below.

The same applies equally in those less common cases where rents have been determined by the court, and are a matter of public record (most obviously on a lease renewal under Part II of the *Landlord and Tenant Act* 1954). A judgment on a rent issue in a lease renewal would not be admissible in a subsequent rent review arbitration, or would carry no weight.

Evidence in previous arbitrations and court proceedings

Potentially more useful is the evidence adduced in a previous arbitration, either to rely upon or to use in cross-examination against the other side's expert. Previous experts' reports are often worth comparison with the report adduced in the current case. However, arbitration confidentiality extends to the evidence, both a party's own evidence and the evidence adduced by the other side. The confidentiality obligation also extends to the lawyers and surveyors, and to the arbitrator himself. This can potentially make it impossible to act if a surveyor has in his files a dynamite piece of evidence which he obtained in a previous arbitration and which would greatly assist his current client. His obligation to his current client is to use the information, but he cannot do so by reason of the arbitration confidentiality, and this conflict may be irreconcilable.

However, the same rule does not apply to evidence adduced in previous court proceedings. It is perfectly permissible to cross-examine an expert witness on inconsistent expert evidence given in other court proceedings.

4.4 Confidential documents in the hands of a third party

A more common occurrence is that confidential evidence is held by third parties – typically incentives offered by landlords to new tenants in comparable properties.

The instinctive reaction of a lawyer tends to be astonishment at the way one can ring up a surveyor, tell him (or her) that there's a rent review on foot, and he will oblige by divulging every detail of the deal he just did for his client on the property next door. However, the *Code of Practice for Commercial Leases in England and Wales (2007)*[5] supports the agent's approach: transparency should be the norm. It is good for the market.

If a client insists on confidentiality, as they are entitled to do, then that confidence must be respected unless overridden in one of the circumstances identified earlier. The section on third party disclosure below is also relevant to this point.

Confidential comparables: *South Tyneside v Wickes Building Supplies*
STBC was the landlord of a DIY warehouse store and Wickes was the tenant. A rent review was referred to arbitration. STBC knew that B&Q and Wickes had competed in the market for a lease of other similar premises, and that B&Q was successful. STBC sought details of the rent payable by B&Q at the other site and of bids by rival retailers. B&Q's lease contained a confidentiality clause.
Disclosure was refused because other comparables and material were available to the arbitrator. The documents were both confidential and acutely commercially sensitive. The confidentiality clause was on those facts of considerable weight.

> **Tipping the wink**
>
> It is a breach of confidence not only to reveal confidential information, but also to '**tip the wink**' about the existence or content of confidential documents.
>
> In *London & Leeds Estates v Paribas (No. 2)* expert A acted for the landlord. Expert B acted for the tenant. Both experts had been involved in a previous arbitration where A acted for the tenant and B was the arbitrator. B told the tenant's legal team that A's proof of evidence in the earlier proceedings was of interest. The 'wink' having been 'tipped' by B to his principal, the tenant issued summonses seeking production of B's proof and expert reports.
>
> The court criticised B for 'tipping the wink' to his client in breach of confidence. However, the court overrode the confidentiality of the arbitration because it was in the public interest that the tenant should be permitted to explore inconsistency in A's expert evidence.

4.5 Quality of evidence

The quality of each piece of rental evidence put forward by the parties will inevitably vary and it is surprising how often evidence that is put forward is inaccurate and/or incomplete.

Often, details of incentives given to ingoing tenants, such as rent-free periods or capital contributions, are not fully disclosed. This obviously has the effect of producing a higher devaluation, which is known as a headline rent (further consideration of the devaluation of incentives is given below).

Other areas where details are often sketchy are on matters such as floor areas, specification and lease terms. All these factors will impact upon the devaluation of transactions and the relevance of those transactions to the subject review.

In order to ensure that these matters are adequately addressed it is important for the valuer to develop a method of ensuring that all the right questions are asked. This can be done by the use of a pro forma for the confirmation of comparable evidence. This can be completed and if necessary sent to an individual involved in the transaction for signature, which will in any event be necessary if the rent review ends up being determined by a third party. An example of such a pro forma is included in Appendix 1. Further guidance about third party referrals is given in Chapters 9–12.

Having gone this far it is often the case that the valuer then blindly relies on the pro forma and fails to agree the facts of the comparable transaction with his opposite number. This is a mistake because if the rent review ends up being determined by a third party then the third party can be faced with the situation of having two conflicting pro formas relating to the same comparable transaction: one pro forma supplied by the tenant and the other by the landlord. Each side will then challenge the factual accuracy of the other side's evidence in counter submissions. This creates obvious problems for the third party and also brings into question the credibility of the valuers. It is therefore much better to disclose the pro forma to your opposite number at an early stage in order that the facts can be agreed. It is usually the case that the parties can eventually agree the facts relating to each of the pieces of comparable evidence and a joint schedule can be produced showing all agreed comparables. However, the parties will often still disagree about the relevance of each piece of evidence, the devaluation of incentives and which of the pieces of evidence is the most pertinent.

The best evidence is that which relates to physically similar properties, in similar location, held on similar lease terms, where the date of the transaction is as close as possible to the subject rent review date. This may sound obvious. Frequently, however, the property that is the best comparison physically may well be held on entirely different lease terms and the property which is subject to an open market letting on the same date as the rent review date of the subject property is in fact physically distinct from the subject property. The valuer must therefore use his skill and judgment to construct a hierarchy of evidence and place the subject property at the appropriate value within that hierarchy. This is where the disagreements occur.

4.6 Weighting applied to different types of evidence

As described above, the commercial purpose of a rent review is to enable the landlord to obtain the market rent for which the property would be expected to let in the open market at the review date. Open market lettings are therefore the best evidence of this. The valuer may wonder how rent review settlements, arbitration awards and lease renewals, etc. rate alongside such lettings. It is suggested that the hierarchy of evidence in descending order is as set out below. (This hierarchy is adopted from the guidance given in the case of *Wallshire v Aarons.*)

Open Market lettings

It should be remembered that a rent review is trying to simulate the open market and therefore Open Market lettings are the best evidence and carry considerably more weight than other categories of evidence.

Agreements between valuers at arm's length upon lease renewal or rent review

Settlements of this nature **should** have been arrived at after both parties had thoroughly researched the market. The settlements should therefore theoretically reflect most of the rental evidence that was available at the review date and potentially a little afterwards if the review was agreed after the relevant date.

At first sight it would appear that evidence of this nature is nearly as good as open market evidence but this is not so. Problems with this sort of evidence can occur in a number of situations:

1   The parties may not have been in possession of all of the rental evidence that was available at the time. One party, for example, may have been unaware of the latest letting. It is therefore possible that the rent review settlement could be out of step with the actual market level.
2   Consideration should be given to whom the parties negotiating the settlement were. Unrepresented tenants, for example, have been known to agree rent reviews at figures out of line with the market level. This is by no means always the case but it is something that the valuer should be aware of as a possibility.
3   In the case of lease renewals, security of tenure can be an issue. For example, the tenant who holds a property on a lease that is contracted out of the *Landlord and Tenant Act 1954* will be in a weak negotiating position at lease renewal and may be persuaded to agree a rent higher than the true market level in order to retain possession of the property and save the cost of moving.

Determinations by an independent expert

The extent to which determinations by independent experts reflect the open market depends to a large extent upon the quality of the independent expert. In most cases the expert will have received submissions from the parties. The expert should therefore be in possession of as much evidence as valuers would have been if they had agreed the review by negotiation. In addition an expert can supplement the evidence presented by the parties with details of any evidence that he is aware of which the parties are not. For this reason expert determinations rank closely behind negotiated settlements.

Arbitration awards

In the case of arbitration awards the valuer must remember that the figure awarded might not be an indication of the arbitrator's personal opinion of the value of the particular property. This may seem odd to those who are not involved in arbitration. The key point to consider, however, is that an arbitrator's award is based solely upon the evidence that is presented to him by the parties. If the parties do not argue a particular point or present a certain piece of evidence then it is not open to the arbitrator to supplement the party's case by introducing those details. The level of the arbitrator's award is therefore entirely dependent upon the quality of the evidence put to him together with the way it is expressed and the manner in which the parties were represented. Accordingly less weight should be awarded to arbitration awards than to those categories above.

Historically, evidence of previous arbitration awards was regarded as not being admissible in subsequent arbitrations (*Land Securities v Westminster City Council*). The principal reason was that arbitration awards in this context were considered hearsay. The importance of this principle has been overridden to a large extent by the *Civil Evidence Act* 1995, which allows for the introduction of hearsay evidence. However, the position remains that the rent figure produced by an arbitrator is of little or no evidential value in a subsequent arbitration. To determine how much weight should be attached to the figure adopted by the earlier arbitrator, it is generally necessary to investigate what evidence he had before him and how he had treated it. Since this effectively means a rehearing of the original arbitration, it is rare that evidence of an earlier arbitration award will be of much assistance. (See, in the context of leasehold enfranchisement, the decision of the Lands Tribunal in *Arrowdell v Coniston Court*.)

The *Arbitration Act* 1996 allows the parties specifically to agree that they will admit arbitration awards. If the parties do not make such a specific agreement then the default position set out in the *Arbitration Act* 1996 is that then the arbitrator has the power to decide whether to admit such evidence or not.

Determinations by the court under Part II of the Landlord and Tenant Act 1954

Determinations by the courts rank below arbitration awards because an arbitrator will usually have particular expertise in the subject area. This expertise will enable an arbitrator better to evaluate the evidence than a non-expert judge.

Hearsay

Since the introduction of the *Civil Evidence Act* 1995 and the *Arbitration Act* 1996 the question is no longer whether hearsay evidence is admissible. The issue is rather one of how much weight should be attached to it.

4.7 Analysis of incentives

When considering the devaluation of the comparable transactions, the valuer must have regard to the effect of any incentives in the context of the overall deal.

The valuer will need to distinguish between incentives that have an impact upon the rent agreed, and those that do not. The question that the valuer should ask himself is 'would the rent agreed have been materially different without the incentive?'. If the answer is yes then the valuer should attempt to analyse the transaction to produce an equivalent rent.

The valuer should remember that there is no single method of analysis agreed within the profession for devaluing incentives. Each case needs to be considered on its own merits. Some valuers use sophisticated discounted cash flow (DCF) techniques but more commonly they adopt a straight line analysis. The period over which incentives should be devalued is also open to interpretation. Again, there is no set rule.

Before going on to look at these issues in more detail it is useful to first consider why incentives might be given and also to consider what form incentives might take.

Reasons for granting incentives

The reasons for a landlord granting an incentive are many and varied and of course will be different in each situation. A non-exhaustive list of situations that might lead to an incentive being offered by a landlord is set out below.

- to achieve a quick letting in an over-supplied market;
- to give the appearance of high rents;
- to maximise capital value;
- to facilitate funding;
- to ease the initial cash flow for the tenant;
- for taxation purposes;
- to secure a tenant of strong covenant standing;
- to secure a long lease; and/or
- to limit liability for empty rates and service charge shortfall.

It should be remembered that there are also situations when a tenant might offer an incentive to the landlord over and above an attractive rental bid. This can occur, for example, where a premium is paid to secure a unit in an under-supplied market.

4.8 Types of incentives

Premium payments

Premiums are capital payments made by one party in the transaction to the other. These payments can occur in various situations and the treatment of them will need to be different in each case.

Premiums paid on assignment

There is an argument to say that if a premium is paid on assignment of a lease then this is an indication that the current passing rent is not at market level. The argument goes that if the premium is paid by the assignee (i.e. the incoming tenant) to the assignor (i.e. the outgoing tenant) then it is an indication that the property is under rented. The outgoing tenant is enjoying a profit rent and it is the benefit of this that he is selling. On the other hand, if the assignor pays the premium to the assignee, then this would illustrate that the property was over rented. The assignor is paying the assignee to take on the liability of an over rented property.

The extent to which this type of transaction can be used to prove that the passing rent is not the market level will, however, depend upon the circumstances of the evidence that is being put forward. If the parties have specifically agreed that the payment represents the capitalisation of the profit rent then the evidence might be useful in supporting other evidence. If only one party relates the premium to the capital value of a profit rent then it will be of less value. If a third party puts an analysis of this nature forward then it should be treated with extreme caution. There may have been other factors at play which lead one party to pay a premium. Such factors might include service charge and rates liability and dilapidation issues.

Premiums paid by a tenant to a landlord on a new letting

At the time of a new letting a premium might be paid by the landlord to the tenant or vice versa. Each situation needs to be treated differently and is considered below.

There has been considerable debate as to whether or not a premium that is paid by an ingoing tenant to a landlord should be devalued to produce an equivalent rent.

Consideration should be given to the motivation behind the payment. The question that should be asked is was the payment in lieu of rent or was it for something else?

In situations where the tenant has derived a particular benefit, such as, for example, an enhanced specification, then the premium payment is not part of the rental transaction. Rather, it can be identified as being a payment for a particular benefit. It should not therefore be devalued into an equivalent rent.

Similarly in situations where a payment of a premium is purely 'key money' then again the premium should not be devalued into an equivalent rent. The expression 'key money' has been defined to mean an over bid, in addition to the market rent, by way of a one-off capital payment, which a tenant is willing to pay to obtain a lease on a particular property. If 'key money' were to be devalued to produce an equivalent rent then this may produce an artificially high figure.

Problems can, however, occur in identifying whether a payment is in fact 'key money' or if it is something else. In some markets, where rental evidence is scarce, premium payments have become common. This is true, for example, in the supermarket sector. It is not unusual for operators to pay substantial capital premiums in order to secure an acquisition. They argue that this is key money. Landlords, on the other hand, have argued that it is not. Landlords claim that it is a payment to secure the property at an artificially low rent and thus the premium should be analysed to produce an equivalent rent.

There is no right and wrong answer to this problem. Each case must be considered on its merits. It is fair to say that if there are a number of parties bidding and the under bidders are also offering substantial premiums, then this adds weight to the argument that the premium payment is not purely 'key money' and therefore that it should, at least in part, be devalued into an equivalent rent. Many independent experts and arbitrators have, however, been reluctant to devalue premiums into an equivalent rent. The courts have also been unwilling to enter into the arena on this issue (*BLCT (13096) Ltd v J Sainsbury plc* and *Safeway Stores v Legal & General Assurance Society*).

Premiums paid by a landlord to a tenant on a new letting

A premium that is paid by a landlord to a tenant at the time of a new letting can generally be regarded as an inducement unless the payment can be shown to be towards something specific. Generally therefore, payments of this nature are analysed to produce an equivalent rent.

Rent-free periods

Rent-free periods are usually granted at the start of the lease but this is not always the case. They can be given at any time during the lease. The timing is important when the incentive is devalued on a net present value basis. A rent-free period at the start of the lease will be of more value to the tenant than a deferred rent-free period.

Stepped rents

The analysis of stepped rents can cause problems if the nature of the steps results in the rent being in excess of market rental levels.

Contributions to fit out

Contributions to fit out may be in the form of a cash payment or alternatively might involve the landlord actually undertaking certain works.

The valuer must separate fit out works into two groups.

The first group of works relates to those that any tenant would need. These should not be regarded as an inducement.

The second group is those works that are more specialist in nature and/or specific to the particular tenant. The valuer will need to decide whether to devalue these into an equivalent rent. In reaching his decision the valuer should consider if 'normal fit out works' are common across all the comparables. If so he may wish to ignore them. He should also consider whether the fit out works are being undertaken as an obligation to the landlord. If so are they to be rentalised at review? If the improvements are to be disregarded at review and would otherwise affect value then the advantage that this gives to the tenant should be devalued over either the life of the improvements, a generally accepted write down period or the lease term or until the next break if earlier.

Purchase of existing interest

This is common where a tenant relocates. The landlord may agree to underwrite the tenant's ongoing liabilities at the former premises or if it is the same landlord may accept a surrender of the existing lease. In such situations the valuer should assess the present value of the liability that the landlord is assuming when determining the equivalent rent.

Lease concessions

Examples of leasehold concessions might include matters such as the capping of a service charge or the relaxation of a particular tenant's obligation under the lease, such as, for example, the repairing obligation. These sorts of concessions need careful consideration because a lease with, for example, a capped service charge may be more advantageous to a tenant than a lease without such a cap. It is, however, difficult for the valuer to quantify this without the knowledge of what the service charge costs are going to be in the future.

Break clauses

When considering the impact of a break clause on the devaluation the valuer should take into account how likely it is that either the tenant or the landlord will activate the break clause. Factors that will affect this include whether there are any penalties for activating the break clause and also the level of rental relative to current market levels.

Other inducements

Other types of inducements include the following:

1   payment of fees;
2   capped rents; and
3   rental concessions.

4.9   Period of devaluation of incentives

Most rent review clauses direct the valuer to assess the open market rental value of the property on the assumption that it is let without inducement, such as those identified above. The valuer must therefore analyse comparables to arrive at an equivalent rent in each case. In doing so he must consider the period over which any inducements are to be devalued and also the method of devaluation to be used.

The equivalent rental outcome of the devaluation of any inducement will be dependent to a large extent on the period over which that inducement is devalued.

Some valuers will write off the benefit over the period up to the first rent review. This approach may well be appropriate where the first rent review coincides with a break clause or where it is anticipated that the tenant will not benefit from the inducement after that date.

In situations where the parties are committed to the lease for a longer period of time without a break, there is no consensus amongst valuers about the proper period over which the incentive should be devalued over the entire term of the lease. The two approaches are illustrated by the examples below.

Devaluation period: two extreme examples

Devaluation 1
Assume that a tenant takes a lease of a 3000 sq. ft. office suite for a term of 15 years with five-yearly upwards only rent reviews and that the rent reserved is £45,000 p.a. Assume also that the tenant receives a rent-free period of five years and that there are no break clauses. If this transaction is devalued over the five years to the first review then the equivalent rent on a straight-line basis can be shown to be nil.

Devaluation 2
The landlord however has taken a longer-term view. He has secured a minimum of 10 years' income at £45,000 p.a. (and in all likelihood his income will be more once the rent reviews have been implemented). Therefore he analyses the deal over the 15-year term of the lease. The landlord will claim that a total rental income of £450,000 has been secured over 15 years and therefore the average rent is £30,000 p.a. or £10 p.s.f.

Clearly these two approaches provide vastly different outcomes. Whilst there is still no consensus throughout the industry as to the correct approach, there has in recent years been some movement amongst rent review surveyors to devalue over a compromise period, midway between the two extremes. In the example above that might be to devalue over ten years. Thus the landlord will have net receipts over the first ten years of £225,000. This averages to £22,500 p.a. or £7.50 p.s.f. p.a.

4.10 Method of devaluation of incentives

In the same way that there is no consensus between valuers about the correct period over which inducements should be devalued, there is also no consensus about what method of devaluation should be used.

The straight-line basis is in practice widely adopted. The approach is to work out the net receipts that are received (after having deducted the value of any inducements) during the devaluation period and then average that over the same number of years to arrive at an average rent over the devaluation period.

The advantage of the straight-line approach is that it is easy to understand and is straightforward. However, it ignores the basic principle of valuation that a pound today is worth more than a pound in five years' time. In view of this it can be argued that a more sophisticated discounted cash flow technique should be adopted.

4.11 Post review evidence

It should be remembered that the commercial purpose of a rent review is to enable the landlord to obtain the market rent for which the property would be expected to let in the open market at the review date. As we have seen above, comparable evidence is used as an indication of market sentiment at the rent review date. Evidence that is created on or slightly before the review date is a helpful indication of market sentiment at that time. It is, however, often the case that a rent review is not settled until some months after the actual review date. By this time, post review date evidence may also be available to the parties. In a rising market the landlord may wish to introduce this evidence whilst in a falling market it is the tenant who will want to include it. The questions are how should this post review date evidence be treated and what, if any, weight should be attached to it? The answers to these questions depend to a large extent upon the nature of the evidence itself.

Post review events and comparables

Evidence of a post review events is inadmissible. The reason for this is that hypothetical parties, at the review date, would not have advance knowledge of the events and therefore would not reflect the post review event in their agreement. (See e.g. *Duvan Estates v Rossette Sunshine Savouries*.)

By contrast, post rent review date comparable transactions **are** admissible as evidence of rent on the valuation date. The weight given to them will decrease with the passage of time.

Post review comparables: *Segama NV v Penny Le Roy*

The tenant held a lease of a shop with a rent review at 1 October 1982. The new rent was determined by an arbitrator in July 1983. In his award, the arbitrator took into account comparable transactions which had taken place after the review date but before the arbitration hearing. The landlord sought permission to appeal. The High Court refused permission. The judge held that the arbitrator had been right to receive evidence of post review date comparables. He suggested that if the comparable transaction had taken place the day after the rent review date of the subject property then that would be a good guide as to market rents at the review date. The longer after the review date the comparable transaction took place then the less reliable it became as a guide to rental levels at that review date and therefore the less weight should be applied to it. The judge suggested that the same was true of comparable evidence from before the review date: the longer before the review date the transaction took place then the less accurate it would become as an indication of the level of market rent at the review date itself.

5

Arriving at a rental value

5.1 Introduction

By this stage the valuer will have accepted the rent review instruction from his client and collected sufficient information to allow him to arrive at an estimate of the rental value of the subject property. He will have:

1 gathered the physical evidence needed at the time of his inspection of the property;
2 considered the legal evidence whilst reviewing the lease; and
3 researched the market, evidenced by comparable transactions.

He may have found, for example, that he is valuing a shop in a prime situation. Further, he will know how big it is and what physical disabilities it suffers from. He will also know if the lease has, for example, a restrictive user clause or alienation provision. The valuer will have collected information in relation to each of the comparable properties and have a similar knowledge in respect of those. He will know what type of transaction has taken place in relation to each. He will know the lease terms, including the rental. He will have physical information on the properties and know how big they are.

It is now a question of drawing the various elements together in order to arrive at an estimate of rental value of the subject property. This is done by constructing a hierarchy of evidence and placing the subject property at the correct point within that hierarchy.

The estimate of rental value can then form the foundation for advice to the client on negotiating tactics and the triggering of the rent review.

5.2 Weighing the evidence

Every valuer will have their own method of weighing the evidence. However, the checklist below is suggested as a basic template which works.

Quality of evidence	Is the evidence clearly so good that it must be a main element in the final determination? Is it so bad that it must be rejected out of hand? If somewhere between, is there any secondary evidence which supports the main evidence or which undermines it?
The experts' opinions	Is there sufficient evidence that the arbitrator does not need to attach much weight to the opinions of the experts on either side?
The 'hierarchy'	There is a well-worn hierarchy of the weight to be attached to various types of evidence. These are: • open market lettings (preferably freely negotiated between parties with professional valuation advice); • negotiated lease renewals (preferably freely negotiated between parties with professional valuation advice); • rent reviews (preferably freely negotiated between parties with professional valuation advice); • expert determinations; • arbitrations; • court decisions (e.g. the initial rent payable in the case of a new lease under the *Landlord and Tenant Act* 1954).
Adjustments for difference	• Size. • Location. • Terms of the lease (open user, alienation, service charges, etc.). • Specification (old building unsuitable for modern IT cabling, heating, air conditioning). • Lease.
Scoring	Each piece of evidence can then be scored from good weight to no weight.
Conclusions	The picture which emerges can then be used to arrive at a conclusion.

5.3 Reporting to the client

Clients' requirements in respect of reporting will vary. Some clients will be happy to receive verbal recommendations whilst others will require a full-blown report. The valuer should, however, be mindful of disclosure. If a written report is given then this may at a later date be discoverable under s. 34(2)(d) of the *Arbitration Act* 1996. It may also be discoverable in any litigation under the *Civil Procedure Rules* 1998.

5.4 Formal reports

Plainly, every surveyor should be familiar with the form of an expert report. A checklist is set out below.

Template index for typical expert report in rent review
1 Identity, qualifications and experience of the expert.
2 Summary of the expert's instructions.
3 Summary of relevant lease terms and in particular the hypothetical transaction which the expert has assumed.
4 Details of the locality of the subject property and the comparables. Any particular general market commentary.
5 The subject property.
6 Comparables.
7 Analysis and opinion.
8 Conclusion.
9 Expert declaration.

Appendices:
- the lease;
- any agreed statement of facts;
- maps and plans showing the locality and locations of the subject property and comparables;
- photographs of the subject property and comparables;
- extracts from relevant RICS guidance, e.g. *Code of Measuring Practice*;
- signed statements of the facts of comparable transactions.

Part C

Implementing the review

6

The machinery of rent review

6.1 Forms of rent review covenants and the alternatives

The overwhelming majority of rent review clauses involve a review of the rent on the rent date to a market rent. However, there are many variations and alternatives to this standard model.

Upwards-only rent review

Because institutional landlords have required a certainty of income over long periods, the upwards-only rent review has become nearly universal practice. Upwards-only reviews also have financial advantages to tenants. (See *United Scientific Holdings v Burnley BC*.) In recent years, the government has backed initiatives to reduce the prevalence of upwards-only reviews in commercial leases. The *Code of Practice for Commercial Leases (2007)*[5], endorsed by RICS and the government, provides that where requested, landlords should offer alternatives to upwards-only review. The RICS/Law Society Model Form of lease includes both upwards-only and upwards and downwards forms of review. Despite these attempts to embrace other forms, a 2004 study of 17,000 commercial leases found that 87 per cent were on an upwards-only basis (*Monitoring the 2002 Code of Practice for Commercial Leases: An Interim Report*[6]).

The upwards-only review clause will require that if the open market rent arrived at after the review is less than the passing rent, the passing rent continues to be payable. Various words can be used to achieve this effect:

- A statement that the rent can be increased but not decreased.
- A statement that the rent after review will be 'the greater' or 'the higher' of the passing rent and the reviewed rent.
- A statement that the question to be referred to a third party was 'whether any and if so what increase' there should be in the rent (*Royal Insurance Property Services v Cliffway*).
- Machinery which enables only the landlord to trigger a review of the rent. This is not a true upwards-only review since there is at least the possibility that the rent will be lower after the review, but a properly advised landlord will not of course trigger the review if the market rent is likely to be lower than the passing rent. For this reason, the market rent for the property should be carefully assessed before the landlord serves a trigger notice under such a clause.
- Some other indication in the lease. For example, a late review provision may indicate that the parties intended an upwards-only pattern. If the tenant is required to pay any excess of the revised rent over the passing rent to the landlord without any corresponding obligation on the landlord to repay any excess of the passing rent over the reviewed rent, this suggests an upwards-only pattern (*Brimicam Investments v Blue Circle Heating* and *Great Bear Investments v Solon Co-operative Housing Services*). Similarly, frequent references in the lease to the rent increasing on review without any references to the rent falling suggest an upwards-only review provision (*Standard Life Assurance v Unipath*).

Upwards and downwards rent review

Here the rent may go up or down at review. Although favoured by tenants, it may mean that it will pay a premium to the rent for the benefit of such a review clause. An upwards and downwards review can be achieved in a number of ways:

- By not using any of the words set out above in relation to an upwards-only clause.
- A provision entitling the tenant to propose a new rent. This is not determinative if the clause also expressly provides for an upwards-only pattern.
- An obligation on the landlord to repay any excess of the passing rent over the reviewed rent in the event of late review.

Threshold (or floor) rent review

This is a hybrid between the upwards-only and the upwards and downwards review clause. Here there is a level below which the rent may not fall, typically the initial rent payable under the lease. With such a clause, the rent will not automatically revert to the threshold rent in the event that the landlord fails to trigger a review (*New Zealand Post v ASB Bank*). A provision in the lease that the reviewed rent will not fall below 'the rent hereby reserved' gives rise to an upwards-only review rather than a threshold review (*Secretary of State for the Environment v Associated Newspapers Holdings*).

Indexation

Gearing the rent to an index occurs where rental evidence is very scarce or where the property is unique. The index is typically the Retail Prices Index, although in one case the rent was geared to an index of the rents payable for other properties (*British Railways Board v Mobil Oil Co*). The rent may well be reviewed much more frequently than the typical five-year pattern. The lease will often include express provisions for rebasing or changes in the index. Hybrid versions allow for a review to market rent at intervals.

Stepped rent

This occurs where at the outset of the lease the parties agree a fixed increase in rent at intervals. Rents may also be increased by a fixed percentage at intervals or have a fixed increase at the first review before reverting to a traditional upwards-only rent review thereafter.

Turnover rent

A turnover rent means a rent all or part of which reflects the annual turnover (or sometimes the annual net profit) of the tenant. (Examples of turnover rents are *Debenhams v Sun Alliance & London Assurance Co* and *Berthon Boat Co v Hood Sailmakers*.) They arise in several situations where a straight market rent is considered inappropriate. For example, many shops in the London main rail termini have been let on turnover rents for over a century and shopping malls sometimes adopt a turnover rent for their 'keystone' retail tenants. It is common for the turnover rent to be only an element of the rent or for there to be a threshold element. Turnover rents present valuers with particular difficulties in finding comparables.

Rent as a proportion of rent in headlease

Where there is a headlease, it sometimes occurs that the rent reviews and the rents for both the sublease and headlease are co-ordinated. The rent payable under the sublease may be stated as a proportion of the rent payable under the headlease. The rent review for the sublease is therefore a fairly simple exercise, although difficulties may arise where the headlease is surrendered (*Lorien Textiles (UK) v SI Pension Trustees* and *Millett (R&A) v Leon Allen International Fashions*).

6.2 Setting the review in motion

Traditional forms of rent review provision require the process to be started by one party (usually the landlord) serving a notice on the other party. There has been an increasing trend in recent years towards forms of review which take place automatically without any trigger notice.

Automatic review

Where the clause in the lease simply states that the review will take place on a specified date or on the occurrence of a particular event no notice is required (*Edwin Woodhouse Trustee Co v Sheffield Brick Co*). However, if the lease states that one party may 'require' a rent review, by implication notice must be given before the process begins (*Stylo Shoes v Weatherill Bond Street*).

There is no presumption that the rent review machinery has to be operated at each review date or that the machinery must be capable of being operated by both parties to the lease (*Hemingway Realty v Clothworkers' Co*).

Form of trigger notice

The lease will ordinarily specify what formalities are required to initiate the rent review. If the word 'notice' is used, it is probably implicit that this must be in writing. In any event, most modern leases specifically state that the notice must be in writing or expressly incorporate s. 196(1) of the *Law of Property Act* 1925.

Where the lease does not set out what should be included in the trigger notice, the notice should be in sufficiently clear terms to bring home to the other party that the server is exercising its rights under the lease. It is probably irrelevant whether or not the recipient believes that the document is intended to be a trigger notice. (The various formulations of this test were reviewed by the Court of Appeal in *Lancecrest v Asiwaju*.)

Out of an overabundance of caution, some surveyors and lawyers routinely head rent review notices with the words 'without prejudice' and/or 'subject to contract'. There is no need to attach such labels, and the practice may invalidate the notice. The test is whether in the light of these words, the document is still sufficiently clear to bring home to the recipient that it is intended to exercise the server's rights under the lease. There are several examples where the inclusion of these labels in rent review notices have nullified them.

Without prejudice / subject to contract labels

Shirlcar Properties v Heinitz	Trigger notice	'Subject to contract'	Invalid
Norwich Union Life Assurance Society v Waller	Trigger notice and counter-notice	'Without prejudice' and 'without prejudice subject to contract'	Invalid
British Rail Pension Trustees v Cardshops	Counter-notice	'Subject to contract'	Valid
Royal Life Insurance v Phillips	Trigger notice	'Subject to contract and without prejudice'	Valid
Maurice Investments v Lincoln Insurance Services	Trigger notice	'Subject to contract without prejudice'	Invalid

Contents of trigger notice

If the lease sets out what should be included in the trigger notice, the professional adviser should comply with these requirements. It is not uncommon for surveyors to have standard forms of rent review notices which they use in all cases, but since the requirements of leases vary, this is a risky practice.

The omission of some required matters is not necessarily fatal. These requirements may be treated as not being 'of the essence' of the lease. For example, if the lease requires the notice to inform the tenant of its right to serve a counter-notice and to draw the tenant's attention to the consequences of not serving a counter-notice, it is not essential for the trigger notice to include these matters (*Taylor Woodrow Property v Lonrho Textiles*). However, most requirements of the lease in relation to trigger notices are of the essence and they should be strictly observed. If there is any doubt about whether the contents of the notice comply with the requirements of the lease, the test will be whether the notice, fairly read, does communicate that information (*Norwich Union Life Insurance Society v Sketchley*).

If the lease does not require the notice to give a figure for the new rent, it is unnecessary to do so. However, it is more usual for the lease to require the trigger notice and/or the counter-notice to give a rent figure. The requirements vary. Some leases state that the rent must be 'specified' or require the landlord to state its 'proposed' rent or give an 'opinion' as to the new rent.

If the lease requires the notice to give a rent figure, and the rent figure is omitted, the omission is not usually fatal (*Dean & Chapter of Chichester Cathedral v Lennards*; *Taylor Woodrow Property v Lonrho Textiles*; *Patel v Earlspring Properties* (a counter-notice case)). However, if the language of the lease is sufficiently clear and time is of the essence of the agreement, a requirement for the trigger notice to specify a rent may be held to be mandatory (*Commission for the New Towns v Levy & Co*).

Must the rent stated in the notice be a genuine figure, or may any figure legitimately be included? The general position is that the figure in the notice need not be a genuine pre-estimate of the rent (*Amalgamated Estates v Joystretch Manufacturing*; *Rey v Ordnance Estates*). Indeed, a trigger notice which specified a rent of four times the market rent has been held valid (*Fox & Widley v Guram*). There is a possible exception to this where the lease requires the rent to give the landlord's 'opinion' of the market rent, and a wholly unrealistic figure is stated. It has been held in Canada (*Canadian National Railway Co v Inglis*) that such a notice is wholly fraudulent, but to date there is only one (unreported) first instance decision where this argument has prevailed (*Tudor Evans (Swansea) v Long Acre Securities*).

If there is an error on the face of the notice which is both obvious and which would not mislead a reasonable recipient, this may be saved by the rule in *Mannai Investment Co v Eagle Star Life Assurance Co.*

As with all rent review notices, a note of caution should be sounded about relying too heavily on reported decisions of the courts. Judges have repeatedly stressed that it is hazardous simply to compare one notice with another which has been previously considered in another court case. Each case may well involve subtle differences of fact or differently worded provisions of the lease. This does, however, reinforce the simple message that advisers should carefully check the individual requirements of the lease and follow them before drafting and serving a rent review notice.

Examples of trigger notices in various forms appear in Appendix 1. However, the surveyor should carefully check that the relevant notice complies with the requirements of the lease and adapt the notices accordingly.

6.3 Responding to the review – counter-notices

It is common for a lease to require the tenant to serve a counter-notice if it contests the landlord's proposed rent.

The form of counter-notice will be that specified in the lease, and similar rules apply to those which apply to trigger notices. The valuer must be careful not simply to adopt pro forma counter-notices in every case, but should always check the provisions of the lease to see what is required. This is perhaps more important than in the case of trigger notices, since time will often be of the essence for serving a counter-notice, and failure to use the correct form may result in the tenant paying the rent specified by the landlord.

The general rule is that a counter-notice must be sufficiently clear to bring home to the landlord that the tenant is exercising its right to serve a counter-notice (*Amalgamated Estates v Joystretch Manufacturing*). Where the lease stipulates that the counter-notice must challenge the landlord's proposed rent, a general challenge to the review is sufficient (*Lancecrest v Asiwaju*). Even if the lease requires the counter-notice to specify a proposed rent, the omission of this may not be fatal (*Patel v Earlspring Properties*).

Examples of a counter-notice appear in Appendix 1.

Notice electing for third party determination

A variation on the above is a requirement for the tenant (and sometimes the landlord) to serve notice electing for the rent to be determined by an expert or arbitrator.

In earlier cases, the courts tended to require such notices to comply strictly with any requirements in the lease. For example, a notice which simply disagreed with a proposed rent and called on the other side to negotiate was held insufficient (*Amalgamated Estates v Joystretch Manufacturing*). However, the test is now firmly established to be the same as for counter-notices. The notice must be sufficiently clear to bring home to the other party that an election has been made to go to a third party determination.

An example of a notice electing for third party determination appears in Appendix 1.

6.4   Service of notices

The general rule is a notice is given by causing it to be received by the other party to the lease. This rule is subject to any alternative method provided for in the lease or under statute and in practice almost every rent review notice is served by one of these alternative means.

Express stipulations

As far as express stipulations as to service in a lease are concerned, some are likely to be mandatory. Where a trigger notice was required to be served (a) by a recorded delivery letter (b) addressed to the tenant and (c) at its registered office, only the second and third requirements were held mandatory (*Midland Oak Construction v BBA Group*). If the notice has to be 'left' at an address, it is sufficient if the notice is left at a customer service desk rather than with a manager (*Warborough Investments v Central Midlands Estates*). Equally, a notice is 'received' when it is delivered to an address specified in the lease, even though the tenant and its agent may not be there (*Wilderbrook v Oluwu*).

The position with agents can be hazardous. Where the notice is given by an agent, it should be in the name of the party not the agent. The agent should only sign with the express permission of the party and the notice should state that it is signed by the agent on behalf of the party. Failure to do so may invalidate the notice (*Dun & Bradstreet Software Services (England) v Provident Mutual Life Assurance Association*). Where the notice is to be given to an agent, this should only generally be done if the lease permits it. An adviser should not generally serve a notice on the other party's surveyor, solicitor or any associated company without such authority. The only safe method is to serve the notice at the party's home or registered office. Otherwise a complex legal question may arise as to whether the agent had express implied or ostensible authority to accept service.

Law of Property Act 1925, s. 196

It is common to find an express provision that s. 196 of the *Law of Property Act* 1925 applies to notices served under the lease. Even if s. 196 is not expressly incorporated, it is probable that it applies to rent review notices in any event (*Blunden v Frogmore Investments*).

'196. Regulations respecting notices

(1) Any notice required or authorised to be served or given by this Act shall be in writing.

(2) Any notice required or authorised by this Act to be served on a lessee or mortgagor shall be sufficient, although only addressed to the lessee or mortgagor by that designation, without his name, or generally to the persons interested, without any name, and notwithstanding that any person to be affected by the notice is absent, under disability, unborn, or unascertained.

(3) Any notice required or authorised by this Act to be served shall be sufficiently served if it is left at the last known place of abode or business in the United Kingdom of the lessee, lessor, mortgagee, mortgagor, or other person to be served, or, in case of a notice required or authorised to be served on a lessee or mortgagor, is affixed or left for him on the land or any house or building comprised in the lease or mortgage, or, in case of a mining lease, is left for the lessee at the office or counting-house of the mine.

(4) Any notice required or authorised by this Act to be served shall also be sufficiently served, if it is sent by post in a registered letter addressed to the lessee, lessor, mortgagee, mortgagor, or other person to be served, by name, at the aforesaid place of abode or business, office, or counting-house, and if that letter is not returned through the post office undelivered; and that service shall be deemed to be made at the time at which the registered letter would in the ordinary course be delivered...'

Essentially, s. 196 allows two additional means of service in addition to personal service and any other method of service permitted by the lease.

- Under s. 196(3), the notice may be left at the last known place of abode or business address. If it is 'left' at such an address, it is irrelevant whether the person actually received it; indeed, the court will not intervene even if the recipient can prove it did not receive the notice (*Blunden v Frogmore Investments*). The 'last known' place of abode or business requires the sender to make reasonable enquiries about the recipient's whereabouts. One cannot simply rely on the address in the lease (*Arundel Corporation v Khokher*).
- Under s. 196(4), the notice may be served by recorded delivery. This provision is much used in practice, and it is equally frequently misunderstood. Section 196(4) contains two limbs: a permitted method of service and a deeming provision for the date of service. The operation is illustrated by one case which provides a salutary example for surveyors (*WX Investments v Begg*). The tenant's surveyor sent a counter-notice to the landlord's surveyor, just before expiry of the period permitted by the lease. The latter was away when the counter-notice arrived, and the Royal Mail re-delivered after expiry of the time limit. On appeal, it was held that the counter-notice had been served (it had been 'sent by post' by special delivery and not 'returned'). The counter-notice was deemed to have been served on the date when it would have been delivered had it been sent by ordinary first class post. It was therefore properly served in time.

The Royal Mail has an online tracking system to confirm receipt of special delivery items. Advisers are strongly advised to use this facility.

In addition, s. 196(2) of the *Law of Property Act* 1925 allows notices to be addressed to 'the lessee' without giving a name, although it is obviously better to give the proper name.

Insolvent or dead parties

Insolvent or dead parties also pose problems, often because the adviser is not aware of the difficulty until after an attempt has already been made to effect service.

Dead and insolvent parties: methods of service

Individual /company?	Bankrupt /insolvent?	Serve on
Individual	Bankrupt	Trustee in bankruptcy
Individual	Deceased (with will)	Executors
Individual	Deceased (no will)	Public Trustee
Company	Insolvent (lease not disclaimed under s. 656 of the *Companies Act 1985*)	Liquidator
Company	Insolvent (disclaimed)	Notices cannot be served* (consider applying to vest lease in original tenant if there is one). *If this is a landlord's trigger notice, and the insolvent party is not the original tenant, it may be that the only option for the landlord is to serve on the original tenant who remains liable: *Beegas Nominees v BHP Petroleum*.
Company	Dissolved (lease not disclaimed under s. 654 of the *Companies Act 1985*)	The Crown
Company	Dissolved (disclaimed)	The Crown and the dissolved company (consider seeking court order restoring party to register)

6.5 Deficiencies in the machinery

In some circumstances, the courts are prepared to intervene where it can be said that the machinery of the rent review has broken down. It may do so by supplying missing words in the agreement as a process of construction, by implying terms or by rectifying the lease. The legal principles which apply to each of these remedies differ, but there is a common thread. The court will give effect to the intention of the parties at the time of the lease.

With upwards/downwards reviews one party may frustrate the review process by refusing to co-operate in the joint appointment of a third party valuer. The court may make the appointment itself (*Sudbrook Trading Estate v Eggleton* and *Royal Bank of Scotland v Jennings*). Furthermore, if only the landlord can apply to appoint the valuer, a term will be implied that it must apply to RICS within a reasonable time (*Barclays Bank v Savile Estates*). The process of appointment is treated as mere machinery which has broken down.

However, there are limits. If the step is an essential part of the process, the courts will not intervene. For example, they have consistently refused to require a landlord to trigger an upwards/downwards rent review where the parties have expressly reserved that power to the landlord alone under the terms of the lease (*Hemingway Realty v Clothworkers' Co*).

7

Time limits

7.1 Introduction

All rent review provisions will include stipulations about dates or time limits.

Words	Meaning	Example
'from' or after' X date	X date is excluded and the period starts the next day (*Trow v Ind Coope*)	'Three months after 17 June 2008' means on any date between and including 18 June 2008 and 17 September 2008
Period 'begins' or 'commences' on X date	X date is included and the period starts on that date	'Three months commencing on 17 June 2008' means on any date between and including 17 June 2007 and 16 September 2007
'not later than [a specified period] after' X date	corresponding date rule: means before or on the last date of the period (*Dodds v Walker*)	'Not later than 3 months after 17 June 2008' means on any date before and including 17 September 2008
'within' a specified period	corresponding date rule: means 'before or at expiry' of the period (*Manorlike v Le Vitas Travel Agency*)	'Within three months of 17 June 2008' means on any date between and including 17 June 2008 and 17 September 2008
'clear days'	exclude the first and last day of the period (*East v Pantiles (Plant Hire)*)	'Three clear days after 17 June 2008' means 21 June 2008

'before the expiration of the [Xth] month/year of the term'	at any date before the anniversary (*Supasnaps v Bailey*)	'Before the expiration of the third month of the term' for a lease starting on 17 June 2008 means any date up to and including 16 September 2008
'not less than' a specified period after X date	the act may be done on or after the corresponding date (*EJ Riley Investments v Eurostile Holdings*)	'Not less than 3 months after 17 June 2008' means on or after 17 September 2008
'at any time not earlier than [a specified period] before' X date	at any time during that specified period ending on X date (*London & Manchester Assurance v GA Dunn & Co*)	'At any time not earlier than 3 months before 17 June 2008' means up to and including 17 June 2008

It is common for review dates to be calculated from 'the commencement of the term' or during the Xth year of the term. In such a case, the adviser must take care to ensure that the term commencement date is not confused with the date of the lease. By contrast, if the period in the lease is calculated 'from the date hereof', it runs from the date of the lease (*Bisichi Mining v Bass Holdings*).

The rent review provision may also refer to a 'quarter', which can have a number of meanings. The traditional quarter days are 25 March, 24 June, 29 September and 25 December in each year (although the Crown Estate has special quarter days). It has been held that a 'clear period of two quarters' referred to quarters starting on a quarter day, whereas 'not later than two quarters' before the review date meant six months (*Samuel Properties (Developments) v Hayek* and *East v Pantiles (Plant Hire)*).

7.2 Time of the essence – the general rule

Where the rent review provision includes a procedural time limit, the questions frequently arise whether compliance with that time limit is mandatory and whether any failure to comply with the time limit is fatal. The time limit will be mandatory if, in relation to that particular provision, 'time is of the essence' of the agreement. It should be noted at once that time may be of the essence of some periods prescribed by the lease, but not of others.

The general position was settled by the House of Lords in the leading rent review case of *United Scientific Holdings v Burnley BC*. There is a presumption that time is not of the essence of any time stipulation in a rent review clause and that the time limit is not mandatory. There are very significant exceptions to this presumption, recognised in *USH v Burnley* itself and in numerous subsequent decisions of the courts. However, it should be noted that the presumption is a strong one, and only the clearest evidence can displace the presumption that failure to comply with time limits in a rent review clause is not fatal (*Starmark Enterprises v CPL Distribution*).

7.3 Time of the essence – exceptions to the rule

The recognised exceptions were summarised in *USH v Burnley* and have been developed in subsequent case law.

The rent review provision states that time is of the essence

Leases frequently state that 'time is of the essence' in respect of steps to be taken at rent review. Such a provision will displace the presumption and make time of the essence of that step.

The main difficulty is that conveyancers frequently attempt to make time of the essence of only some periods in the rent review clause but not others. This is typically intended to give an advantage to the landlord by making time of the essence only in relation to the steps to be taken by the tenant. If the drafting does not succeed in achieving this outcome it may not be clear precisely which time stipulations are made of the essence. For example, the apparently clear words 'time is of the essence of this provision' beg the question exactly what provision they apply to. These words have been held to apply to a clause requiring an arbitrator to give his opinion within a specified period but not to an associated clause dealing with the time the parties were to apply to the arbitrator. (See *Shuwa Ashdown House Corporation v Graygrigg Properties* which reviewed (and doubted) these decisions.) Similarly, a general statement that 'as respects all periods of time referred to in this Schedule time shall be deemed to be of the essence of the contact' was held ineffective in relation to specific steps which followed in a proviso (*Wilderbrook v Oluwu*). Moreover, a specific reference to time being of the essence of one clause is a good indication that time is not of the essence of other clauses (*Lancecrest v Asiwaju*).

However, subject to these reservations, an express statement in the lease that time is of the essence is the most certain way of making a period for taking a step in the rent review process mandatory.

The rent review provision uses emphatic language

It is recognised that the draftsman may use sufficient emphatic language without specifically using the words 'time is of the essence'.

Words	Time of the essence?	Case
'shall' (e.g. 'shall give notice before 17 June 2008')	No	USH v Burnley
'in any event' (e.g. 'give notice in any event before 17 June 2008')	No	Touche Ross v Secretary of State of the Environment
'condition precedent' (e.g. 'It shall be a condition precedent to give notice by 17 June 2008')	No	Chelsea BS v R & A Millett (Shops) Ltd
'but not otherwise' (e.g. 'give notice before 17 June 2008 but not otherwise')	Yes	Norwich Union v Sketchley
'but not at any other time' (e.g. 'give notice by 17 June 2008 but not at any other time')	Yes	First Property Growth Partnership v Royal & Sun Alliance Property Services

The rent review provision has contra-indications

Apart from emphatic language, there may be contra-indications in the rent review machinery itself. A complex rent review scheme which gives the landlord several different opportunities to seek rent reviews, each on a different date, may envisage that time is of the essence for each step once the next date has arrived (*Kirkland Properties v GRA Developments*). However, such arguments generally fail.

There are other contra-indications in the lease

Where the landlord serves its trigger notice late, the tenant frequently overlooks an opportunity to argue that it is too late for the landlord to initiate the review. If a lease has a break clause exercisable after the date of a review, it has been held that this makes time of the essence for the review itself. (This was an example given in *USH v Burnley* itself.) The reasoning is that the parties must have intended the tenant to know the rent it would have to pay when deciding whether to exercise the break.

There must, however, be a close relationship between the break clause and the timing of the rent review. If the break coincides with the review, that is ordinarily sufficient (*Al Saloom v Shirley James Travel Services*). However, if the timetable for the review is vague or the review is outside the landlord's control time will not be of the essence for triggering the rent review (*Edwin Woodhouse Trustee Co v Sheffield Brick Co* and *Metrolands Investments v JH Dewhurst*).

Where the lease provides for what will happen in the event of a particular time limit not being complied with

If the lease provides for the consequences of failure to comply with a time limit, this may indicate that time is of the essence for complying with that time limit. What is required is a default clause which adds something to what would have been implied anyway. The clearest example would be a clause which provides that in default of serving a notice in time any late notice will be void and of no effect (*Power Securities (Manchester) v Prudential Assurance*).

This also applies to deeming provisions. Frequently leases provide that if the tenant fails to serve a counter-notice the rent stated in the landlord's trigger notice is treated as the reviewed rent. The position has been firmly settled by the Court of Appeal in the case of *Starmark Enterprises v CPL Distribution*. Time is of the essence for service of a tenant's counter-notice if the lease provides that in default it is deemed to have agreed the rent specified in the landlord's trigger notice. Similarly, where the lease states that if the tenant fails to serve a counter-notice the rent will be 'conclusively fixed' at the figure in the trigger notice, this also makes time of the essence for service of the tenant's counter-notice (*Mammoth Greeting Cards v Agra*).

Although the above cases involve the validity of tenants' counter-notices, the same applies to landlords who are in default. Where the lease states that the trigger notice is 'null and void' if the landlord fails to apply for a third party determination, time is of the essence (*Lewis v Barnett*, also see *Iceland Frozen Foods v Dangoor*).

7.4 Serving a notice making time of the essence

A party may in some circumstances make time of the essence for a time limit by serving a formal notice on the party in default. This concept is familiar to conveyancing lawyers, but it is now firmly established that the remedy also applies to rent review (*Barclays Bank v Savile Estates*).

A notice may be served making time of the essence if the following conditions are met:

1   there is a stipulated time limit for taking some step;
2   only one party may carry out that step; and
3   there is no procedure for the other party to take that step.

It is unlikely that the tenant may make time of the essence in the situation where it most frequently would like to do so, namely where a landlord refuses to serve a trigger notice in an upwards and downwards review. This is because the first condition will not be met. A lease will almost invariably permit the landlord to serve a trigger notice at any time rather than requiring him to serve notice at a specified date (*Power Securities (Manchester) v Prudential Assurance Co*). However, a notice making time of the essence may be served in other circumstances, such as where a landlord has not applied for the third party determination within a stipulated time limit. The notice would require the application to be made within a reasonable period. Three months has been suggested as a reasonable period under the notice (*Lancecrest v Asiwaju*).

7.5 Application to court to extend time for arbitration

The court has no general equitable power to extend time. If time is of the essence for any step in the review process, it may however be possible to apply to the court to extend time for reference to arbitration.

Section 12 of the *Arbitration Act* 1996 provides that where an arbitration agreement states that a claim will be barred or extinguished unless the party begins arbitral proceedings by a specific date the court may by order extend the time for taking that step. The court may do so only if it is satisfied that:

(a)   the circumstances are such as were outside the reasonable contemplation of the parties when they agreed the provision in question, and that it would be just to extend the time; or

(b)   the conduct of one party makes it unjust to hold the other party to the strict terms of the provision in question.

The fact that the rent proposed by the landlord is unrealistically high or that the time limit was overlooked by inadvertence would not be grounds for invoking this provision. (*Fox & Widley v Guram* [1998] 1 EGLR 91)

This power is in addition to the other powers to extend procedural time limits under the 1996 Act.

7.6   Estoppel, waiver and election

It is sometimes contended that it would be inequitable to allow a party to rely on the strict wording of the rent review clause as a result of some act it has done during the course of the review. These arguments involve the three linked concepts of estoppel, waiver and election. Each has various subcategories and has been formulated in different ways. (For a fuller treatment of the law of estoppel, election and waiver, see *Snell's Equity*[7].)

Estoppel. A must have altered its position to its detriment in reliance on B's unambiguous representation. That representation may be express or implied.
Waiver. A must have expressly or impliedly waived a stipulation in the rent review machinery which exists for its benefit alone. What is required is an unambiguous concession with knowledge of all the material circumstances and B must act in reliance on the concession.
Election. Where A was at liberty to adopt either of two mutually exclusive courses of action in relation to B and it elected to adopt one of them and to reject the other and B was influenced by that election to alter its position to its detriment.

In the context of rent review, these arguments rarely succeed, since a rent review is to the mutual benefit of both parties. However, it has been held that a landlord who continues to negotiate after a tenant failed to serve a counter-notice (the time for service of which was of the essence) waived its right to rely on the tenant's default (*Fifield v W & R Jack (New Zealand) Ltd*).

7.7 The review date

The review date is commonly specified in the lease, even where a range of dates are permitted for initiating and determining the review. However, the review date is not necessarily the date when the reviewed rent is valued. Where there is any ambiguity, the valuation is likely to take place on the review date, but not in every case. The lease may provide for the valuation to be by reference to prevailing market values when the determination is carried out. (See e.g. *Webber v Halifax Building Society*.)

7.8 Delayed reviews

It is common for the parties (usually the landlord) to seek a review some time after the review date. Indeed, the opportunity for a retrospective review regularly features in auction sales particulars of commercial properties.

Is it ever too late?

If time is of the essence of initiating a review, it will obviously not be possible to review the rent after the period specified in the lease has expired. In relation to cases where time is not of the essence, the case of *Amherst v James Walker Goldsmith & Silversmith (No. 2)* has now firmly established that mere unreasonable delay (even when coupled with injustice to the other party) will not result in abandonment or loss of the right to review. Although *Amherst* stated that a party might be estopped from initiating the review as a result of an estoppel, it appears that even this possibility is limited. A statement that the landlord believes its right to review has been lost will not be enough to prevent a late review, nor will acceptance of the old rent over a period of time (*Chartered Trust v Maylands Green Estate Co*; *London & Manchester Assurance v GA Dunn & Co*). It has been held in Scotland that a delay in implementing the review during which the passing rent was demanded and accepted waived the landlord's right to review (*Banks v Mecca Bookmakers (Scotland)*; *Waydale v MRM Engineering*). Whether these cases would be followed in England and Wales is at least doubtful.

Part D
Concluding the review

8
Negotiations and settlements

8.1 Introduction

The review having been triggered, the valuer will then be tasked with agreeing the rent with the other side.

After the initial correspondence it is often easiest to start negotiations by way of a meeting with the other side on a 'without prejudice' basis.

8.2 The first meeting

If professional valuers represent both parties then it is usually straightforward to arrange a first meeting. In situations where the tenants are not represented there can often be a reluctance to deal with the matter. In these situations the landlord's valuer is often left with no alternative but to apply for the appointment of a third party to determine the rental value. This usually encourages the tenant to appoint his own valuer.

The venue for the first meeting is not really important. The meeting could take place at the offices of one valuer or at the subject property.

The valuers for each side should go to the meeting with a clear idea of what their objectives are. It is unusual to get the other side to agree to your estimate of rental value at the first meeting. Start by indicating that the meeting is on a without prejudice basis. There are then three principal steps that need to be considered to get to the value and these can form the basis of initial discussions.

1 Compare floor areas. Floor areas are a matter of fact and it should be the case that they can be agreed.

2   Compare your interpretation of the lease with that of the other side.
3   Compare comparable evidence and be prepared to give details of each comparable to your opposite number.

The first meeting: tips and tricks
- Take a calculator and a scale rule.
- Review the floor plans and calculations prior to the meeting.
- Go to the meeting armed with survey drawings (if available), scale plans and two copies of your calculation of the floor areas.
- Remember that silence is a good negotiating tool. Let the other side speak and listen to what they say. You might find that they are prepared to offer something that is, from your perspective, better than what you were going to ask for. So let them speak first.
- Similarly, if possible, let the other side disclose their measurements first. If they are more advantageous than your own you can simply accept them. If you are acting for the tenant then always ask the landlord's agent for his areas first. It is after all for him to prove his case. If you are acting for the landlord then it should be harder to get the tenant's agent to disclose his areas before you have shown him yours.
- There are bound to be small discrepancies between the parties' surveys but the valuer should ask himself whether these actually matter in the overall valuation. If not then do not get too distracted by them. Often valuers will argue over 10 sq. ft of ancillary space, which is in the end valued at £3 per sq. ft. This makes £30 per annum difference to the valuation. At the end of the negotiation the valuers then round the valuation by £250. Was it really worth the joint inspection?
- You are well advised to compromise on the areas that are of little value such as, for example, ancillary space, whilst holding firm on the areas of greater value such as the 'zone A' space. If there are areas of disagreement that make a large difference to the valuation then the only way to proceed may be by way of a joint inspection to identify any errors in measurement that have occurred.
- Go through the review clause in detail before the meeting and understand exactly how the review clause works and which bits affect value. Know your case law on this.
- Summarise the lease prior to attending the first meeting. A well-organised lease summary should identify the salient lease terms and identify the page number and clause number for each covenant. This will allow you quickly to find the appropriate place in the lease. It is surprising how this gives the well-prepared valuer the upper hand in negotiation over the less well-prepared valuer who finds himself desperately flicking through the lease in an attempt to find the relevant section. As we have seen above, there are many clauses that can affect value. Go to the meeting with a clear idea of which clauses you feel impact upon value and have some evidence to support your view. It may be that the other side agrees with your interpretation. If not then you need to be able to argue your case.

- Go to the meeting with a comprehensive schedule of comparable evidence.
- If your opposite number puts forward evidence that you are unaware of then ask him for contact details of the parties involved and check out with those involved what your opposite number has told you. As highlighted above, watch out for the devaluation of incentives as this can make a huge difference to the effective rent.

At the end of the meeting take stock of where you are and confirm what has been agreed and what remains in dispute. Agree to take instructions on these matters from your client.

8.3 Updating the client

After the first meeting check out the information that your opposite number has given to you and update the client on how negotiations are proceeding. The same three areas will need to be addressed.

Floor areas

Have the floor areas been agreed? If they have then are the agreed areas in line with the areas that you reported to the client prior to the review being triggering? If they are not as previously advised then explain why not. Had you made a simple error? If so say so. Was there something more fundamental? Did the tenant's agent, for example, produce a licence for alteration that you had previously been unaware of. If so ask your client for a copy of it and check it out.

New interpretation of lease

Was the interpretation of the lease the same on both sides? If not then explain why not. If you disagree with your opposite number on a particular issue, then consider what impact that is going to have on value. If it is material then it may be worth advising your client to seek a legal opinion on that matter but if there is little or no impact on value, then do not waste time and money on it.

Comparables

There are potentially three areas to consider in relation to comparables.

1 **'New' comparables.** These are comparables that may not have been available when you first reported. New lettings, rent review settlements or lease renewals could have occurred in the period between when you originally reported to the client and the time of the first meeting.

2 **'Unknown' comparables** that warrant further consideration. These are comparables that were simply not known to the valuer prior to the other side raising them.

3 **'Updated' comparables.** These are transactions which you were aware of but the information that had been relied upon subsequently proved to be either incorrect or incomplete. For example, you may not have been aware of substantial incentives on the letting of a key comparable.

Obviously the introduction of any of these three types of information could lead the valuer to change his opinion of value. If your opposite number introduces such evidence then it is critical that you advise your client of this as soon as possible. Ignoring the problem will not make it go away. Advise upon what impact this is likely to have on value and if necessary revise your estimated rental value. There is no point in being unrealistic. This will simply delay the settlement of the rent review and in all likelihood increase the cost of doing so.

The key point is to keep the client up to date. Explain what is happening and take instructions. This will help to manage the client's expectations.

8.4 Can agreement be reached?

Following on from the initial meeting there are likely to be further rounds of negotiations either by way of further meetings, over the telephone, in correspondence or in all likelihood a combination of all. It may be that agreement can be reached after those exchanges in which case after confirming instructions from the client the valuer will need to consider the requirements for documenting the agreed rent which may be set out in the lease.

Always keep an eye on the timetable specified by the lease. Do not leave it until the last moment to serve a counter-notice or to apply to RICS for the appointment of an arbitrator because you hope the matter can be resolved by negotiations.

8.5 Negotiations 'without prejudice' or 'subject to contract'

The parties will frequently wish to conduct negotiations privately without compromising the 'open' position of each side. To achieve this, there is a tendency to refer to mark every piece of correspondence with the other side 'without prejudice' and 'subject to contract'. However, these two formulae are frequently misunderstood, and the marking of documents in this way does not always have the intended effect.

Without prejudice

Genuine 'without prejudice' negotiations (whether written or verbal) are privileged from disclosure in any court or arbitral proceedings. The privilege applies to anything forming part of negotiations intended to settle a dispute.

The marking of a document as being 'without prejudice' indicates that it is intended to be privileged. However, the rule does not apply to communications which have a purpose other than settlement of the dispute (e.g. discussions between surveyors who are trying to agree details of a comparable). Even if correspondence on such issues is marked 'without prejudice' it will not be protected.

Similarly, the **privilege**, where it exists, covers not only the particular letter or conversation itself but also all subsequent parts of the same correspondence on both sides, even those not expressed as being 'without prejudice'. However, the safest course of action is always to mark without prejudice correspondence clearly as such.

Furthermore, the privilege only applies to the particular rent review. Once the deal is done, the negotiations become open, even if the review has not yet been formally documented. For the same reason, what is without prejudice between parties A and B is not protected from disclosure between B and C or C and D. Without prejudice negotiations in comparable transactions are therefore not privileged. A surveyor who had acted for a party on a rent review could therefore be required to divulge what he has said 'without prejudice' if he subsequently acts on a review on a nearby unit involving different parties.

An offer to settle a matter made 'without prejudice' does not in itself prevent a binding agreement arising from it. If an offer to settle a new rent is made 'without prejudice' and this is accepted by the other side, the agreement is binding, subject to the matters set out below. In order to make a non-binding offer, the offer has to be made 'subject to contract'.

Subject to contract

Anything concluded in correspondence or a discussion which is genuinely marked 'subject to contract' or 'subject to lease' is not binding until a formal document is executed by the parties. The mere fact that one document in a series is not marked 'subject to contract' does not make it an unqualified offer if it is clear from reading the correspondence that that is the case (*Henderson Group v Superabbey*).

'Off the record' conversations

Note there is legally no such thing as an 'off the record' conversation. Either something is without prejudice or it is not. Lawyers are under a professional obligation to report to their clients the contents of any 'off the record' conversation, and it is probable that a surveyor is under the same obligation.

In a trial of a *Landlord and Tenant Act* 1954 lease renewal, a dispute emerged during the expert evidence as to the area of the landlord's best comparable. The judge sent the surveyors off in the evening to re-measure. During this exercise, the landlord's surveyor entered part of the comparable property and remarked '**what a sh**hole**'. No prizes for guessing the first question in cross examination the following day about that comparable (this is not a joke, it really happened).

8.6 Offers 'without prejudice save as to costs' ('Calderbank' offers)

A Calderbank offer is an offer made by one party to the other offering to settle the review but reserving the express right to show the offer to the judge or arbitrator at a later stage when the latter is considering costs.

The offer is made (and should be expressly marked) 'without prejudice save as to costs'. The 'without prejudice' element ensures that the recipient cannot show the offer to the court or arbitrator before the tribunal has reached its decision. The 'save as to costs' element permits either party to show the offer to the tribunal during any subsequent argument as to who should bear the costs. This second element is critical: an offer which is simply 'without prejudice' may not be referred to at any stage of the dispute.

The advantage of a Calderbank offer is that if a party makes such an offer, and 'beats' that offer before a tribunal, it will generally be entitled to its costs after the time for accepting the offer has elapsed. It is therefore an incentive to the other party not to reject a fair offer of settlement.

Example of Calderbank offer

The tenant states in 'open' correspondence that rent should be £60,000 p.a. The landlord contends in open correspondence that the rent should be £100,000 p.a. The tenant makes a Calderbank offer at £72,500 p.a. The rent is determined by the arbitrator at £70,000. The tenant has therefore 'beaten' his Calderbank offer. He has a good claim to his costs from the date he made the offer, even though he has failed to succeed on his open position of £60,000 p.a.

Calderbank offers need not be complicated; indeed in the context of rent review, the simpler they are, the better. If the offer is to confer any realistic protection on the offering party, the offer will be pitched at a level more favourable to the other side than the rent for which offering party is openly contending. In the courts, Calderbank offers have largely been replaced by offers under Part 36 of the *Civil Procedure Rules* 1998.

If well advised, each party may make a Calderbank offer. As may happen, neither party may beat their offer, with the award being somewhere between the two offers. In such a case, no order for costs is the usual result.

Any Calderbank offer should be made at as early a stage as possible. This is because the award of costs in favour of a party which has beaten its Calderbank offer ought not to be made in respect of any costs incurred before the date when the offer should have been accepted. By analogy with the position under the *Civil Procedure Rules*, 21 days is likely to be considered to be an appropriate period for an offer to be accepted.

A draft Calderbank letter is included at Appendix 1.

Tips and tricks
- Be careful how keenly a 'without prejudice save as to costs' offer is pitched: the offer could be accepted!
- Ensure that the offer has an expiry date after which it cannot be accepted; otherwise it could be accepted at a late stage when it may have become fairly clear what the result is likely to be.

8.7 Binding agreements

Whether there has been a binding agreement as to the new rent may become an issue. Many rent review clauses provide that the reviewed rent will be such rent as is 'agreed' by the parties in default of which all or part of the review machinery applies. If there is a binding agreement there will be no right to apply for a third party determination.

A mere agreement by surveyors to recommend a rent figure to their clients is not 'binding' agreement (*Esso Petroleum Co v Gibbs Financial Services*). Similarly, if the rent review provision requires the agreement of the 'parties' to the lease, the approval of any surety is needed before the agreement is binding (*Cressey v Jacobs*). All conditions attached by one party to the agreement must be satisfied before it binds the parties. There is no reason why the parties should not agree the new rent orally unless the lease requires otherwise (*J Schruyer & Son v Lexington Securities*).

Provided any agreement about the rent is in accordance with the terms of the lease, it will bind any original tenants or sureties. If the rent is not in accordance with the terms of the lease (e.g. the parties agree a stepped rent) it will not (*Beegas Nominees v BHP Petroleum*).

The surveyor's authority

A surveyor is able to negotiate but he can only reach a binding agreement if he is authorised to do so. The authority may be actual (i.e. the surveyor's retainer authorises him to reach an agreement) or ostensible (i.e. the client has represented to the other side that the agent is authorised to reach an agreement). Generally, a surveyor does not have ostensible authority to conclude an agreement on behalf of its client. Any agreement as to the new rent should therefore preferably be signed by the client, or the surveyor should get express instructions from the client that he is able to agree the new rent on the client's behalf. The surveyor who makes an agreement as agent without the express permission of his client runs a risk. By making the agreement as agent, the surveyor is representing to the other party that he has authority to bind the client. If it later emerges that the surveyor did not have authority to make the agreement, the surveyor may be personally liable to pay damages to the other party for breach of warranty of authority.

8.8 No settlement

If it becomes apparent that agreement is not going to be reached, it may be necessary to refer the matter to a third party for determination. The process for both arbitration and independent expert determination is considered in Chapters 9–11.

Obviously, most rent reviews are concluded without recourse to the courts or third party determination. Many rent review express provide for a period during which the parties are to attempt to reach a negotiated settlement. Typically, the lease provides that the parties 'shall attempt to agree', 'shall use their best endeavours to reach agreement' or 'shall consult' and then states that in default of agreement the matter may be referred to third party determination. These clauses do not impose any obligation to negotiate in good faith or at all and they do not make negotiations a condition precedent to a reference to a third party (*Essoldo v Elcresta*; *Patel v Earlspring Properties*).

If time is made of the essence of the negotiating period this simply means that after expiry of the period the matter can be referred to third party determination without the need to conclude the negotiations (*Kings (Estate Agents) v Anderson*).

9
Reference to third party

9.1 Introduction

Disputes arise under all commercial agreements, but a rent review is more than most an invitation to a dispute. The 'right' rent on review is essentially a matter of opinion and differences in opinion are inevitable. For that reason, rent review clauses in any properly drawn lease will include a provision for the resolution of disputes by a third party.

9.2 Arbitrator or expert?

The principal mechanism for third party determination found in rent review clauses is a reference to arbitration. Less common is a provision for expert determination. The two methods are entirely different. So the first question which must be asked when a dispute arises is, 'what is the dispute resolution procedure?'. That in turn requires examination of the relevant clause in the lease.

An arbitration clause is usually easy to spot. It will almost always refer to 'arbitration' or the appointment of an 'arbitrator'. Frequently it will include a reference to the *Arbitration Act* 1996 or (in older leases) to its predecessor the *Arbitration Acts* 1950 and 1979. Expert determination clauses are more varied in their drafting. Sometimes one sees the formula that the rent is to be determined 'by a surveyor acting as an expert ...', or 'acting as expert not arbitrator'.

Hybrid provisions

The example given below is of a hybrid provision which neatly demonstrates the difference between the two methods of dispute.

A 'hybrid' arbitration clause

'If the amount of the market rent shall not have been agreed between the landlord and the tenant by the relevant date of review, then the same shall at the landlord's option be determined either:

   (i) by the award of an arbitrator to be nominated in the event of the parties failing to agree upon one by the President for the time being of the Royal Institution of Chartered Surveyors on the application of either party the costs of such arbitration to be in the award of the arbitrator whose decision shall be final and binding on the parties hereto and in accordance with the provisions of the *Arbitration Act* 1996 or any statutory modification or re-enactment thereof or

   (ii) by the decision of an independent valuer acting as an expert and not an arbitrator such valuer failing agreement to be nominated by the President for the time being of the Royal Institution of Chartered Surveyors aforesaid on the application of either party the decision of any such valuer to be final and binding on the parties hereto and the fees of such valuer to be in his award.'

Unclear cases

Sometimes it is unclear whether a determination should be by an arbitrator or an expert. In these cases, the clause will be construed according to ordinary legal rules of construction.

Unclear cases: examples

1 The rent is to be 'determined by a chartered surveyor nominated by the President of the RICS ... '. However, there is another clause elsewhere in the lease which uses the word 'arbitrator'. This probably means the rent is to be settled by an expert: *Langham House Developments v Brompton Securities*.

2 The mere fact that the new rent is to be determined by a 'surveyor' is neutral. However, if his decision is to be 'final and binding', this points towards it being an expert: *Fordgate Bingley v Argyll Stores*.

The differences between an expert and an arbitrator

Arbitration
- Governed by *Arbitration Act* 1996
- Adversarial procedure
- Oral hearing where appropriate
- Reasoned award unless agreed otherwise
- Statutory rights of appeal

> **Expert determination**
> - No statutory basis
> - Procedure is a matter for the expert
> - Usually no oral hearing
> - Usually no reasons given for determination
> - Very limited prospects of having the determination set aside by the court

9.3 Failure of dispute resolution machinery

Very occasionally, the usual dispute resolution machinery is omitted from a rent review clause, or the machinery provided is for some reason inoperable. As long as it is clear upon what basis or criteria the rent is to be fixed, the court will not permit that agreement to be frustrated by a breakdown in the machinery for determining the rent (*Sudbrook Trading Estate v Eggleton*).

In the example of the hybrid clause set out above, it is for the landlord alone to choose which method of dispute resolution shall be used, although either party may apply for the appointment of the arbitrator or expert as the case may be. In this situation, the court would probably not permit the landlord to choose between the two methods by a refusing to make an appointment so as to frustrate the tenant's rights.

If extreme circumstances, where there has been a wholesale omission or breakdown of the machinery, the court itself will determine the rent. A judge is quite capable of doing so as he will do with lease renewals under Part II of the *Landlord and Tenant Act* 1954.

10
Arbitration

10.1 Introduction

This chapter gives guidance to surveyors acting for one of the parties in a rent review arbitration.

Arbitrations are subject to the provisions of the *Arbitration Act* 1996, and much of the 'correct' terminology derives form this legislation.

Terminology
The arbitrator is also referred to as 'the tribunal', particularly in the *Arbitration Act* 1996. The term encompasses tribunals made up of a number of arbitrators and/or an umpire (neither of which is common in rent review arbitrations).
In the context of a rent review, the tribunal may become involved when there is a 'dispute' or 'difference' capable of being referred to arbitration (*Arbitration Act* 1996, s. 82(1)).
The body which appoints the arbitrator in default of agreement by the parties (usually RICS) is known as and 'arbitral institution'.

The surveyor will first have to address whether he should act at all, and if so, whether he should act as both expert and advocate.

10.2 Duties when acting as an expert

Obligations to the tribunal

A surveyor or other expert witness owes duties to the tribunal independent of his specific obligations laid down by RICS or another professional body. These duties are summarised in the leading case of *The Ikarian Reefer*.

The *Ikarian Reefer* principles

I Expert evidence should be, and should be seen to be, the independent product of the expert uninfluenced as to the form or content by the exigencies of litigation.

2 An expert witness should provide independent assistance by way of objective unbiased opinion in relation to matters within his expertise. An expert witness in the High Court should never assume the role of an advocate.

3 An expert witness should state the facts or assumption on which his opinion is based. He should not omit to consider material facts which could detract from his concluded opinion.

4 An expert witness should make it clear when a particular question or issue falls outside his expertise.

5 If an expert's opinion is not properly researched because he considers that insufficient data are available, this must be stated with an indication that the opinion is no more than a provisional one. In cases where an expert witness who has prepared a report could not assert that the report contained the truth, the whole truth and nothing but the truth without some qualification that qualification should be stated in the report.

6 If, after exchange of reports, an expert witness changes his view on the material having read the other side's expert report or for any other reason, such change of view should be communicated (though any legal representative) to the other side without delay and when appropriate to the court.

7 Where expert evidence refers to photographs, plans, calculations, analyses, measurements survey reports or other similar documents, these must be provided to the opposite party at the same time as the exchange of reports.

The *Ikarian Reefer* principles have been adopted and adapted by RICS and many other professional bodies.

RICS practice statement and guidance note: Surveyors acting as expert witnesses

RICS provides its members with a mandatory practice statement and a guidance note relating to their conduct when acting as an expert witness. The latest edition of the practice statement is found at Appendix 3. It is a professional duty of any member of RICS to comply with any applicable RICS practice statement. Disciplinary action may follow a breach of the statement. Equally seriously, breaches may be the focus of an attack at the hearing on the credibility of a surveyor acting as an expert witness and/or may be a central allegation in a claim for professional negligence.

The practice statement applies in arbitrations, unless the parties to the arbitration agree it will not, or the arbitrator directs it should not. It is difficult to see why any party would wish not to apply the practice statement; this must to some degree undermine the integrity and hence the value of the expert evidence. The authors have not encountered any arbitration where such a dispensation has been agreed. The practice statement does not apply to a surveyor appointed to determine a matter as an independent expert (unless the parties agree it should) or to a surveyor acting for a party in a mediation.

Strictly speaking, the practice statement *Surveyors acting as expert witnesses* does not apply to the situation where the surveyor acts in the dual role of both expert witness and advocate; the RICS applies the separate practice statement *Surveyors acting as advocates* to this situation (see below). However, parts of the practice statement on expert witnesses are incorporated into the latter as an Appendix, and the surveyor advocate should therefore generally have regard to both practice statements when acting.

Core principles

The principal message of the practice statement is that a surveyor's expert evidence must:

- be, and be seen to be, the independent unbiased product of the surveyor, and fall within his expertise, experience and knowledge;
- state the main facts and assumptions it is based upon;
- not omit material facts that might be relevant to the expert's conclusions; and
- be impartial and uninfluenced by those instructing or paying the surveyor to give the evidence.

Conflicts of interest

In addition to various administrative requirements designed to ensure the existence of proper written records of the terms of the surveyor's retainer and instructions, the practice statement provides that a surveyor must notify his client of any potential or actual conflict of interest. Furthermore, a surveyor aware of an actual or potential conflict of interest who considers the tribunal/court might attach less weight to his evidence must advise the client of that fact.

The practice statement does not bar the usage of contingency/conditional fees as a method of remuneration for expert witnesses. However, it recognises that courts of law will only in exceptional circumstances accept evidence from an expert witness acting under a conditional fee arrangement, and that, even where admitted, the court may well give such evidence little weight. Where the fee arrangement for a surveyor's instructions is intended to be a conditional fee, the surveyor must, prior to accepting instructions to act as an expert witness, advise the prospective client in writing of the risk that the tribunal at hand may view evidence given under a conditional fee arrangement as being tainted by bias, and may attach less weight to it; it may even refuse to admit it at all, or find the whole conditional fee arrangement void. The express consent of the client in writing is required before being able to proceed on such a fee arrangement, and the practice statement also requires the surveyor to make a declaration to the tribunal in respect of conditional fee arrangements.

The provisions of the practice statement do not prevent a surveyor who is engaged as an expert witness from advising his client about the merits or defects in either party's case. It is therefore entirely legitimate for the surveyor to help prepare points for cross-examination by any advocate acting for the surveyor's client. These do not form part of the surveyor's expert evidence.

Independence

Most experts justify their opinion by an analysis of the facts to which they apply their particular experience and expertise. They would consider the opinions they offer are 'independent' at least in the sense that those opinions are not unduly biased in favour of their client to the extent that they cannot be defended. The fact that a conclusion drawn from that expertise is justified would not automatically mean that that conclusion is independent in the sense defined by the practice statement. It is precisely because two conflicting opinions can both be justified that many cases turn on a conflict of opinion between experts.

A useful definition of 'independence'

'Experts should provide opinions which are independent, regardless of the pressures of litigation. In this context, a useful test of "independence" is that the expert would express the same opinion if given the same instructions by an opposing party. Experts should not take it upon themselves to promote the view of the party instructing them or engage in the role of advocates.' (Practice Direction to Part 35 of the *Civil Procedure Rules* 1998 at paragraph 4.3)

10.3 Duties when acting as an advocate

Most routine rent review arbitrations and third party determinations are conducted by a surveyor without the use of a separate professional advocate. By contrast, it is rare for surveyors in more significant rent review arbitrations to undertake their own advocacy. Apart from the size and complexity of a matter, and whether significant legal issues are involved, there are a number of practical matters to be taken into account. The decision whether a surveyor should act as an advocate is often not a simple one.

Should the surveyor act as both expert and advocate? Practical issues

Advantages

- Saving expense
- Avoiding delay
- Surveyor/advocate 'speaks same language' as surveyor/arbitrator

Disadvantages

- Adverse impact on the weight attributed to the expert's evidence
- Surveyor's duty to act independently as expert may hinder surveyor advancing client's 'case' as an advocate
- Communications between surveyor advocate and lay client not subject to legal privilege
- Agreements by an advocate (whether a lawyer or a surveyor) bind client where an agreements between expert witnesses do not bind client
- Possible difficulties with points of law

The surveyor should therefore at an early stage decide whether a separate advocate is required and advise the client accordingly.

If the surveyor concludes that advocacy should be handled by someone else, he may turn to a range of other professionals – for example, a solicitor or solicitor-advocate, another surveyor, or a barrister. Members of RICS are approved under the Bar

Council's Direct Licensed Access Scheme and they may therefore instruct barristers directly without the need for a solicitor. The employment of specialist landlord and tenant barristers for rent arbitration advocacy under the scheme is becoming increasingly common.

RICS practice statement and guidance note: Surveyors acting as advocates

RICS provides its members with a separate mandatory practice statement and a guidance note relating to surveyor-advocates. The latest edition of the practice statement is found at Appendix 3. The practice statement applies to a surveyor acting as an advocate/party representative whether in writing or orally, before any arbitrator or third party expert. The giving of advice or the provision of assistance to an advocate falls outside the practice statement.

The first step to be taken is to ensure that it is appropriate to act both as an expert and an advocate under practice statement.

Surveyors acting as advocates: pre-conditions
- A surveyor who decides to take on both roles must explain the dual roles to the client in writing.
- When acting in both roles the surveyor must clearly distinguish between the two roles at all times, whether orally or in writing.
- No surveyor should ever attempt to advocate the merits of his client's case when preparing for or giving oral or written expert evidence.

Surveyors acting as advocates: general principles
- A surveyor must advance his client's case by all fair and proper means.
- A surveyor must act with independence in the interests of the tribunal's process, assist the tribunal in the maintenance of the integrity of its process and comply with any applicable rules, directions, orders or procedures of the tribunal.
- A surveyor must not conduct himself in a manner which is discreditable, or prejudicial to the integrity of the tribunal's process.
- A surveyor must not allow his integrity or professional standards to be compromised.
- A surveyor must not deceive or mislead the tribunal or any opposing party.

The practice statement deals with conflicts of interest and the decision whether to act in the dual roles of expert and advocate in much the same way as the practice statement *Surveyors acting as expert witnesses*. The principal difference is that a surveyor may continue to act as an advocate when there is an actual conflict of interest – provided that the client has confirmed in writing that the surveyor may continue to act (after having been adequately appraised of the relevant facts).

The remainder of the practice statement includes a number of specific duties and obligations relating to the conduct of proceedings:

Surveyors acting as advocates: specific obligations

- A surveyor must advise his client as to the merits of his case.
- If a surveyor considers it would be in the interests of the client to be represented by a lawyer/other professional advocate he shall immediately advise the client of this.
- A surveyor must not attempt to advocate on matters beyond his professional competence. This *may* include particularly complex points of law, evidence or procedure.
- A surveyor must not prepare a statement of case or similar document unless properly arguable.
- A surveyor must not rehearse or coach a witness, nor encourage a witness to give untruthful or partially truthful evidence.
- A surveyor has a duty to assist the arbitrator.
- A surveyor must not give expert evidence to an arbitrator when acting as an advocate, unless permitted to do so.
- A surveyor must draw the tribunal's attention to all relevant legal decisions and legislative provisions he is aware of, whether supportive of the client's case or not.
- A surveyor must advise the tribunal of any procedural irregularity or error which may occur.

10.4 Arbitration clauses

For there to be a valid reference to arbitration, there must be a valid arbitration agreement. The agreement is generally the arbitration clause in the lease itself – although on occasions the parties may agree to refer to an arbitrator a disputed rent review where there is no arbitration clause in the lease.

Pre-conditions to arbitration

Some leases will include a provision that reference to arbitration cannot be made unless the parties have attempted to agree the rent, often during a fixed period (say two months after service of a trigger notice). In the example of the hybrid clause set out in section 9.2 above, no valid reference to arbitration can be made unless it is the landlord who has opted for arbitration. Such a pre-condition is binding, even if there is no possibility of agreement. The pre-arbitration steps set out in the lease must be followed.

10.5 Commencing an arbitration

An arbitration begins when one party serves on the other party a notice requiring him to appoint an arbitrator or to agree to the appointment of an arbitrator. Under s. 14(4) of the *Arbitration Act* 1996, that notice must be in writing.

Leases will generally provide for the parties to agree a single arbitrator or in default for the appointment of an arbitrator by the President of RICS or another body.

Choosing an arbitrator

A surveyor should first attempt to agree the identity of the arbitrator with the other side. You may suggest a single name or a give a list of a number of names and invite the other side to choose one from the list.

Advantages of agreeing an arbitrator
- A known person with whom the parties will be content
- Less risk of an unsuitable appointment being made
- The agreed arbitrator will have the necessary expertise (this is particularly important if the property is unusual or special)
- Saving of time
- Saving of fee to appointing body

It is tempting to reject all candidates suggested by the other side simply because they have been put forward by the other party. This can be a mistake. Arbitrators value their reputations, and an arbitrator who is in any way partial to one of the appointing parties will quickly lose his reputation. The effect of simply refusing to agree all of the other side's suggestions may be to exclude all the best candidates.

Application to the arbitral institution

Not all leases permit both parties to apply for the appointment of an arbitrator. If the lease provides that only the landlord can apply, then the tenant cannot apply and the tenant cannot force him to (*Hemingway Realty v Clothworkers' Co*).

Most leases provide that in default of agreement the arbitrator will be a surveyor appointed by RICS. The procedure for appointment by other potential appointing bodies, such as the Chartered Institute of Arbitrators, is broadly similar.

Application to the President of RICS is made by submitting the appropriate form accompanied by the appropriate fee. The appropriate form DRS1 together with guidance notes may be downloaded free of charge from the RICS website. A copy is reproduced at Appendix 1. The guidance notes are very helpful and filling out the form is largely self explanatory. It is worth noting that:

- The information given about the lease, the property and the parties is critical to the efficiency of conflict-checking procedures.
- It is crucial that any express requirements about the qualifications of the arbitrator are given **using the precise words used in the lease**. This is because it is no longer the practice to enclose a copy of the lease with the application form. If the express contractual requirements are lengthy, set them out on a separate continuation sheet. Failure to do this may result in RICS appointing an arbitrator who does not meet the requirements of the rent review clause and whose appointment will therefore be invalid.

Conflict checking by arbitrator

Under the RICS procedures, the checking of whether the arbitrator has a conflict is carried out in two stages:

- RICS itself seeks a declaration of potential conflicts of interest from each candidate it is considering appointing;
- if the potential candidate declares a potential conflict which RICS does not consider disqualifies him from acting, RICS will further disclose it to the parties for comment.

Defects in the appointment procedure

Very occasionally, a problem arises in the appointment procedure. One example is where the arbitration clause is defectively drafted. For example, the clause may omit any provision for the appointing body to appoint the arbitrator in default of agreement. If agreement cannot be reached, an application may be made to the court to appoint an arbitrator under s. 18(3) of the *Arbitration Act* 1996. Consequently an agreement to arbitrate a rent review can never be frustrated by inability to appoint an arbitrator. If the court does appoint an arbitrator itself, the *Arbitration Act* sets out the procedure which will be adopted (s. 19). In such a case, it is obviously better to involve a solicitor.

Notification of appointment by arbitral institution

The President of RICS or other appointing body then writes to the parties confirming the appointment of a named arbitrator. In the case of RICS, this letter comes from the Dispute Resolution Service in Coventry. The appointee follows this by writing to the parties directly to confirm his appointment and, most importantly, to set out his fees. An example of a letter of appointment is at Appendix 1.

Communicating with the arbitrator – some 'Dos and Don'ts'
- Always communicate in writing. Never telephone the arbitrator.
- Every letter or fax to the arbitrator **must** be copied to the other side **and** must indicate on its face that it has been copied to the other side.
- The arbitrator similarly will communicate with both sides at the same time.

The arbitrator is addressed as 'Sir' or 'Madam' as the case may be. An arbitrator is a tribunal exercising a quasi judicial function and needs to be treated with respect.

10.6 The arbitrator's fees

It is vitally important to understand that the liability of each party to the arbitrator for his fees is quite separate from any issue which might arise later about whether one side or the other should be directed to pay the arbitrator's fees as a result of losing the case.

Express agreement as to fees

Where an arbitrator is to be appointed by a party or by agreement, the arbitrator will first require an express agreement about his fees. This agreement can provide for the arbitrator to be paid an hourly rate, a daily rate, a fixed fee or a combination of any of these (depending on the stage of the arbitration concerned). A wise arbitrator refuses to accept an appointment without such agreement.

Any party which agrees the arbitrator's fees becomes liable for those fees. If both parties agree, they will be jointly and severally liable to the arbitrator. This means that the arbitrator can sue either party for the whole of his fee, whatever the outcome of the arbitration. Between themselves, the parties will usually be liable in equal shares. Such expressly agreed fees cannot be reduced by the court (*Arbitration Act* 1996, s. 28(5)).

Problems frequently occur where one party is reluctant to go to arbitration or is effectively taking no part in the process. In such a situation, the *Arbitration Act* 1996 contains detailed provisions to prevent the arbitration. If no one agrees the arbitrator's fees, any party may apply to the court for an order as to how the arbitrator's fees should be calculated. Where only one party agrees the arbitrator's fees, the parties are jointly and severally liable to pay a reasonable fee to the arbitrator (*Arbitration Act* 1996, s. 28). The effect of this is that the party which has agreed the fees is liable to the arbitrator for the agreed fees, but the other party is liable for a reasonable proportion of those fees.

10.7 Procedure and directions

The procedure to be adopted in the arbitration by the arbitrator is determined by the arbitrator (subject to the right of the parties to agree their own procedure) (*Arbitration Act* 1996, s. 34(1)). There is no default standard procedure. The parties should therefore attempt to agree the procedure, in the same way that many cases proceed through the courts on the basis of directions agreed between the parties.

Typical directions and a timetable appear in Appendix 1.

In a straightforward rent review, sensible parties should have no difficulty in agreeing a simple set of directions. Even if it is not possible to agree everything, the parties should be able to agree certain matters, leaving only a few disputed items for the arbitrator to determine. Such an approach will assist the arbitrator and limit the amount of time (and therefore fees) incurred by the arbitrator in dealing with procedural matters.

If directions cannot be agreed, they will have to left for the arbitrator to determine in accordance with the broad principles set out in s. 33(1) of the *Arbitration Act* 1996. The arbitrator must act impartially, must give each party a reasonable opportunity to put their case and must adopt suitable procedures which avoid unnecessary delay and expense. The Act itself states that 'the object of arbitration is to obtain the fair resolution of disputes by an impartial tribunal without unnecessary delay or expense'. That principle looms large when the procedure of the arbitration is to be decided.

Preliminary meeting

In more difficult cases, the arbitrator may decide to hold a preliminary meeting at which directions for the conduct of the arbitration can be set.

Advantages of a preliminary meeting
- The parties and the arbitrator can meet (possibly for the first time) face to face, which is an opportunity to build confidence
- The arbitrator may be able to build a better picture of the needs of the case at a meeting
- Questions can be posed and answered
- It can be quicker in terms of time costs to deal with matters at a short meeting than by exchanges of correspondence

Disadvantages of a preliminary meeting
- Possible delay pending all parties and the arbitrator being able to find a mutually convenient time slot
- Potential increased costs if parties need to travel or if the disputed matters are narrow in scope
- In a straightforward rent review, there may not be much the arbitrator can learn from a face to face meeting

---

Hearing or written representations?

The vast majority of rent review arbitrations are dealt with using written representations only and without a hearing. The content of these representations is dealt with at section 5.4 above.

However, the question whether or not there should be a hearing is the most fundamental issue in procedural terms. This is a matter for the arbitrator (*Arbitration Act* 1996, s. 34(2)(h)). The choice can be a difficult one. Ideally, there would be a hearing in every case. However, hearings are expensive. In low value rent review cases, or where the difference between the parties is not great, the amount at stake will simply not justify the expense of an oral procedure. In high value cases, or where the parties are a very long way apart, an oral hearing may well be regarded as essential. Complexity is also a factor. Many rent reviews (even those where significant sums are involved) turn on an evaluation of a small number of comparable transactions, common to each side's expert and the facts of which are not in dispute. In such a case, the arbitrator may be able to reach his decision based on the written reports of the experts and an unaccompanied view of the subject property and the comparables.

Where there is a difference between the factual evidence of witnesses (e.g. whether an alleged comparable transaction really did complete) an oral hearing is almost always essential to enable the facts to be explored in cross-examination. The possibility of side letters or collateral 'sweeteners' may need to be explored in cross-examination.

It is sometimes suggested that where there is a point of law in dispute, there should preferably be an oral hearing as argument can assist the arbitrator to resolve the dispute. This is questionable in the context of rent review. An issue as to the construction of a particular clause in the lease is generally one which the arbitrator can well decide based on written representations and reference to any case law.

Representation of the parties

The arbitrator does not have power to control who represents the parties. There is nothing whatsoever to stop a party representing himself, or from employing an eminent QC and a large legal team to deal with a relatively trivial dispute. The *Arbitration Act* 1996 provides that unless otherwise agreed by the parties, a party to arbitral proceedings may be represented in the proceedings by a lawyer or other person chosen by him (s. 36). Therefore, if one party decides that its expert surveyor will also act as advocate, there is nothing which that party or the arbitrator can do to prevent the other party instructing counsel, if they choose to do so.

Statements of case

A statement of case is what it says it is. This is a written explanation of the position of each party stating what it wants the arbitrator to decide. Whether or not separate statements of case from each side will assist the arbitrator will depend on the nature of the dispute.

In rent review cases, there is usually a big overlap between the matters which would ordinarily appear in a statement of case and what would appear in the expert's opinion evidence about the value of the property. Where the issue is simply about the 'right' rental level, and the parties have set out their position in correspondence, statements of case may therefore be unnecessary. The expert reports will contain all the arbitrator needs. On the other hand, where there are difficult issues of law, statements of case are essential.

Even if there are to be no statements of case, it is essential that the parties set out in correspondence the relief or remedy which they are asking the arbitrator to award. As discussed elsewhere, in many cases this will simply be a declaratory award as to the level of the market rent, but it could include other matters such as the award of interest under s. 49 of the *Arbitration Act* 1996.

Evidence

'Admissibility' of evidence refers to whether comparables or other evidence should be allowed to go before the arbitrator at all. 'Weight' is the significance attached by the arbitrator to the admissible evidence adduced before him. Both these matters are for the arbitrator (*Arbitration Act* 1996, s. 34(2)(f)).

'Hearsay' evidence is evidence given by one of the parties which is not first-hand knowledge. Much (if not most) evidence of comparable transactions is hearsay evidence, because the valuer bases his information on what he has been told by the agent who dealt with the transaction.

Hearsay evidence now generally admissible

Hearsay evidence used to a major problem area in rent review arbitrations. Valuers were technically required to provide direct evidence from someone involved in every comparable transaction about what had happened.

Since the *Civil Evidence Act* 1995, hearsay evidence has generally become admissible in court proceedings, subject to certain safeguards. There is no good reason to apply any different rule in rent review arbitrations.

Unless there is a serious dispute over the facts of a comparable transaction, it is unlikely to be helpful to attempt to exclude or limit hearsay evidence. In many cases, it is simply disproportionate to require each comparable to be proved to a high degree.

A more productive approach is for the directions to permit hearsay evidence on the same basis as it is admitted in court.

Another useful approach is to deal expressly with the method by which evidence of comparable transactions is to be adduced (if not agreed).

> **Typical directions relating to comparable evidence**
> - A requirement that each party provide details of all comparable transactions to the other side at an early stage, in order that the facts can be checked.
> - A direction for the parties' experts to attempt to agree the facts of the comparable transactions and reduce those agreed facts to an agreed statement of facts.
> - A requirement that any comparable evidence involving a transaction of which the expert does not have first-hand knowledge is supported by a statement of the facts of such transaction signed off by the party (or agent) who does have direct personal knowledge of the transaction.

In the rare cases where this kind of procedure still leaves facts in dispute, it may be necessary to cross-examine the party or agent(s) concerned. The powers to summon witnesses in arbitrations are dealt with below.

The means by which one party may force the other to disclose documents is dealt with below.

Documents and disclosure by the other party

'Disclosure' is the process by which each party must reveal documentary evidence to the other party in advance of the arbitrator's determination. Obviously, one party may not have access to all the documents that the other has (e.g. information about alterations to the property or rent concessions made at the start of the lease) and will need access to them before making submissions.

In court proceedings, the *Civil Procedure Rules* 1998 lay down elaborate standardised procedures for general disclosure of certain categories of documents (r. 31.6). However, since there are no standard directions which apply to arbitrations, the parties must ask for a specific direction if they want disclosure of documents. Whether there should be disclosure (and the extent of that disclosure) is matter for the arbitrator (*Arbitration Act* 1996, s. 34). There is no longer any deemed disclosure obligation implied into the arbitration clause.

In many cases, disclosure will be entirely unnecessary. Many experienced arbitrators consider such an order for general disclosure to be too blunt a direction for a rent review. (See e.g. *Handbook of Rent Review*[8], at paragraph 7.6.9.) Even where disclosure is necessary, orders framed in very general terms requiring disclosure of all relevant documents are likely to be disproportionate and contrary to the duty under s. 33 to adopt 'suitable' procedures and to avoid unnecessary delay and expense. The best advice is to work out what categories of document exist, or probably exist, and to ask for them specifically.

If the arbitrator does order disclosure, the extent of what is required will vary from case to case. Standard disclosure in court proceedings requires the parties to provide to the other parties all the documents on which they rely and all documents which adversely affect or support the case of any party.

Some documents need not be disclosed at all. Confidentiality and privilege are dealt with in Chapter 4.

A fundamental issue will always be the relevance of any document to the rent review in question. There is no duty to disclose a document which is irrelevant. For example, if the rent review clause directs the parties to disregard tenant's improvements, the tenant's records of what work was carried out may assume considerable importance, whereas if there is no such disregard, the evidence becomes and outside the scope of disclosure.

Confidentiality may also affect relevance, because confidentiality can be argued to render documents irrelevant on the ground that confidential documents would not be available to the hypothetical tenant in the hypothetical transaction at the review date.

Documents held by third parties

There is no direct power to order an unco-operative third party to give disclosure in an arbitration (*Tajik Aluminium Plant v Hydro Aluminium AS*). However, where there are relevant documents in the hands of a third party, there are indirect powers to obtain these documents by requiring a witness to attend the hearing and produce what he has.

The power to issue a witness summons is exercisable by the court rather than the arbitrator. The power adapts the court's own procedures for securing the attendance of a witness to give oral testimony and produce other documents. The relevant procedure is set out in r. 34.2 of the *Civil Procedure Rules* 1998. Since these procedures may be used in an arbitration with the permission of the tribunal or the agreement of the other parties, you and the other side may simply agree that a witness be summoned. (For an example of the witness summons procedure in action, see *London and Leeds Estates v Paribas (No. 2)*.)

Obviously, it is inconvenient for the parties to have to wait until the arbitration itself to know what documents the witness will produce. However, there is no reason why a preliminary hearing could not be specifically ordered by the arbitrator, to which a third party could be ordered to bring documents. Such 'Khanna' hearings are possible in litigation before the court (*Khanna v Lovell White Durrant*).

The court has power to order the preservation of evidence held by third parties (*Arbitration Act* 1996, s. 44). Although this cannot be used as a short cut to requiring a third party to disclose documents in an arbitration, the third party can be ordered to allow the documents to be inspected and photocopied (*Assimina Maritime Ltd v Pakistan Shipping Corporation*).

Expert evidence

In rent reviews, the main directions will relate to expert evidence. A checklist of matters which will have to be considered is set out below.

Checklist of matters to be considered for expert witness direction
Proof of comparable evidence
Written reports
Form of report (declaration)
Timing of reports
Exchange or sequential?
Without prejudice meeting
Written questions of expert
Supplemental reports/reports in reply
Attendance for cross examination

The form of report is dealt with in Chapter 5. The biggest problem is often the difficulty in avoiding advocacy. Even if the expert also acts as advocate (see below), the expert report itself should not include that advocacy. Classic indications of this difficulty occur where a report:

1 makes statements as to the legal implications of provisions in a lease;
2 purports to answer the overall/ultimate issues in the case rather than being confined to the valuation issues; or
3 addresses the issues in the case only on the basis that the position argued for on behalf the client is correct and fails to address or acknowledge the implications of the other side's arguments being correct.

An expert adopting such a report risks (at the very least) annoying the arbitrator and (more likely) undermining the weight which will be attached to his evidence. These matters can be dealt with by the arbitrator in his statement of case. If there is no statement of case, it is best to avoid any advocacy in the expert report.

Costs capping

'Costs capping' (also referred to as the use of 'pre-emptive costs orders') is presently a fashionable issue in civil litigation.

Unless otherwise agreed the tribunal may direct that the recoverable costs of the arbitration or any part of the arbitral proceedings shall be limited to a specified amount (*Arbitration Act* 1996, s. 65). A costs capping direction may be made at any stage, but this must be done sufficiently in advance of the time when the costs will be incurred for the limit to be taken into account.

Such orders are very difficult to apply in practice. Save in the very weightiest and most complex rent reviews, it is to be doubted whether there is any merit in exploring costs capping. The parties themselves are of course free to agree a limit on recoverable costs (*Arbitration Act* 1996, s. 63(1)).

Access to premises

Under the *Arbitration Act* 1996, the court has a statutory power to require inspection of property (s. 44). This means the tenant must give access to the subject premises and, arguably, that the landlord must give access to any comparables which it controls. There is no power under the Act or any other power to permit the arbitrator to direct that a third party give access to a comparable property for the experts to inspect.

10.8 Points of law

Most legal issues are likely to have been identified by the directions stage. There are essentially two ways of dealing with points of law.

First, and most commonly, the arbitrator will decide the point of law in his award. The losing party may then attempt to appeal to the court on the basis that there has been an error of law (under *Arbitration Act* 1996, s. 69).

The arbitrator may choose to appoint a legal adviser to report to the arbitrator and the parties to help him decide the point of law (*Arbitration Act* 1996, s. 37). If a point of law has arisen, and a party is not content that it be determined by the arbitrator, they may apply to the arbitrator inviting him to appoint such a legal adviser (e.g. a Queen's Counsel experienced in Landlord and Tenant law) to advise as to the point of law. Most arbitrators would agree to such an application if made jointly; an application by one party which is resisted by the other would have to be determined on the merits. The use of legal advisers is comparatively rare in low value rent reviews.

Secondly, it is open to the parties to agree not to refer a point of law to arbitration and instead to seek a decision of the court. This may be done once the rent review has been referred to arbitration (*Arbitration Act* 1996, s. 45(1)). If only one party wishes to refer a point of law to the court, he must obtain the agreement of the arbitrator **and** satisfy the court that the determination of the question by the court is likely to produce substantial savings in costs and that the application was made without delay. This is a test which is deliberately difficult to satisfy.

10.9 Applications to the arbitrator

It is frequently necessary to apply to the arbitrator for an order or direction. Fortunately, in arbitrations such applications can be made relatively informally.

Making an application to the arbitrator
- The application is by letter to the arbitrator, copied to the other side.
- The application letter must clearly identify the relief or directions(s) sought and the grounds for them.
- It is helpful to summarise the grounds in a few lines before embarking on a detailed explanation.
- The letter should state whether the arbitrator is asked to convene a meeting to deal with the application.

A sample letter making an application to an arbitrator appears in Appendix 1.

10.10 Compliance with directions

The parties are required to do all things necessary for the proper and expeditious conduct of the arbitration, which specifically includes complying with any of the arbitrator's directions 'without delay' (*Arbitration Act* 1996, s. 40).

Extensions of time

The arbitrator may fix the time within which any directions are to be complied with and give the parties extensions of time to comply with these limits whether or not the time limit has already expired (*Arbitration Act* 1996, s. 34(3)). The directions will always contain time limits for taking each procedural step.

If it becomes impossible to comply with a step within the time allowed, then it is by far the best tactic to seek an extension of time as soon as possible. The consent of the other side should be sought before referring the matter to the arbitrator. Reasons given for delay before a time limit has expired almost always appear more genuine than an excuse produced for the first time after the event. Making an application for an extension of time also retains the initiative – which is far better than reacting to an application by the other side for a sanction against the defaulting party.

Arbitrator's powers in case of a party's default

Where a time limit is not complied with, arbitrators vary in their approach. Some will be proactive and write to the defaulting party seeking an explanation. Others will take the view that because arbitration is a consensual process which the parties have chosen, it should be left to one of the parties to make an application in respect of the default.

Unless the parties have agreed otherwise, arbitrators have significant powers to impose sanctions under s. 41 of the *Arbitration Act* 1996.

In case of a failure to comply with directions, the usual first step would be for one party to seek a 'peremptory order' (*Arbitration Act* 1996, s. 41(5)). Such an order fixes a further period within which the direction must be complied with. Failure to comply within that further period gives the arbitrator and the court further powers to deal with the default under the Act.

Powers of arbitrator to punish non-compliance with directions under *Arbitration Act* 1996, s. 41(7)(a)
- direct that the party shall not be entitled to rely upon any allegation or material which was the subject matter of the order;
- draw adverse inferences;
- proceed to an award on the basis only of the material properly provided; and
- make an order for costs.

If a party does not comply with directions for expert evidence, the arbitrator may therefore, for example, exclude any expert evidence from that party and proceed on the basis of the other party's expert evidence alone.

The court has (unless excluded by agreement of the parties) concurrent power under s. 42 to order compliance with a peremptory order made by an arbitrator. However, the court may not act unless the applicant has exhausted any available arbitral process. In most instances of default in rent review arbitrations, there will be an appropriate sanction open to the arbitrator under s. 41 and so recourse to the court will not be appropriate.

10.11 Hearings

If a hearing is to be held, an oral hearing is the defining moment of the rent review arbitration process. It is the culmination of the many hours of preparatory work and the point at which each side tests the other's case.

There is a good deal of administrative work involved in setting up an arbitration hearing. The date (even if fixed at an earlier stage) must remain convenient for the parties, their witnesses and the arbitrator. A venue must be found, agreed, booked and paid for. Lunch and refreshments must be laid on. The documents must be collated into convenient agreed form. These matters can usually be dealt with in correspondence between the parties and the arbitrator without the need for formal directions.

Attendance at the hearing

An arbitration is by its nature, confidential. It follows that persons not connected with the matter may not be permitted to attend. Attendees on each side would be expected to be the advocate, the expert and (although not always) a representative of the party. The attendance of extra people, such as trainees, should be expressly cleared in advance with the other side. Where a party is a company or similar, attendance should be limited to a representative(s) who is directly responsible for the matter.

Where third party witnesses are to give evidence, they will be expected to wait outside the hearing room until called to give evidence.

Bundles of documentation

In a straightforward rent review, all the relevant documentation may be contained in the experts' reports and their appendices and it may be convenient to work from the two reports. Often, however, there are other relevant documents, and if so a hearing bundle should be prepared. This should be paginated. Duplication of documents within each bundle should be avoided. There must be copies for the witnesses to use when giving evidence and for the arbitrator as well as the parties themselves.

Arbitration room layout (two-party arbitration)
Number of rooms
Normally, a minimum of three rooms is required: a hearing room (which can double as the arbitrator's room) plus a retiring room for each party. Ideally, there would be a further room available for the arbitrator, as that leaves the hearing room free to allow the parties to access documents left there and/or allows a neutral room for negotiation. Fewer than three rooms means one surveyor may have to take instructions in a corridor.

Layout of the hearing room
The hearing room needs to be large enough to accommodate the parties' team on each side and the arbitrator. Ideally there will be separate tables for the parties and the arbitrator; a 'horseshoe' layout of tables often works well. In smaller rooms the parties can sit on either side of a long table with the arbitrator at the end.
Ideally there is a separate table for witnesses giving evidence; alternatively, the witness could sit at the opposite end of the long table to the arbitrator. Conventionally, the claimant party (the party which commenced the arbitration) sits to the arbitrator's right.

Order of events

The procedure is a matter for the arbitrator, but usually the arbitrator will follow a variation of the sequence adopted in the court.

Typical sequence of hearing
1   Arbitrator's introduction, housekeeping, list of attendees taken.
2   Applicant's opening address. In a straightforward rent review this may be short or dispensed with altogether.
3   Applicant's factual evidence (if any):
   (a)   examination in chief (this may be limited to confirming name and address of the witness, correcting any errors in the witness statement and otherwise confirming that the witness statement is true);
   (b)   cross-examination;
   (c)   re-examination;
   (d)   questions by the arbitrator (if any, and bear in mind the arbitrator may have asked questions during examination in chief or in cross examination);
   (e)   questions by either party arising out of answers given to the arbitrator.
4   Applicant's expert evidence:
   (a)   examination in chief (this may be limited to confirming name and address of the witness, correcting any errors in the expert report and otherwise confirming the expert declaration. If there have not been supplemental reports the expert may be permitted to comment on the other side's expert evidence);
   (b)   cross-examination;
   (c)   re-examination;
   (d)   questions by the arbitrator (if any, and bear in mind the arbitrator may have asked questions during examination in chief or in cross examination);
   (e)   questions by either party arising out of answers given to the arbitrator.

5 Respondent's factual evidence (if any).
6 Respondent's experts evidence.
7 Respondent's closing address.
8 Applicant's closing address.

Variations
Disputed factual evidence may well concern comparable transactions and involve third parties attending, perhaps under witness summons. It may be convenient to deal with all the factual witnesses first, before hearing from the experts. Busy witnesses are frequently 'interposed' out of order to enable them to attend at a specific time and then return to their work. The arbitrator may wish to hear all evidence and submissions on one issue before moving on to another. The arbitration hearing is infinitely adaptable and intentionally flexible.

Dealing with evidence during the hearing

As a general rule, arbitrators prefer not to rule any evidence inadmissible; rather they would admit the evidence which a party wishes to adduce but give it such weight as it deserves – which may be none at all. The reason for this is a sound one: to refuse even to consider a piece of evidence risks causing a sense of injustice to the adducing party and may ground a challenge to the award in due course alleging that the exclusion of the evidence was serious irregularity. Admitting evidence but giving it little weight is a decision with which the court will rarely interfere.

This issue can arise with comparable evidence. One party's expert may seek to rely on the terms of a particular transaction. However, he may be unable to prove the facts other than by second-hand hearsay and/or by relying on evidence in breach of a direction as to how comparable evidence is to be adduced. Although the other side may seek a direction excluding the evidence, the arbitrator may well be better advised to admit the comparable evidence but attach no weight to it when making his award.

Some 'dos' and 'don'ts'

Do

- Observe formality. An arbitration hearing is a serious matter.
- Address the arbitrator as 'Sir' or 'Madam' as the case may be.
- Ensure that the parties, the arbitrator and the witnesses are all working from the same agreed set of documents. There is nothing worse than discovering after 40 minutes that the arbitrator's bundle has different pagination.
- Ensure that there are decent quality refreshments/lunch provided. A hungry arbitrator is a tetchy arbitrator.

Don't

- Discuss the case with any witness while they are in the middle of giving evidence.
- Talk while a witness is being sworn – there must be complete silence during the oath or affirmation.
- Interrupt the arbitrator or (save in extreme circumstances) anyone else.
- Use a 'Blackberry' or other PDA to access emails, etc. during the hearing. You may think it won't be noticed, but it will.

Failure to attend the hearing/make written representations

If a party without sufficient cause fails to attend a hearing (or make written representations in a written arbitration procedure), the arbitration can still continue in the absence of the defaulting party (*Arbitration Act* 1996, s. 41(4)).

10.12 Arbitrator's inspection

The arbitrator will usually wish to inspect the subject property and may wish to carry out an external or internal inspection of some or all of the comparables (subject to gaining access). This is essentially a matter for the arbitrator. (*Arbitration Act* 1996, s. 34(2)(g) is usually taken as being the relevant power.) Whether it is necessary or cost effective to do so will depend on the case, the subject property, the arbitrator's familiarity with the subject property/properties of a similar kind/the locality and so on. If the subject property has unusual features, it may be worthwhile to have an inspection.

Inspections may be accompanied by the representatives of each party or unaccompanied. It is unwise to generalise, but a surveyor-arbitrator may well prefer the freedom of an unaccompanied inspection.

The timing of inspections generally comes down to convenience. There is no 'right' time. The earliest realistic date is after exchange of expert evidence. Subject to that, the inspection could be before, during or after any oral hearing.

As stated above, neither the arbitrator nor the court can require third parties to give access to comparable properties if they will not agree.

10.13 The arbitration award or awards

The arbitration award is the determination of the issues put before the arbitrator. Unless agreed otherwise it will be a reasoned written award, setting out the basis upon which the arbitrator has reached his decision. The only other formal requirements are that the award is signed by the arbitrator (or all of them if there is more than one), that it gives the date and that it states the 'seat' of the award (i.e. the legal jurisdiction where the award is made, which will, in rent review cases, inevitably be England and Wales) (*Arbitration Act* 1996, s. 52).

The remedy

In the vast majority of rent reviews, the arbitrator need only declare the rent at the review date.

The *Arbitration Act* 1996 states that the arbitrator also has a range of other powers to order a party to do something or even to rectify the lease subject to any agreement of the parties to restrict or extend his powers (*Arbitration Act* 1996, s. 52). Of more practical benefit is that if there is any doubt about the date from which the new rent is payable, the arbitrator may make a declaration of that date. If the rent review clause does not specifically require the tenant to pay the additional rent which has accrued since the review date, the arbitrator has power (if asked to exercise it) to order payment of a sum of money (*Arbitration Act* 1996, s. 48(4)).

Interest

Unless excluded by agreement of the parties, the arbitrator has wide powers to award interest (*Arbitration Act* 1996, s. 49).

Unless otherwise agreed by the parties, interest may be simple or compound and may be awarded for periods before the arbitration was commenced and continuing after the award is made. Importantly, the statutory power to award interest is exercisable even where the substantive award is simply to declare what the market rent is as at the review date. The arbitrator therefore has power to award interest in cases where it is the rent review clause which provides for the level of the new rent (as is the case with most upwards-only review clauses) and for payment of any backdated arrears.

There is no authority in the rent review context as to the exercise of the power to award interest. However, the lack of any contractual interest clause in the lease will plainly not disentitle a party to claim interest under the Act (by analogy with the decision in *Lesotho Highlands Development Authority v Impregilo SpA*). However, a tenant will want to contend that it is unjust to award interest on any reviewed rent that a rent review clause backdates to the review date. Future interest, payable if the backdated sums go unpaid for a period after the award is made, is a different matter.

More than one award

It is common practice for there to be more than one award, a practice provided for in the legislation (*Arbitration Act* 1996, s. 47).

It is not unusual for there to be three separate awards. For example, if the arbitrator first decides a preliminary point of law (e.g. whether the trigger notice was served in time), then goes on to determine the rent, and then makes an award dealing with costs, each counts as an 'award' under the Act. This is particularly important when it comes to appeals. Time for appealing runs form the date of each separate award – not the date when the last award is made.

Confusion over terminology – 'interim' and 'final' awards

Under the *Arbitration Act* 1996, s. 47 (unless the parties agree otherwise) the arbitrator may make more than one award at different times on different aspects of the matters to be determined. Each of those awards has the same status and each of them is simply an 'award'.

However, the previous *Arbitration Acts* used different terminology. It was common to describe the award on the rent as an 'interim award' but which left the issue of costs to a 'final award' at a later date. Unfortunately, some arbitrators continue to use these terms.

Do not be misled into thinking that the statutory time limits for challenging a so-called 'interim' award is not running until after the 'final' award is made.

10.14 'Taking up' the award

Under the Act, the arbitrator himself decides on the date of the award. Otherwise, the date of the award is the date when it is signed (*Arbitration Act* 1996, s. 56(1)). The date of the award is important for calculating the time each party has to appeal. The parties themselves will not be present at that time and they are unlikely to know that the award has been made.

Unlike a judgment in court, the result of the arbitration award is not automatically disclosed to the parties. Instead, it must first be formally 'taken up' by one or other of the parties.

Almost invariably the arbitrator will exercise his right to withhold the award until he is paid his fees. The reason for this is obvious. A party will be less inclined to pay the fees once it has the award – particularly if it is the losing party. Once the fees are paid and the award is taken up, the arbitrator is under a duty to notify the parties of the award (*Arbitration Act* 1996, s. 55).

Arbitration Act 1996

'55(1) The parties are free to agree on the requirements as to notification of the award to the parties.

(2) If there is no such agreement, the award shall be notified to the parties by service on them of copies of the award, which shall be done without delay after the award is made.

(3) Nothing in this section affects section 56 (power to withhold award in case of non-payment).

56(1) The tribunal may refuse to deliver an award to the parties except upon full payment of the fees and expenses of the arbitrators.'

The way things work in practice

1 The arbitrator makes the award.
2 The arbitrator writes to both parties informing them the award is ready and that it may be taken up on payment of his fees and expenses in the sum of £X.
3 One or both parties pay the fees and ask for service of the award.
4 The arbitrator sends the award to the parties as soon as the fee payment has cleared.

It should be repeated that the statutory time limits for challenging an award run from the date of the award, not the date it is taken up (*Arbitration Act* 1996, s. 70(3)). Delay in taking up an award therefore eats into the time available for any challenge.

10.15 Disputes as to fees

The amount of room for manoeuvre open to a party which wishes to dispute the fees claimed by the arbitrator will of course depend on the fee arrangements made at the outset (see above). It should be remembered that the party which wishes to take up the award may not be the party which appointed the arbitrator. In case of any dispute with the arbitrator about how much the arbitrator's fees should be, an application may be made to the court (*Arbitration Act* 1996, s. 56(2)).

10.16 Costs and Calderbank letters

The parties' initial obligation to pay the arbitrator's fees and expenses in order to procure the arbitrator's appointment and the taking up of the award are discussed above. However, the separate issue of how much each party must eventually pay towards the arbitrator's costs and the costs and disbursements incurred by the other party is covered by s. 59(1) of the *Arbitration Act* 1996. These costs are collectively known as the 'costs of the arbitration'.

Agreement as to costs

It is possible for the parties to agree how costs should be allocated or apportioned (*Arbitration Act* 1996, s. 61(1)). Such an agreement may be found in the arbitration agreement or it may be agreed later. For example, the parties may agree at the time that the disputed rent is referred to arbitration that there will be no order for costs, regardless of the result. Such an agreement is valid and binding. However, the parties cannot rely on any allocation of costs made in the rent review provisions of the lease itself. Any provision in a rent review clause which states that one side or the other will pay the other party's costs in any event will be void (*Arbitration Act* 1996, s. 60).

> **Costs terminology in awards**
> **'No order for costs'** means each party bears their own costs of the arbitration or a part of it.
> **'X's costs in the arbitration'** is an order which may be made at a preliminary stage. This means that X's costs of the preliminary stage (such as an application for disclosure) will be payable by the other party subject to whatever order is made in the final award.
> **'Costs in the arbitration'** is another order which may be made at a preliminary stage. This means that whoever 'wins' the arbitration will also get their costs of the preliminary stage.
> **'X's costs in any event'** is a further order which may be made at a preliminary stage. This means that X will get his costs of the preliminary stage (such as an application for disclosure) regardless of the eventual outcome of the arbitration.

Interim and interlocutory costs orders

If an application is made and determined during the course of an arbitration (e.g. an application for disclosure), the arbitrator may at the time of determining that application direct how the costs of it are to be dealt with. However, this is not effective actually to award costs: those costs must in due course be dealt with in that part of the arbitrator's award which deals with costs.

> **Terminology: 'interlocutory' and 'interim'**
> **'Interlocutory'** is the traditional term for an order made during the course of proceedings on the way to a final award. In the courts, this term was replaced in the *Civil Procedure Rules* 1998 by the 'Plain English' term 'interim'.
> Some arbitrators do not like to refer to **'interim'** costs awards because the word may suggest the award is only temporary (which it is not). Nevertheless, 'interim' and 'interlocutory' costs awards may now be regarded as interchangeable terms.

The award of costs

Section 61(2) of the *Arbitration Act* 1996 provides a presumption that the losing party pays the winner's costs. The principle is usually truncated into the simple proposition that 'costs follow the event'. The difficulty in rent review cases lies not in the principle, but in determining 'the event' or 'the successful party'. In the vast majority of cases, the arbitrator will find a rent somewhere between the rent suggested by both sides – even if he comes very close to accepting the entirety of one side's arguments. Unless the award is spot on, or very close to, one side's figure, the arbitrator may well conclude that neither party has 'succeeded' and that the just award is no order for costs. The problem can be illustrated by the examples below.

Costs – three examples

Say the tenant contends that the revised rent should be £60,000 p.a. and the landlord seeks £100,000 p.a.

Example 1: If the arbitrator determines either £60,000 or £100,000 there will be clearly successful party and an unsuccessful party.

Example 2: If the figure determined is £80,000, it might be said both parties have succeeded or equally that neither party has succeeded.

Example 3: If the figure determined is £65,000 or £95,000, it might be said both parties have succeeded or equally that neither party has succeeded. Yet it still cannot be said that the party which has done better has been 'successful' since they have only established part of their case.

For this reason, a practice has grown up of making 'without prejudice save as to costs offers', also known as 'Calderbank offers' after the case of *Calderbank v Calderbank* in which the use and effectiveness of such offers was confirmed by the Court of Appeal. These are discussed in Chapter 8.

Issue based offers

'Issue based' costs orders are also open to the arbitrator. Such an award of costs may be appropriate where, although in the end one party has succeeded, along the way that party has lost on one or more identifiable points. An example could be where a party has raised an unsuccessful challenge to jurisdiction, or where a party lost on a preliminary point of law but went on to succeed overall. In such cases, the arbitrator may deal with the costs of such issue separately.

Assessment of costs

If an award is made that one party pays some or all of the other party's costs, a dispute may arise as to how much of bill is actually recoverable against the paying party. For example, the parties frequently argue about whether it was reasonable for the other side to have incurred substantial legal fees where the legal issues were straightforward.

Although the *Arbitration Act* 1996 provides that the parties can agree the recoverable costs of the arbitration, such agreements are rare in rent review cases (s. 63(1)). Once the winning party has calculated his costs, it will often therefore be left to the arbitrator to determine the recoverable costs by an award under s. 63 of the Act.

Such an award is an award in itself, despite the fact that arbitrator will already have issued the final award in the arbitration itself.

Technically, the arbitrator can decline to assess the costs. If he declines the task, the power devolves to the court (*Arbitration Act* 1996, s. 63(4)).

Basis of assessment of costs

When assessing costs, the arbitrator should normally allow a reasonable amount in respect of all costs reasonably incurred. Any doubt about whether costs were reasonably incurred or whether they were reasonable in amount will be resolved in favour of the paying party (*Arbitration Act* 1996, s. 65(5)). This equates to the 'standard basis' of assessment before the courts under the *Civil Procedure Rules* 1998. Typically, a winning party will get back only 80–90 per cent of the costs it has incurred on this basis, since some items of expenditure will not be reasonable. Surveyors will therefore often agree a compromise that this proportion of the winning party's costs should be paid to avoid further recourse to the arbitrator.

However, in an appropriate case, the arbitrator can award costs on the more generous 'indemnity costs' basis. This effectively means that the receiving party gets all its costs back. In proceedings before the court, indemnity costs are only awarded in cases of misconduct. Losing the arbitration, even very heavily (e.g. the other side achieves exactly the rent for which it contended) will not by itself justify an award of costs on an indemnity basis.

11

Correcting and challenging an arbitration award

It is sometimes said by surveyors that they need not know much about how the challenge an award, since any such challenge is likely to be handed over to the client's legal advisers. This would be a mistake. A thorough working knowledge of the appeal and challenge process always helps in negotiating settlements and compromises. Furthermore, the actions of the surveyor may dramatically improve or indeed ruin his client's chance of a successful challenge to an award. This chapter therefore deals with the various means of challenging an award.

11.1 Challenges to jurisdiction

In the context of rent review, jurisdiction issues usually mean whether the lease gives the arbitrator the power to make an award. Other jurisdiction issues are set out below. Section 30(1) of the *Arbitration Act* 1996 provides that the arbitrator himself may rule on his own jurisdiction.

Time to challenge jurisdiction

Under the Act, any party who objects to jurisdiction must raise the objection 'no later than the time he takes the first step in the proceedings to contest the merits of any matter' (*Arbitration Act* 1996, s. 31(1)). In short, if there is a potential objection to the arbitrator's jurisdiction, failure to take the point immediately will mean that the right to take the point is lost. Although technically s. 31(3) allows jurisdiction points to be taken late, any well-advised party must assume that the arbitrator will not allow a late challenge to jurisdiction.

The mere fact that a party participates in appointing an arbitrator does not mean it loses the right to challenge jurisdiction. A party may therefore agree to appoint Mr X or Miss Y as arbitrator while expressly reserving its objection to jurisdiction. Parties to a rent review arbitration can correspond to some degree with the arbitrator on preliminary matters. However, they must be cautious. In many rent reviews there will be no exchange of statements of case. It may therefore be more difficult to identify the 'first step ... to contest the merits'. If a surveyor wishes to contest jurisdiction, the best advice is to write a clear letter of objection to the arbitrator at the earliest possible stage setting out the challenge to jurisdiction and the grounds.

Example

Athletic Union of Constantinople v National Basketball Association
R contended that the arbitrator had no jurisdiction because the arbitration clause was invalid under the Greek law which applied to the disputed contract. C contended that the right to challenge had been lost because, before serving its statement of case, R had written to the arbitrator complaining that the time limit for serving its statement of case was too short. C's contention failed. R's letter to the arbitrator only concerned preliminary matters and not the merits.

There are a number of grounds on which jurisdiction may be challenged.

Invalid arbitration agreement

This issue needs little further explanation. The question of the validity of arbitration agreements (in rent reviews, usually the arbitration clause in the lease) is dealt with below.

Improper constitution of the arbitral tribunal

This ground of objection under s. 30(1)(b) of the Act includes matters such as whether there has been a valid reference to arbitration, whether all the procedural steps required by the arbitration clause to be taken have in fact been taken and whether any time limits have been complied with.

> **Improper constitution of tribunal: examples**
> - An arbitration clause which permits only the landlord to refer a disputed review to arbitration. Any attempt by the tenant to appoint an arbitrator would not be valid.
> - A provision requiring the tenant to serve a counter-notice disputing the rent proposed by the landlord, failing which the rent proposed by the landlord is deemed to be agreed. Failure to serve a valid counter-notice will disentitle any party from referring the rent review to arbitration. This prevents a reference to arbitration by either a tenant who thinks the rent specified in the landlord's trigger notice was too high or a reference by a landlord who considers that the rent he specified in the trigger notice was too low.
> - A clause which provides that a review may be referred to arbitration if the parties have been unable to agree after two months from a trigger notice. An application by either party within the two months would be premature.

Improper appointment of the arbitrator

This is also a matter which falls within s. 30(1)(b). Where the appointment has been made by an appointing body after a valid application to that body, the issue is unlikely to arise. However, issues can arise where the arbitrator has been appointed in some other way, for instance, where one party contends that the arbitrator they proposed was agreed by the other party. If the second party asks for the President of RICS to appoint an arbitrator, a situation can arise where there are 'competing' appointments, one by each side.

Matters outside the arbitration clause

This is essentially a question as to the scope of the arbitration agreement. Since in most rent reviews the rent review clause usually includes a bespoke arbitration clause, this ground of objection is unlikely to be an issue. However, in complex reviews, issues can arise where the tasks necessary to fix the rent are split. For example, a rent review clause might make turnover a relevant factor to be taken into account in assessing the new rent. If the clause specifies that the tenant's turnover is to be certified by an accountant whilst the rent itself is to be referred to arbitration, the arbitrator lacks jurisdiction to assess the turnover.

Ruling on jurisdiction by arbitrator

The consequence of a ruling by an arbitrator that he lacks jurisdiction is that the arbitration is a nullity. Therefore, it usually makes sense for the arbitrator to issue an award as to jurisdiction before proceeding with the case on the merits of the dispute. However, the arbitrator can, if he thinks fit, deal with jurisdiction issues in his substantive award. This course could be appropriate where the jurisdictional point is plainly a bad one but procedural fairness would dictate that the aggrieved party be heard fully on the issue, thus causing delay and wasting money if the issue is dealt with separately.

Reference of jurisdiction issues to the court

Section 32 of the *Arbitration Act* 1996 provides that the court may determine any question as to the substantive jurisdiction of the arbitrator. Applications other than by agreement of the parties have to cross various hurdles set out in s. 32(2)(b) before the court will even hear the application and these hurdles may not be easy to surmount. In particular, the applicant will have to show a 'good reason' why the arbitrator should not deal with the jurisdiction issue himself. In practical terms, an application to the court is unlikely to be cheaper than having the arbitrator deal with the matter, even if the other party threatens to appeal to the court.

11.2 Removal of the arbitrator

Although clients (particularly those who lose) frequently complain about the conduct of arbitrators, it is comparatively rare for the arbitrator to be removed.

An arbitrator may have his authority to act revoked by agreement between the parties (*Arbitration Act* 1996, s. 23(3)). Any party to an arbitration may also apply to the court for the removal of the arbitrator on the grounds specified in s. 24(1) of the *Arbitration Act* 1996.

> **Grounds for removal of arbitrator under s. 24(1) of the *Arbitration Act* 1996**
> - justifiable doubts as to impartiality;
> - arbitrator does not possess qualifications required by lease;
> - arbitrator physically or mentally incapable of conducting the proceedings (or justifiable doubts as to capacity to do so);
> - arbitrator refused or failed properly to conduct proceedings and substantial injustice caused to the applicant; and
> - arbitrator refused or failed to use all reasonable despatch in conducting proceedings or making award and substantial injustice caused to the applicant.

As stated above, such applications rarely succeed. In particular, an allegation of bias or mental incapacity would have to be based on clear evidence. As to lack of qualifications, rent review clauses do sometimes provide that the arbitrator must possess certain qualifications (e.g. that the arbitrator has 'experience in lettings or valuations in X locality'). However, in practice the RICS appointment process avoids most such mistakes.

Apart from the above, an arbitrator has no right to resign without the agreement of the parties.

11.3 Correcting an arbitration award

Section 57 of the *Arbitration Act* 1996 permits the correction of an award. 'Correcting' an award is a narrow concept and it is limited to situations where there has been a clerical or other similar error. It does not include direct challenges to the arbitrator's decisions or reasoning. An example of the sort of error which might legitimately be the subject of a corrective award would be a simple arithmetical error: perhaps the arbitrator determines that the reviewed rent per square metre is £X but mistakenly multiplies that by the wrong Gross Internal Area for the subject property and so awards the wrong figure for the market rent.

The arbitrator may make the correction of his own initiative. However, if one party seeks a correction, the proper procedure is first to bring the error to the attention of the other party and invite them to agree on a joint approach to the arbitrator to correct the award. If that is rebuffed, a formal application to the arbitrator should be made. An application must be made within 28 days of the award unless the parties agree otherwise (*Arbitration Act* 1996, s. 57(4)).

11.4 Challenging an arbitration award

Introduction

Since the *Arbitration Act* 1996, the tendency to treat rent review arbitrations as a 'domestic' matter and a case apart has largely disappeared. One has to keep abreast of developments in arbitration in the wider commercial world – what applies to an international arbitration about oil fields in Kazakhstan may well impact on a rent review arbitration in England and Wales. The trend in the wider world is in favour of restricting the intervention of the courts. This is reflected in the policy underlying the *Arbitration Act* 1996 and there is no doubt that it is now much harder to challenge a rent review award than it used to be before the 1996 Act came into force. Pre-1996 Act cases need to be treated with a good deal of caution.

There are three main avenues for a challenge:
- want of jurisdiction (s. 67);
- serious irregularity causing substantial injustice (s. 68); and
- appeal on a point of law (s. 69).

There are no appeals on the facts simply on the basis that 'the arbitrator got it wrong'.

Common restrictions on the rights to challenge an award

The three avenues for challenge share certain common restrictions are set out in s. 70 of the *Arbitration Act* 1996.

Common features
- need to exhaust any procedure within the arbitration for correction of the award;
- 28-day time limit for any challenge; and
- right to challenge may be lost if the point is not taken at the first opportunity.

Section 70 of the *Arbitration Act* 1996 provides the main 28-day time limit for challenging an award. The 28-day time limit is capable of extension, but parties should assume that no extension will be granted. As stated above, the time limit runs from the date of the award even if a party only saw the award at a later date.

Reckoning of time limits and extensions of time

Any appeal on this basis must be made by way of an arbitration claim form. Provided that this is issued by the court within the 28-day time limit, the challenging party then has to serve the claim form within four months. Time limits are reckoned using the detailed rules laid down by the courts (*Arbitration Act* 1996, s. 80(5)). The court also has power to extend these time limits, but an application for an extension of time to serve an arbitration claim form must be made before the time period expires (*Civil Procedure Rules* 1998, r. 7.6(3)). (A, probably non-exhaustive, list of the relevant principles applicable to an application for an extension of time is set out in *Kalmneft v Glencore International*.) The only proper course to be taken is therefore that a challenge should be mounted as soon as possible, and well before any time limits involved will expire.

Loss of the right to object

Section 73 of the *Arbitration Act* 1996 also provides that if a party to arbitral proceedings takes part, or continues to take part, in the proceedings without making any objection, he will lose the right to object. The key therefore is to object at the earliest possible stage.

Want of jurisdiction

If the arbitrator has made a preliminary award accepting jurisdiction at an early stage, this decision may be may be challenged in the court under s. 67 of the Act. The arbitrator may continue with the rest of the arbitration while preparing to deal with the challenge to jurisdiction. Once again, such an award has to be challenged there and then; the aggrieved party cannot wait and see what the outcome of the arbitration is before mounting a challenge to an earlier award as to jurisdiction.

Serious irregularity

Section 68 of the *Arbitration Act* 1996 provides that a party to arbitral proceedings may challenge an award in the proceedings on the ground of 'serious irregularity affecting the tribunal, the proceedings or the award'. 'Serious irregularity' means something which the court considers has caused or will cause substantial injustice – such as a failure by the tribunal to follow its own procedures or to give each party a fair hearing.

The Act sets out an exhaustive list of irregularities (*Lesotho Highlands Development Authority v Impregilo SpA*). Section 68 is a longstop, for an extreme case only, and in practice such challenges rarely succeed.

Appeals based on non-disclosure

Perhaps surprisingly, the prospect of a successful challenge to an award on the grounds of non-disclosure by the other side of relevant documents is poor. This applies even if the document is important, at any rate if the non-disclosure is innocent (*Profilati Italia SRL v Painewebber International Futures*).

Use of personal knowledge or experience

An issue which can arise in rent reviews is the extent to which the arbitrator can use his personal knowledge or experience when reaching his decision.

It is regular for the arbitrator to use his expert knowledge and experience to assess the parties' cases and weigh the evidence and for him to use his personal expert knowledge and experience to make adjustments, provided that the type or adjustment has been raised by the parties in the evidence. However, it is irregular for the arbitrator to use his personal expert knowledge or experience (in effect) to introduce new evidence or for him to use his personal expert knowledge or experience to introduce new valuation points or adjustments. It is also irregular for him to apply the evidence introduced by the parties in a different way to the way the parties did, unless he first identifies the points to the parties so that they may comment/introduce further evidence of their own. (For a useful discussion of the principles, see *St George's Investment Co v Gemini Consulting Ltd*.)

Use of arbitrator's own knowledge: examples
Checkpoint v Strathclyde Pension Fund. The landlord's valuer relied on a number of comparables. The tenant's valuer relied on a single comparable in an area known as the 'Winnersh Triangle'. The arbitrator relied on his personal knowledge and experience as the basis for accepting the landlord's valuation evidence and rejecting that of the tenant. A s. 68 challenge failed in the High Court, and the award was upheld by the Court of Appeal.
Although the arbitrator had used his special knowledge, there was no serious irregularity. The parties had appointed the arbitrator especially for his expertise of lettings in this area.

Guardcliffe Properties Ltd v City and St James Property Holdings Ltd. The arbitrator decided in his award to adjust the rent downwards to reflect a hypothetical rent-free period and to reflect the tenant's ongoing liabilities. These issues had not been raised by either party. The award was set aside for serious irregularity and remitted to the arbitrator. There was a substantial injustice to the landlord because the landlord's surveyor had been denied the opportunity to comment on the appropriateness of the proposed adjustments to the rent.

Appeals on a point of law

Under s. 69 of the Act, the parties may appeal against the arbitrator's award on a question of law. It cannot be emphasised enough that a 'question of law' means what it says, and that the courts are vigilant to dismiss what are really attacks on the arbitrator's findings of fact or treatment of the evidence, dressed up as points of law.

Issues of construction of the lease will usually be treated as a point of law. (For example, *Bisichi Mining v Bass Holdings Ltd* where the arbitrator had to decide whether a reference in a review clause to 'of the said term' of a lease was calculated from the date of grant of the lease or the date from which the term was expressed to run. He decided on the latter, and his award on that issue was reversed on appeal under s. 69.)

Procedure on an appeal

Challenges to rent review arbitrations are usually made in the Chancery Division of the High Court. They are known as arbitration proceedings rather than 'appeals'. Arbitration proceedings are governed by Part 62 of the *Civil Procedure Rules* 1998.

All challenges to arbitration awards (whether or not they are appeals under s. 69 of the Act) are brought by issuing a claim form in the special prescribed form N8. It is crucial to note that under r. 62.4 of the *Civil Procedure Rules* 1998, the claimant has only one month to serve the arbitration claim on the other side. If the claim form expires, the time limit can only be extended in very limited circumstances.

12
Expert determination

12.1 Introduction

The key points to appreciate are that:

1 how an expert determination is conducted is a matter of the contract between the parties (i.e. the rent review clause);
2 the *Arbitration Act* 1996 does not apply and there is no statutory underpinning for the process; and
3 as long as the expert conducts the determination in accordance with the contract, it is effectively impossible to challenge the result.

12.2 Commencing an expert determination

Initial steps

The initial steps to be taken in an expert determination are largely the process for initiating an arbitration.

One must always follow the requirements of the rent review clause. As with arbitration clauses, any contractual pre-conditions to a reference to expert determination must be observed. In broad terms, section 10.5 above is equally applicable to commencing an expert determination, save that there is no statutory power vested in the court equivalent to s. 18 of the *Arbitration Act* 1996. Where the clause provides that in default of agreement, the expert will be appointed by the President of RICS, the application may be made on a form DRS1 in the same way as for an arbitration: see Appendix 1. The surveyor expert and surveyor advocate in an expert determination must have regard to the relevant RICS practice statements set out above.

Expert's fees

Unless the expert determination clause provides for the expert's fees, those fees are a matter for agreement at the time of the expert's appointment. This may mean that the appointing party has to bear the expert's fees come what may. There is no mechanism for having the expert's fees assessed by the court.

A competent expert will invariably require that his retainer permits him to withhold delivery of his determination until his fee has been paid (or insist that he is paid in advance).

12.3 Conduct of an expert determination

Subject to any requirements laid down by the expert determination clause, the procedure and conduct of the determination is entirely a matter for the expert.

Unless the rent review clause confers specific powers on the expert, the expert has no power to direct disclosure, no power to order inspection of documents or of property, no power to examine witnesses, etc. The panoply or rights and powers set out in the *Arbitration Act* 1996 are simply unavailable.

Experts usually invite the parties to make submissions in writing. Although an expert need not do so, there is little advantage in closing out the parties and relying solely on the expert's own investigations. An expert surveyor will be familiar with formal expert reports and will expect to see evidence in the same form, even though he cannot order it. It is therefore in the parties' own interest that expert evidence follows the form discussed earlier in respect of arbitrations above.

Oral hearings are a rarity.

12.4 Duty of the expert

Even where the parties do make submissions, it remains central to the concept of an expert determination that the expert will make his own investigations and seek out his own evidence. As a result, an expert surveyor will almost inevitably wish to inspect the subject property and (so far as possible) the comparables, and he will generally wish to do so unaccompanied.

It follows that experts may investigate the comparable evidence for themselves, take into account such evidence that they have unearthed, apply valuation methods or adjustments not relied upon by the parties and so forth. Unlike an arbitrator, an expert is acting properly in undertaking such tasks.

12.5 The determination

In a rent review, the determination will often be limited to a bare determination or certification of the rent to be paid from the review date.

Unless the lease makes express provision for the content of the determination, there is no particular form. It is only necessary for the expert to reduce his determination to writing, and in order that the document can be identified as the expert determination, it will have to identify the lease, the property, the parties, the date of reference to the expert and his determination itself. It should be dated and signed by the expert.

Unless the agreement expressly requires it, an expert is not required to give reasons for his determination. Such an unreasoned determination is often referred to as 'non-speaking'. Because the parties will usually not know how the expert arrived at his figure, it follows that there will rarely be any material upon which any challenge to the result could be based.

If reasons are required, the duty to give reasons is not as extensive as would be required in an arbitration award. The reasons can be stated briefly so long they contain an explanation as to the result on key issues and how particularly controversial points have been dealt with (*Halifax Life Ltd v Equitable Life Assurance Society*). In case of failure to provide any or any adequate reasons, the court would direct the expert to state his reasons (similar to the statutory power in arbitrations under s. 70(4) of the *Arbitration Act* 1996) (*Halifax v Equitable Life*).

Costs of an expert determination

Sometimes an expert determination clause confers on the expert a power to award costs, or to order one party or other to bear his fees, or both. In the absence of such a contractual provision the expert has no power to make orders.

12.6 Enforcing an expert determination

Unlike the position in arbitration, there is no procedure for converting an expert determination into a judgment of the court. Usually the rent review clause itself will provide the contractual basis for requiring the other party to honour the determination and default in payment of the reviewed rent is a breach of the lease. If in any case it becomes necessary to attempt to enforce the determination directly, the only way to do so is to commence a claim in court relying on the determination, alleging breach of contract, and seeking a judgment based on that contractual claim.

12.7 Challenging an expert determination

Challenging an expert determination is far more difficult than challenging an arbitration award. (If a challenge to an expert determination is contemplated, the Court of Appeal decision in *Jones v Sherwood Computer Services plc* will be required reading.) A challenge to an expert determination is a common law claim. (The principal grounds for challenge are summarised in *British Shipbuilders v VSEL Consortium plc*.)

Grounds for intervention of the court in expert determination

1 If the expert adopts a role, remit or jurisdiction which does not comply with the rent review provision in the lease. However, the court will generally refuse to intervene until after the determination has been made (because until then the point is purely hypothetical).
2 Where the expert fails to carry out instructions or departs from his instructions in a material respect or goes outside of his remit, the court can declare the determination to be not binding.
3 Where the arbitration agreement provides that a determination is to be binding 'save in cases of manifest error', the court can declare the determination to be not binding on the ground that there is a manifest error.
4 Fraud or collusion.

Role, remit or jurisdiction

The court will probably grant an injunction restraining an expert from acting where he was not appointed in accordance with the agreement. A possible example would be where the agreement provided for the President of RICS to appoint the expert in default of agreement by the parties, and such an appointment was made despite the parties having previously agreed on an expert (one party having changed their mind).

Another example would be where the expert did not possess some qualification required by the lease, for example, that he be a partner in a large firm in London.

Failure to carry out instructions/departing from instructions in a material respect

Departing from instructions in a material respect means that the expert has not done what he was appointed to do, and therefore his determination is not binding (*Jones v Sherwood Computer Services plc*). As long as the expert carried out the appointed task, then the determination is binding even if a mistake was made. This is so even if the mistake was a mistake of law.

It is unnecessary to establish any injustice to set aside a determination where instructions have been departed from, and the determination is not binding even if it can be established that the result would have been the same in any event.

Departure from instructions: *Veba Oil Supply & Trading GmbH v Petrotrade Inc*
(See also *Jones v Jones*)
The contract required the expert to make a determination by applying a prescribed method. The expert adopted a more modern, more accurate method. His determination was held to be not binding because he had departed from his instructions.

Misconstruing the lease

Whether misconstruing the lease is a departure from instructions is a difficult question, and the case law is not entirely consistent.

Misconstruing the lease: examples
In *JT Sydenham v Enichers Elastomers Ltd*, an expert determination of a reviewed rent was declared a nullity on the ground that the expert had misconstrued the user clause.
In *Pontsarn Investments v Kansallis-Osake-Pankki*, an application for such a declaration was refused. It was held that there was a disputed construction of part of the lease, and that it was part of the expert's remit to resolve that dispute. Therefore it was not open to either party to challenge the expert's conclusion, right or wrong.

In rent review cases, the key is to examine what it is that is to be decided by the expert. Where the rent review clause directs that the rent is to be reviewed on express assumptions and disregards, the construction of those assumptions and disregards is a matter which remains within the jurisdiction of the court. If there is evidence to demonstrate that the expert has misconstrued them, his determination may be declared not to be binding. (*National Grid v M25 Group Ltd*, see also *Morgan Sindall v Sawston Farms (Cambs) Ltd* and *Level Properties v Balls Brothers Ltd*.)

Manifest error

This is, in reality, a sub-type of failure to follow instructions and may arise where the expert determination clause provides something along the lines of 'determination by an expert whose certificate shall be final and conclusive save in cases of manifest error ...'.

The true meaning of this sort of provision is that the parties have agreed that the expert must not make a 'manifest error' and that if he does, the determination is not binding. As a result, the courts will intervene if 'manifest error' can be shown. A 'manifest error' means an oversight or a blunder so obvious and obviously capable of affecting the determination as to admit of no difference in opinion (*Veba Oil Supply Trading v Petrotrade Inc*). This will be a difficult test to meet unless the determination is a reasoned one, and most often there will not be reasons.

Fraud or collusion

This ground speaks for itself. It requires a lack of good faith on the part of the expert and would, if proven against a surveyor, signal the end of his career. An error honestly made, no matter how awful, is not within this head. The authors are not aware of any case in the rent review context where an expert determination has been set aside for fraud or collusion.

Non-speaking determinations

The mere fact that the expert fails to give full reasons is not generally a reason for challenging an award by an independent expert. The purpose of a non-speaking determination is to keep the expert's workings 'behind the curtain' and the courts will not encourage any attempt to infer what may be happening behind that curtain (*Morgan Sindall v Sawston Farms*).

Prior application to the court

From the above, it is plain that it is difficult to challenge an expert's determination on the grounds of error of law/misconstruction of the lease. If it becomes apparent that the parties are in dispute as to the meaning of a clause or clauses in the lease, the parties may be well advised to issue proceedings in court. They may seek a declaration as to the true meaning and effect of the disputed provisions before the expert determination procedure is invoked. (The mere fact that the parties have agreed to an expert determination does not stop them applying to the court to construe the lease: *P&O Property Holdings v Norwich Union Life Insurance*.)

Negligence

It is sometimes said that there is a further route of challenge, namely that the expert may be sued for negligence. Arbitrators are immune from suit for negligence, independent experts are not. It is now established that an expert appointed by parties to an agreement to determine an issue owes a duty of care to the appointing parties and that he does not enjoy an arbitrator's immunity from suit. However, even if such a claim succeeds, the determination stands. It is not therefore really a method of challenging the determination.

It is not clear whether the expert's duty of care extends beyond the appointing parties to others who may be affected by the determination, for example, sureties or (in pre-*Landlord and Tenant (Covenants) Act* 1995 leases), original tenants.

Negligence: *Zubaida v Hargreaves*

The relevant principles were conveniently summarised:
1 No immunity from suit.
2 A duty of care is owed to both parties.
3 The court will not substitute its own judgment. The expert is not negligent as long as he has acted in accordance with proper professional practice.
4 If the rent determined is significantly outside the bracket which the evidence suggests is acceptable, that may be evidence of negligence.

The independent expert is treated as being in the same position as a valuer retained by one of the parties to value the property. Provided he does what a reasonably competent surveyor would do in valuing the property, he will not be held negligent. In order to establish negligence, the rent arrived at would have to be shown by the claimant to be a determination which no reasonably competent surveyor could have reached (*Currys Group v Martin*).

If a claim in negligence is upheld, the court will award damages against the expert to compensate the claimant for its loss. The determination itself will stand.

12.8 Procedure for challenging an expert determination

There is no particular part of the *Civil Procedure Rules* 1998 which applies. The usual procedure is to bring proceedings under Part 8 of the *Civil Procedure Rules* 1998 seeking a declaration from the court that the expert determination is not binding. The grounds will elaborated in a supporting witness statement. In the rent review context, such proceedings may be taken in the county court or, in more substantial cases, the Chancery Division of the High Court.

12.9 Intervention during the expert determination

In rare cases, it may be appropriate for the court to intervene during the course of the expert determination process. (See e.g. *Shell UK v Enterprise Oil plc*, where the court intervened to order an expert not to use a particular data processing package when to do so would be a manifest error.)

13

After the review

13.1 Rent pending review

The rent review clause will almost invariably state the date from which the new rent is payable. Generally, the lease provides that the passing rent is payable until the new rent is determined, and that in the event of a late review, the reviewed rent is backdated to the rent review date. If the lease fails to state what rent is payable pending the review, the court is likely to imply that the new rent is payable from the review date (*CH Bailey v Memorial Enterprises*; and *United Scientific Holdings v Burnley BC*) and that the passing rent is payable in the interim (*Weller v Akehurst*).

Some leases provide that in the event of a late initiation, the rent is payable from the date of the trigger notice or even that the landlord has no right to a reviewed rent for the period before the determination.

Another matter normally expressly provided for is payment of a balancing sum in the event the reviewed rent is determined after the review date. If the lease is silent as to when this should be paid, it is likely to be payable on the next quarter day after the determination (*South Tottenham Land Securities v R & A Millett (Shops)*).

13.2 Interest

Most modern leases also provide that if the reviewed rent is determined after the review date, the tenant is to pay interest on the balancing payment. If there is no interest provision, none will be implied. As to the arbitrator's power to award interest, see Chapter 10.

13.3 Enforcing an arbitration award or expert determination

In most cases, the question of enforcement of an award by an arbitrator or expert will not arise. This is because a well-drawn rent review clause will provide for the third party reference to be limited to the narrow issue of the (usually) market rent at the review date on the assumptions and disregards set out in the review clause. The award simply declares what that rent is. In those circumstances, the tenant is required to pay any rent shortfall under the lease rather than the award. In case of non-payment, the landlord sues the tenant for arrears of rent under the lease itself, rather than under the award.

However, in rare cases where the lease is not well drawn and the award is not confined to a declaration, it may be necessary to enforce an arbitration award directly. For example, such an application might concern an award of costs or interest under s. 49 of the *Arbitration Act* 1996.

13.4 Recording the review

Some clients insist that their lawyers should prepare a rent review memorandum in every case and attach it to the lease. However, unless the lease requires it, there is no reason why a memorandum is necessary. In any event, in most cases the valuers can prepare the memorandum. An example of a suitable memorandum is included below.

If the lease specifies a prescribed format, then one should use that prescribed format. Generally there are three possible forms of memorandum.

No provision

The lease may by silent on the need to document the review. In cases where the review has been referred to a third party then the award or determination will stand as evidence of the revised rent. In situations where agreement is reached then the review could be documented by a simple exchange of letters. However, the authors would suggest that it is good practice to draw up a memorandum of rent review and to document what has been agreed formally. This will avoid any dispute at a later date.

Memorandum as evidence

The lease may require a memorandum to be signed by the parties as evidence of the review having taken place. In this case a memorandum should obviously be prepared. If the lease prescribes a particular form, that form should be adopted. If there is no prescribed form then a standard format may be used.

Memorandum required

The lease may require a memorandum to be signed as a prerequisite to the reviewed rent becoming payable. This is rare, but if the lease requires documentation on this basis then the memorandum should be completed as soon as possible.

Appendices

Appendix 1A: Specimen pro forma for confirmation of rental evidence

PRO FORMA FOR CONFIRMATION OF RENTAL EVIDENCE		
Address of property:		
Landlord	Name:	
	Agent:	
	Contact name:	Tel:
	Email:	Branch:
Tenant	Name:	
	Agent:	
	Contact name:	Tel:
	Email:	Branch:
Type of transaction	[Open market letting/rent review/lease renewal]	
	Date:	
	Incentives offered?: [y/n]	Details:
Rent	Current rent:	Effective date:
	Previous rent:	Effective date:
	Next review:	
Lease terms	Date:	
	Lessor:	
	Lessee:	
	Term:	
	From/to:	
	Review pattern:	
	Insurance:	[L/T] [insurance rent]
	Repairs:	

	Decorating:
	Alterations:
	Alienation:
	User:
	Service charge:
	Break clauses:
	VAT payable on rent: [y/n]
	Contracted out of 1954 Act?
	Other terms?
Rent review assumptions (if relevant)	Upwards only: [y/n] Vacant possession: [y/n] Willing parties: [y/n] Hypothetical term: All covenants complied with: [y/n] Fit for immediate use and occupation: [y/n] Other terms as per existing lease save as to rent: [y/n] Other:
Disregards	T occupation: [y/n] T goodwill: [y/n] T improvements: [y/n] Other: Expert or arbitrator: Time of the essence:
Interest provisions:	

Appendix 1A: Specimen pro forma for confirmation of rental evidence

Floor areas / [GIA/NIA] **Analysis**	
	Agreed by both parties? [y/n]
NOTES	
Signed:	
Name:	
Qualifications:	
Firm:	
Agent for landlord/tenant:	
Date:	

Appendix 1B: Specimen trigger notice A

This is an example of a simple notice initiating a rent review where the lease requires the landlord to specify a rent.

The precise form of this notice will depend on the requirements of the rent review provision and the wording of the notice should be adapted accordingly.

Date: [*date*]

Dear Sir,

Re: [address of property]

We act as agents for [*name of landlord*], the reversionary owner of the above premises. I am instructed that you are the tenant under a lease of the above premises dated [*X*] made between [*original landlord*] and [*original tenant*].

In accordance with clause [*X*] of the lease, your landlord GIVES NOTICE to you requiring the rent payable under the lease to be reviewed to the yearly rent of **£[X]** (*SPELL OUT PROPOSED RENT IN CAPITAL LETTERS*) from [*review date*], being a review date provided for in the lease.

Yours faithfully,

[*signed*]

[*agent's name*]

For and on behalf of [*name of landlord*]

156

Appendix 1C: Specimen trigger notice B

This is an example of a simple notice initiating a rent review where the lease requires the landlord to specify a figure which is in its opinion the market rent.

The precise form of this notice will depend on the requirements of the rent review provision and the wording of the notice should be adapted accordingly.

Date: [*date*]

Dear Sir,

Re: [*address of property*]

We act as agents for [*name of landlord*], the reversionary owner of the above premises. I am instructed that you are the tenant under a lease of the above premises dated [*X*] made between [*original landlord*] and [*original tenant*].

In accordance with clause [*X*] of the lease, your landlord GIVES NOTICE to you specifying that the yearly sum of **£[*X*]** (*SPELL OUT PROPOSED RENT IN CAPITAL LETTERS*) is in your landlord's opinion the open market value of the above premises at [*review date*], being a review date provided for in the lease.

Yours faithfully,

[*signed*]

[*agent's name*]

For and on behalf of [*name of landlord*]

Appendix 1D: Specimen counter-notice A

This is an example of a simple tenant's counter-notice responding to a landlord's rent review trigger notice where the lease requires the tenant to specify a rent.

The precise form of this notice will depend on the requirements of the rent review provision and the wording of the notice should be adapted accordingly.

Date: [*date*]

Dear Sir,

Re: [address of property]

We act as agents for [*name of tenant*], the tenant of the above premises. We acknowledge receipt of the notice initiating a rent review dated [*X*].

In accordance with clause [*X*] of the lease, the tenant GIVES NOTICE to you specifying the rent payable under the lease to be reviewed to the yearly rent of **£[X]** ([*SPELL OUT PROPOSED RENT IN CAPITAL LETTERS*]) from [*review date*], being a review date provided for in the lease.

Yours faithfully,

[*signed*]

[*agent's name*]

For and on behalf of [*name of tenant*]

Appendix 1E: Specimen counter-notice B

This is an example of a simple tenant's counter-notice responding to a landlord's rent review trigger notice (which does not require the tenant to specify a rent) electing for third party determination.

The precise form of this notice will depend on the requirements of the rent review provision and the wording of the notice should be adapted accordingly.

Date: [*date*]

Dear Sir,

Re: [*address of property*]

We act as agents for [*name of tenant*], the tenant of the above premises. We acknowledge receipt of the notice initiating a rent review dated [*X*].

In accordance with clause [*X*] of the lease, the tenant GIVES NOTICE to you that it objects to the rent proposed by the landlord and requires the annual rent to be determined by an [*independent expert*] [*arbitrator*].

Yours faithfully,

[*signed*]

[*agent's name*]

For and on behalf of [*name of tenant*]

Appendix 1F: Draft Calderbank offer

This is an example of a simple Calderbank offer to compromise a rent review made by the landlord after the matter has been referred to arbitration.

Date: [*date*]

<u>Without prejudice save as to costs</u>

Dear Sirs,

Re: [*address of property*]

As you are aware, we act for the landlord in the pending rent review arbitration arising from the lease dated [*X*].

On behalf of our clients, we hereby offer to compromise the rent review arbitration on the following terms:

1. The rent payable from the rent review date shall be £[*X*] per annum.

2. Save that each party shall bear one half of the fees and disbursements of the arbitrator and one half the cost of drawing up and signing a rent memorandum to be annexed to the lease, there shall be no order for costs.

3. This offer remains open for acceptance until 4.00 p.m. on [*date*].

Yours faithfully,

[*signed*]

[*agent's name*]

For and on behalf of [*name of landlord*]

Appendix 1G: Request for Arbitration – Expert Determination

RICS Form DRS1 and guidance notes*

*See
www.rics.org/Services/Disputeresolution/EnglandandWales/
drs_application_forms.htm

REQUEST FOR ARBITRATION – EXPERT DETERMINATION

Please refer to explanatory notes (EN1) for assistance on how to complete this form.

PROPERTY

Address	
Town/City	
Post Code	
Description	
User Category	

LEASE

Date of lease	
Alleged date of review	
Amount of passing rent	£
Arbitrator or Independent Expert	
Special requirements (if any)	

PARTIES

Landlord	
Company Name	
Address	
Town/City	
Post Code	
Original landlord	
Parent or subsidiary Co.	

Tenant	
Company Name	
Address	
Town/City	
Post Code	
Original tenant	
Parent or subsidiary Co.	

Landlord representative	
Name	
Company	
Address	
Town/City	
Post Code	
Telephone	
Fax	
Email	

Tenant representative	
Name	

Company	
Address	
Town/City	
Post Code	
Telephone	
Fax	
Email	

Application submitted by		
Name		
Company		
Acting for	Landlord / Tenant	(Delete as appropriate)
Dated		

FEES

I enclose cheque for £320 payable to RICS

Or:

Debit my account No. ☐☐☐☐☐☐

Please return the completed form by email, fax or post to:

RICS Dispute Resolution Services   **T +44 (0) 020 7334 3806**
Surveyor Court, Westwood Way   **F +44 (0) 020 7334 3802**
COVENTRY, CV4 8JE   **E drs@rics.org**

Appendix 1H: Specimen letter of appointment by arbitrator

Date: [*date*]

Dear Sirs,

Re: [*address of property*]

Arbitration Act **1996**

You will have been notified by the President of RICS that on [*date*] I was appointed as arbitrator in the above rent review.

I have not been provided with a copy of the lease. I direct that the parties should by 4.00 p.m. on [*date*]:

(a) agree the terms of the lease which applies to the arbitration and to provide me with a copy;

(b) advise me of the state of negotiations between the parties (if any). Please note your obligations under s. 40 of the *Arbitration Act* 1996 in this regard;

(c) advise me of the rental sums in dispute.

If I do not hear from before the above date, or one of you writes to me asking me to proceed earlier, I will after that date proceed to issue a notice for a preliminary meeting and directions.

You may, of course, agree procedures, but if you have already agreed any procedures, please let me know as soon as possible.

All communications with me should be copied to the other party and I would be grateful if you could ensure that no copies of privileged 'without prejudice' material are sent to me. I do not intend to take any telephone calls from the representatives of the parties or the parties themselves unless this is agreed by both sides in advance and I have given the appropriate formal direction.

My fees for dealing with the review will be charged at the rate of £[X] per hour plus VAT and any disbursements. This will cover the award itself, any further award and any post-award matters.

If the matter settles before the award:
(a)   Please inform me as soon as possible, giving details of the agreed sum and any agreement as to costs (including my fees and any fees due to RICS).
(b)   My fees will be due from date of my appointment.

Please note that the matter cannot be closed until my final award (including any further award as to costs or any agreement by the parties as to costs).

I look forward to hearing from you by the date specified above.

Yours faithfully,

[*signed*]

Appendix 1I: Sample directions for arbitration

Manual for Rent Review Arbitrators, Appendix 8

The following text is reproduced from the *Manual for Rent Review Arbitrators*[9].

Possible directions – **These Directions should not be considered as appropriate for every arbitration reference.**

DIRECTIONS NO:

In respect of

(ADDRESS)

IN THE MATTER OF THE ARBITRATION ACT 1996 AND IN THE MATTER OF AN ARBITRATION BETWEEN

Landlord/Tenant – Claimant and Landlord/Tenant – Respondent

FACTS:

By lease dated (...) the above premises were demised by the (...) to the (...). Under the terms of the lease, the rent fell to be reviewed on (...).

The parties having failed to agree the revised rental value, I was by letter dated (...) appointed by the President of the RICS to act as Arbitrator.

A preliminary meeting was held at (...) on (...) as a result of which, by agreement, I now make the following directions:

DIRECTIONS

1.   The landlord is to be the Claimant/Respondent and the tenant is to be the Respondent/Claimant. The Claimant is to be represented by (...) of (...). (See the comment in Chapter 6, 6.5.1. It may be more practical to defer the allocation of the roles of Claimant and Respondent.)

2.   The parties have confirmed to me that there are no other matters dealing with procedure or evidence agreed between them which are not recorded in the arbitration agreement or in these directions.

3.   I understand that no point of law affecting this rent review has been identified at this point. If subsequently the position changes in respect of a legal point or upon any other matter I will discuss with the parties the best procedure for settling the dispute.

4.   The reference is to be by way of written representations from the respective surveyors. The procedure will comprise a statement of agreed facts including agreed comparable transactions, written representations and written replies.

5.   The programme is to be as follows, adopting in each case the close of business at 5pm on the appropriate date.

Action	Date
(i) statement of agreed facts in relation to the subject premises	
(ii) schedule of agreed comparable transactions including agreed proformas	
(iii) initial representations	
(iv) replies	

6.   The Statement of Agreed Facts is to be a single document or bundle signed by both parties and is to include:

   (a) An agreed copy of the lease and of the lease plan(s) coloured in accordance with the lease.

   (b) A schedule of tenant's improvements and alterations to the property and an indication whether any such improvements or alterations are to be taken into account or disregarded in assessing the open market rental value.

   (c) Copy licences and other documents as appropriate.

   (d) A description of the demised premises.

   (e) An agreed statement of the hypothetical transaction.

   (f) The agreed floor areas (including agreed dimensions of a typical floor) measured in accordance with the

RICS *Code of Measuring Practice* and identifying any areas in respect of which there are differences of opinion.

    (g) Floor plans as available.

    (h) Rating assessment.

    (i) Service charge if any for the last three years.

    (j) VAT status of the building.

    (k) A note of any matters of fact upon which the parties are unable to agree and if possible the reasons for the disagreement.

7.   Evidence supplied in respect of comparable transactions will include the following so far as is practical:

    (a) Description of the property including floor areas (measured in accordance with the RICS *Code of Measuring Practice*).

    (b) Type of transaction (for example, open market letting, rent review, third party determination, etc.).

    (c) The terms of the transaction including in the case of an open market letting a note of the date when solicitors were instructed together with date of exchange of contracts and of possession and in the case of rent reviews or third party determination, a copy of the rent review clause or if not possible a note of the main assumptions.

    (d) VAT status of the building.

    (e) Any other matters which are considered likely to affect the open market rental value or the rent payable for the property, including details of rent free periods, capital payments, etc.

8.   As required under the RICS Practice Statement for surveyors acting as expert witnesses, the parties will make every effort to agree the facts of the comparable transactions and to produce as part of the statement of agreed facts agreed proformas in relation to each comparable transaction on which either party seeks to rely. If it is not possible to agree all the relevant facts relating to each comparable transaction, the parties should advise me as soon as possible whereupon I will consider what further action should be taken.

9.   Arbitrator's awards and the determinations of independent experts shall [not] be admissible as evidence in this arbitration but I will decide what weight to give them.

10.   Unless otherwise agreed by the parties, privileged material will not be accepted, whether or not marked 'without prejudice'.

11. Replies are to be confined to matters of rebuttal only. If either party comes into possession of fresh evidence during the course of the reference application for leave to present that evidence may be made to me and I shall give such directions or make such orders as I think fit in all the circumstances.

12. Two copies of the representations and replies are to be exchanged privately between the parties on the dates set out above in paragraph 5 with each party forwarding the spare copy to me by close of business on the third working day thereafter. The interval is to allow any objections as to privileged or otherwise inadmissible material to be brought.

13. All paragraphs of the Statement of Agreed Facts, representations and replies shall be numbered. This requirement is required to assist both me and the parties in connection with the parties' counter representations.

14. Each representation and reply is to comply with the RICS Practice Statement for surveyors acting as expert witnesses (second edition) and is to include a declaration in accordance with paragraphs 3.1 (a) and 5.3 (c) of the Practice Statement.

15. I may direct questions to either or both parties on their representations or replies or on any other matter which I consider relevant. The other party will be informed of any such questions and the replies thereto.

16. I may wish to appoint experts or legal advisors or to take the advice of leading counsel and would give the parties notice accordingly. Any opinions, reports, or advice obtained will be made available to the parties and in that connection I shall give directions as to the time by which any representations or counter representation shall be made. The costs involved in obtaining the opinions, reports, or advice shall form part of my costs and will be incorporated in my final award. Prior to taking any such advice, I will inform the parties of the identity of the advisors and of the estimated costs and will be willing to receive any representations.

17. I shall reserve the right to call for a hearing if in my discretion the circumstances justify it or either party request it. All the costs incurred will form part of the cost of the award.

18. All correspondence with me is to be copied simultaneously to the other party by the same means and all letters are to be marked accordingly.

19. In due course I shall require the parties to make arrangements for me to inspect the subject premises and also the properties cited as comparables.

20. Following my consideration of the matter I shall notify the parties that my reasoned interim award is available. My Award will deal with the question of costs unless either party requests beforehand that I should defer an Award on Costs pending further representations. If such a request is made, I will issue a partial Award final on all issues of principle and valuation, and will reserve the question of costs to a later date.

21. My fees are to be agreed by way of separate correspondence. The award will be issued on receipt of my fees in full.

22. I reserve the right to issue further directions as may appear to me to be necessary and desirable with liberty to the parties to apply.

23. The parties agree that on completion of the reference I may report to the RICS any breach of the RICS Practice Statement for surveyors acting as Expert Witnesses.

[Name]

ARBITRATOR

[Plus Date]

Appendix 1J: Specimen application to arbitrator

Date: [*date*]

Dear Sir,

Re: [*address of property*]

I continue to act on behalf of the applicant in this matter.

I refer to paragraph [*X*] of the Directions made on [*date*] which required the parties to exchange and file their representations by no later than [*date*]. The applicant seeks a short extension of the time for exchanging and filing the tenant's representations.

The reason for the application is that there appears to be a question about the letting terms of a comparable open market letting at [*address*]. I attach pro formas completed by the respective agents who represented the parties to that letting. This shows a discrepancy over whether a two-year rent free period was granted in relation to that letting, a matter which would substantially affect the annual letting value of the comparable. The agents were originally unable to locate their files in respect of that transaction. However, I have now been assured by Messrs [*agent*], the landlord's agent in that letting, that their file has been requested from storage and that a copy of the lease and other information will then be available to resolve the apparent dispute. I attach a copy of letter from Messrs [*agent*] dated [*date*] to this effect.

In the circumstances, I seek an extension of 14 days to [*date*] for exchange and filing of my representations. The evidence may well be of great significance, and no prejudice will be caused to either party by a short delay. Please note that the applicant has complied in all respects with the directions given so far.

On [*date*] I wrote to the respondent requesting an agreed extension, but I have as yet had no reply. Again, I attach a copy of that letter.

As directed, I have copied this application to the respondent's representative.

Yours faithfully,

[*signed*]

[*agent's name*]

For and on behalf of [*name of tenant*]

Appendix 1K: Specimen rent review memorandum

Rent Review Memorandum

DATED:	
THE LANDLORD:	*[Name]* *[Address]*
THE TENANT:	*[Name]* *[Address]*

By this Memorandum the Landlord and the Tenant record the fact that the rent reserved in the Lease brief particulars whereof appear below has been reviewed in accordance with the provisions therein contained and is £*[X]* per annum from *[date]*.

EXCLUSIVE OF VAT

THE LEASE

DATE	PARTIES	PROPERTY	TERM
[DATE]	[NAME] (Lessor) and [NAME] (Lessee)	[ADDRESS]	[ ] years commencing [DATE]

Signed for and on behalf of the Tenant

Signed:

Signed for and on behalf of the Landlord

Signed:

Name (Print): _____ Name (Print): _____

Position: _____ Position: _____

Appendix 2: Arbitration Act 1996

1996 CHAPTER 23

Crown copyright material is reproduced with the permission of the Controller of HMSO and the Queen's Printer for Scotland.

An Act to restate and improve the law relating to arbitration pursuant to an arbitration agreement; to make other provision relating to arbitration and arbitration awards; and for connected purposes.

17th June 1996

Part I: Arbitration Pursuant to an Arbitration Agreement

Introductory
1 General principles

The provisions of this Part are founded on the following principles, and shall be construed accordingly:
(a) the object of arbitration is to obtain the fair resolution of disputes by an impartial tribunal without unnecessary delay or expense;
(b) the parties should be free to agree how their disputes are resolved, subject only to such safeguards as are necessary in the public interest;
(c) in matters governed by this Part the court should not intervene except as provided by this Part.

2 Scope of application of provisions

(1) The provisions of this Part apply where the seat of the arbitration is in England and Wales or Northern Ireland.

(2) The following sections apply even if the seat of the arbitration is outside England and Wales or Northern Ireland or no seat has been designated or determined:
(a) sections 9 to 11 (stay of legal proceedings, &c.), and
(b) section 66 (enforcement of arbitral awards).

(3) The powers conferred by the following sections apply even if the seat of the arbitration is outside England and Wales or Northern Ireland or no seat has been designated or determined:

(a)   section 43 (securing the attendance of witnesses), and

(b)   section 44 (court powers exercisable in support of arbitral proceedings);

but the court may refuse to exercise any such power if, in the opinion of the court, the fact that the seat of the arbitration is outside England and Wales or Northern Ireland, or that when designated or determined the seat is likely to be outside England and Wales or Northern Ireland, makes it inappropriate to do so.

(4) The court may exercise a power conferred by any provision of this Part not mentioned in subsection (2) or (3) for the purpose of supporting the arbitral process where:

(a)   no seat of the arbitration has been designated or determined, and

(b)   by reason of a connection with England and Wales or Northern Ireland the court is satisfied that it is appropriate to do so.

(5) Section 7 (separability of arbitration agreement) and section 8 (death of a party) apply where the law applicable to the arbitration agreement is the law of England and Wales or Northern Ireland even if the seat of the arbitration is outside England and Wales or Northern Ireland or has not been designated or determined.

3 The seat of the arbitration

In this Part "the seat of the arbitration" means the juridical seat of the arbitration designated:

(a)   by the parties to the arbitration agreement, or

(b)   by any arbitral or other institution or person vested by the parties with powers in that regard, or

(c)   by the arbitral tribunal if so authorised by the parties,

or determined, in the absence of any such designation, having regard to the parties' agreement and all the relevant circumstances.

4 Mandatory and non-mandatory provisions

(1) The mandatory provisions of this Part are listed in Schedule 1 and have effect notwithstanding any agreement to the contrary.

(2) The other provisions of this Part (the "non-mandatory provisions") allow the parties to make their own arrangements by agreement but provide rules which apply in the absence of such agreement.

(3) The parties may make such arrangements by agreeing to the application of institutional rules or providing any other means by which a matter may be decided.

(4) It is immaterial whether or not the law applicable to the parties' agreement is the law of England and Wales or, as the case may be, Northern Ireland.

(5) The choice of a law other than the law of England and Wales or Northern Ireland as the applicable law in respect of a matter provided for by a non-mandatory provision of this Part is equivalent to an agreement making provision about that matter.

For this purpose an applicable law determined in accordance with the parties' agreement, or which is objectively determined in the absence of any express or implied choice, shall be treated as chosen by the parties.

5 Agreements to be in writing

(1) The provisions of this Part apply only where the arbitration agreement is in writing, and any other agreement between the parties as to any matter is effective for the purposes of this Part only if in writing.

The expressions "agreement", "agree" and "agreed" shall be construed accordingly.

(2) There is an agreement in writing:
(a)   if the agreement is made in writing (whether or not it is signed by the parties),
(b)   if the agreement is made by exchange of communications in writing, or
(c)   if the agreement is evidenced in writing.

(3) Where parties agree otherwise than in writing by reference to terms which are in writing, they make an agreement in writing.

(4) An agreement is evidenced in writing if an agreement made otherwise than in writing is recorded by one of the parties, or by a third party, with the authority of the parties to the agreement.

(5) An exchange of written submissions in arbitral or legal proceedings in which the existence of an agreement otherwise than in writing is alleged by one party against another party and not denied by the other party in his response constitutes as between those parties an agreement in writing to the effect alleged.

(6) References in this Part to anything being written or in writing include its being recorded by any means.

The arbitration agreement
6 Definition of arbitration agreement

(1) In this Part an "arbitration agreement" means an agreement to submit to arbitration present or future disputes (whether they are contractual or not).

(2) The reference in an agreement to a written form of arbitration clause or to a document containing an arbitration clause constitutes an arbitration agreement if the reference is such as to make that clause part of the agreement.

7 Separability of arbitration agreement

Unless otherwise agreed by the parties, an arbitration agreement which forms or was intended to form part of another agreement (whether or not in writing) shall not be regarded as invalid, non-existent or ineffective because that other agreement is invalid, or did not come into existence or has become ineffective, and it shall for that purpose be treated as a distinct agreement.

8 Whether agreement discharged by death of a party

(1) Unless otherwise agreed by the parties, an arbitration agreement is not discharged by the death of a party and may be enforced by or against the personal representatives of that party.

(2) Subsection (1) does not affect the operation of any enactment or rule of law by virtue of which a substantive right or obligation is extinguished by death.

Stay of legal proceedings
9 Stay of legal proceedings

(1) A party to an arbitration agreement against whom legal proceedings are brought (whether by way of claim or counterclaim) in respect of a matter which under the agreement is to be referred to arbitration may (upon notice to the other parties to the proceedings) apply to the court in which the proceedings have been brought to stay the proceedings so far as they concern that matter.

(2) An application may be made notwithstanding that the matter is to be referred to arbitration only after the exhaustion of other dispute resolution procedures.

(3) An application may not be made by a person before taking the appropriate procedural step (if any) to acknowledge the legal proceedings against him or after he has taken any step in those proceedings to answer the substantive claim.

(4) On an application under this section the court shall grant a stay unless satisfied that the arbitration agreement is null and void, inoperative, or incapable of being performed.

(5) If the court refuses to stay the legal proceedings, any provision that an award is a condition precedent to the bringing of legal proceedings in respect of any matter is of no effect in relation to those proceedings.

10 Reference of interpleader issue to arbitration

(1) Where in legal proceedings relief by way of interpleader is granted and any issue between the claimants is one in respect of which there is an arbitration agreement between them, the court granting the relief shall direct that the issue be

determined in accordance with the agreement unless the circumstances are such that proceedings brought by a claimant in respect of the matter would not be stayed.

(2) Where subsection (1) applies but the court does not direct that the issue be determined in accordance with the arbitration agreement, any provision that an award is a condition precedent to the bringing of legal proceedings in respect of any matter shall not affect the determination of that issue by the court.

11 Retention of security where Admiralty proceedings stayed

(1) Where Admiralty proceedings are stayed on the ground that the dispute in question should be submitted to arbitration, the court granting the stay may, if in those proceedings property has been arrested or bail or other security has been given to prevent or obtain release from arrest:
(a)   order that the property arrested be retained as security for the satisfaction of any award given in the arbitration in respect of that dispute, or
(b)   order that the stay of those proceedings be conditional on the provision of equivalent security for the satisfaction of any such award.

(2) Subject to any provision made by rules of court and to any necessary modifications, the same law and practice shall apply in relation to property retained in pursuance of an order as would apply if it were held for the purposes of proceedings in the court making the order.

Commencement of arbitral proceedings
12 Power of court to extend time for beginning arbitral proceedings, &c

(1) Where an arbitration agreement to refer future disputes to arbitration provides that a claim shall be barred, or the claimant's right extinguished, unless the claimant takes within a time fixed by the agreement some step:
(a)   to begin arbitral proceedings, or
(b)   to begin other dispute resolution procedures which must be exhausted before arbitral proceedings can be begun,

the court may by order extend the time for taking that step.

(2) Any party to the arbitration agreement may apply for such an order (upon notice to the other parties), but only after a claim has arisen and after exhausting any available arbitral process for obtaining an extension of time.

(3) The court shall make an order only if satisfied:
(a)   that the circumstances are such as were outside the reasonable contemplation of the parties when they agreed the provision in question, and that it would be just to extend the time, or
(b)   that the conduct of one party makes it unjust to hold the other party to the strict terms of the provision in question.

(4) The court may extend the time for such period and on such terms as it thinks fit, and may do so whether or not the time previously fixed (by agreement or by a previous order) has expired.

(5) An order under this section does not affect the operation of the Limitation Acts (see section 13).

(6) The leave of the court is required for any appeal from a decision of the court under this section.

13 Application of Limitation Acts

(1) The Limitation Acts apply to arbitral proceedings as they apply to legal proceedings.

(2) The court may order that in computing the time prescribed by the Limitation Acts for the commencement of proceedings (including arbitral proceedings) in respect of a dispute which was the subject matter:
(a)   of an award which the court orders to be set aside or declares to be of no effect, or
(b)   of the affected part of an award which the court orders to be set aside in part, or declares to be in part of no effect,

the period between the commencement of the arbitration and the date of the order referred to in paragraph (a) or (b) shall be excluded.

(3) In determining for the purposes of the Limitation Acts when a cause of action accrued, any provision that an award is a

condition precedent to the bringing of legal proceedings in respect of a matter to which an arbitration agreement applies shall be disregarded.

(4) In this Part "the Limitation Acts" means:
(a)   in England and Wales, the [1980 c. 58.] *Limitation Act 1980*, the [1984 c. 16.] *Foreign Limitation Periods Act 1984* and any other enactment (whenever passed) relating to the limitation of actions;
(b)   in Northern Ireland, the [S.I. 1989/1339 (N.I. 11).] *Limitation (Northern Ireland) Order* 1989, the [S.I. 1985/754 (N.I. 5).] *Foreign Limitation Periods (Northern Ireland) Order* 1985 and any other enactment (whenever passed) relating to the limitation of actions.

14 Commencement of arbitral proceedings

(1) The parties are free to agree when arbitral proceedings are to be regarded as commenced for the purposes of this Part and for the purposes of the Limitation Acts.

(2) If there is no such agreement the following provisions apply.

(3) Where the arbitrator is named or designated in the arbitration agreement, arbitral proceedings are commenced in respect of a matter when one party serves on the other party or parties a notice in writing requiring him or them to submit that matter to the person so named or designated.

(4) Where the arbitrator or arbitrators are to be appointed by the parties, arbitral proceedings are commenced in respect of a matter when one party serves on the other party or parties notice in writing requiring him or them to appoint an arbitrator or to agree to the appointment of an arbitrator in respect of that matter.

(5) Where the arbitrator or arbitrators are to be appointed by a person other than a party to the proceedings, arbitral proceedings are commenced in respect of a matter when one party gives notice in writing to that person requesting him to make the appointment in respect of that matter.

The arbitral tribunal
15 The arbitral tribunal

(1) The parties are free to agree on the number of arbitrators to form the tribunal and whether there is to be a chairman or umpire.

(2) Unless otherwise agreed by the parties, an agreement that the number of arbitrators shall be two or any other even number shall be understood as requiring the appointment of an additional arbitrator as chairman of the tribunal.

(3) If there is no agreement as to the number of arbitrators, the tribunal shall consist of a sole arbitrator.

16 Procedure for appointment of arbitrators

(1) The parties are free to agree on the procedure for appointing the arbitrator or arbitrators, including the procedure for appointing any chairman or umpire.

(2) If or to the extent that there is no such agreement, the following provisions apply.

(3) If the tribunal is to consist of a sole arbitrator, the parties shall jointly appoint the arbitrator not later than 28 days after service of a request in writing by either party to do so.

(4) If the tribunal is to consist of two arbitrators, each party shall appoint one arbitrator not later than 14 days after service of a request in writing by either party to do so.

(5) If the tribunal is to consist of three arbitrators:
(a)   each party shall appoint one arbitrator not later than 14 days after service of a request in writing by either party to do so, and
(b)   the two so appointed shall forthwith appoint a third arbitrator as the chairman of the tribunal.

(6) If the tribunal is to consist of two arbitrators and an umpire:
(a)   each party shall appoint one arbitrator not later than 14 days after service of a request in writing by either party to do so, and
(b)   the two so appointed may appoint an umpire at any time after they themselves are appointed and shall do so

before any substantive hearing or forthwith if they cannot agree on a matter relating to the arbitration.

(7) In any other case (in particular, if there are more than two parties) section 18 applies as in the case of a failure of the agreed appointment procedure.

17 Power in case of default to appoint sole arbitrator

(1) Unless the parties otherwise agree, where each of two parties to an arbitration agreement is to appoint an arbitrator and one party ("the party in default") refuses to do so, or fails to do so within the time specified, the other party, having duly appointed his arbitrator, may give notice in writing to the party in default that he proposes to appoint his arbitrator to act as sole arbitrator.

(2) If the party in default does not within 7 clear days of that notice being given:
(a)   make the required appointment, and
(b)   notify the other party that he has done so,

the other party may appoint his arbitrator as sole arbitrator whose award shall be binding on both parties as if he had been so appointed by agreement.

(3) Where a sole arbitrator has been appointed under subsection (2), the party in default may (upon notice to the appointing party) apply to the court which may set aside the appointment.

(4) The leave of the court is required for any appeal from a decision of the court under this section.

18 Failure of appointment procedure

(1) The parties are free to agree what is to happen in the event of a failure of the procedure for the appointment of the arbitral tribunal.

There is no failure if an appointment is duly made under section 17 (power in case of default to appoint sole arbitrator), unless that appointment is set aside.

(2) If or to the extent that there is no such agreement any party to the arbitration agreement may (upon notice to the other parties) apply to the court to exercise its powers under this section.

(3) Those powers are:
(a)   to give directions as to the making of any necessary appointments;
(b)   to direct that the tribunal shall be constituted by such appointments (or any one or more of them) as have been made;
(c)   to revoke any appointments already made;
(d)   to make any necessary appointments itself.

(4) An appointment made by the court under this section has effect as if made with the agreement of the parties.

(5) The leave of the court is required for any appeal from a decision of the court under this section.

19 Court to have regard to agreed qualifications

In deciding whether to exercise, and in considering how to exercise, any of its powers under section 16 (procedure for appointment of arbitrators) or section 18 (failure of appointment procedure), the court shall have due regard to any agreement of the parties as to the qualifications required of the arbitrators.

20 Chairman

(1) Where the parties have agreed that there is to be a chairman, they are free to agree what the functions of the chairman are to be in relation to the making of decisions, orders and awards.

(2) If or to the extent that there is no such agreement, the following provisions apply.

(3) Decisions, orders and awards shall be made by all or a majority of the arbitrators (including the chairman).

(4) The view of the chairman shall prevail in relation to a decision, order or award in respect of which there is neither unanimity nor a majority under subsection (3).

21 Umpire

(1) Where the parties have agreed that there is to be an umpire, they are free to agree what the functions of the umpire are to be, and in particular:
(a)   whether he is to attend the proceedings, and
(b)   when he is to replace the other arbitrators as the tribunal with power to make decisions, orders and awards.

(2) If or to the extent that there is no such agreement, the following provisions apply.

(3) The umpire shall attend the proceedings and be supplied with the same documents and other materials as are supplied to the other arbitrators.

(4) Decisions, orders and awards shall be made by the other arbitrators unless and until they cannot agree on a matter relating to the arbitration.

In that event they shall forthwith give notice in writing to the parties and the umpire, whereupon the umpire shall replace them as the tribunal with power to make decisions, orders and awards as if he were sole arbitrator.

(5) If the arbitrators cannot agree but fail to give notice of that fact, or if any of them fails to join in the giving of notice, any party to the arbitral proceedings may (upon notice to the other parties and to the tribunal) apply to the court which may order that the umpire shall replace the other arbitrators as the tribunal with power to make decisions, orders and awards as if he were sole arbitrator.

(6) The leave of the court is required for any appeal from a decision of the court under this section.

22 Decision-making where no chairman or umpire

(1) Where the parties agree that there shall be two or more arbitrators with no chairman or umpire, the parties are free to agree how the tribunal is to make decisions, orders and awards.

(2) If there is no such agreement, decisions, orders and awards shall be made by all or a majority of the arbitrators.

23 Revocation of arbitrator's authority

(1) The parties are free to agree in what circumstances the authority of an arbitrator may be revoked.

(2) If or to the extent that there is no such agreement the following provisions apply.

(3) The authority of an arbitrator may not be revoked except:
(a)   by the parties acting jointly, or
(b)   by an arbitral or other institution or person vested by the parties with powers in that regard.

(4) Revocation of the authority of an arbitrator by the parties acting jointly must be agreed in writing unless the parties also agree (whether or not in writing) to terminate the arbitration agreement.

(5) Nothing in this section affects the power of the court:
(a)   to revoke an appointment under section 18 (powers exercisable in case of failure of appointment procedure), or
(b)   to remove an arbitrator on the grounds specified in section 24.

24 Power of court to remove arbitrator

(1) A party to arbitral proceedings may (upon notice to the other parties, to the arbitrator concerned and to any other arbitrator) apply to the court to remove an arbitrator on any of the following grounds:
(a)   that circumstances exist that give rise to justifiable doubts as to his impartiality;
(b)   that he does not possess the qualifications required by the arbitration agreement;
(c)   that he is physically or mentally incapable of conducting the proceedings or there are justifiable doubts as to his capacity to do so;
(d)   that he has refused or failed:
     (i)   properly to conduct the proceedings, or
     (ii)   to use all reasonable despatch in conducting the proceedings or making an award,
    and that substantial injustice has been or will be caused to the applicant.

(2) If there is an arbitral or other institution or person vested by the parties with power to remove an arbitrator, the court

shall not exercise its power of removal unless satisfied that the applicant has first exhausted any available recourse to that institution or person.

(3) The arbitral tribunal may continue the arbitral proceedings and make an award while an application to the court under this section is pending.

(4) Where the court removes an arbitrator, it may make such order as it thinks fit with respect to his entitlement (if any) to fees or expenses, or the repayment of any fees or expenses already paid.

(5) The arbitrator concerned is entitled to appear and be heard by the court before it makes any order under this section.

(6) The leave of the court is required for any appeal from a decision of the court under this section.

25 Resignation of arbitrator

(1) The parties are free to agree with an arbitrator as to the consequences of his resignation as regards:
(a)   his entitlement (if any) to fees or expenses, and
(b)   any liability thereby incurred by him.

(2) If or to the extent that there is no such agreement the following provisions apply.

(3) An arbitrator who resigns his appointment may (upon notice to the parties) apply to the court:
(a)   to grant him relief from any liability thereby incurred by him, and
(b)   to make such order as it thinks fit with respect to his entitlement (if any) to fees or expenses or the repayment of any fees or expenses already paid.

(4) If the court is satisfied that in all the circumstances it was reasonable for the arbitrator to resign, it may grant such relief as is mentioned in subsection (3)(a) on such terms as it thinks fit.

(5) The leave of the court is required for any appeal from a decision of the court under this section.

26 Death of arbitrator or person appointing him

(1) The authority of an arbitrator is personal and ceases on his death.

(2) Unless otherwise agreed by the parties, the death of the person by whom an arbitrator was appointed does not revoke the arbitrator's authority.

27 Filling of vacancy, &c

(1) Where an arbitrator ceases to hold office, the parties are free to agree:
(a)   whether and if so how the vacancy is to be filled,
(b)   whether and if so to what extent the previous proceedings should stand, and
(c)   what effect (if any) his ceasing to hold office has on any appointment made by him (alone or jointly).

(2) If or to the extent that there is no such agreement, the following provisions apply.

(3) The provisions of sections 16 (procedure for appointment of arbitrators) and 18 (failure of appointment procedure) apply in relation to the filling of the vacancy as in relation to an original appointment.

(4) The tribunal (when reconstituted) shall determine whether and if so to what extent the previous proceedings should stand.

This does not affect any right of a party to challenge those proceedings on any ground which had arisen before the arbitrator ceased to hold office.

(5) His ceasing to hold office does not affect any appointment by him (alone or jointly) of another arbitrator, in particular any appointment of a chairman or umpire.

28 Joint and several liability of parties to arbitrators for fees and expenses

(1) The parties are jointly and severally liable to pay to the arbitrators such reasonable fees and expenses (if any) as are appropriate in the circumstances.

(2) Any party may apply to the court (upon notice to the other parties and to the arbitrators) which may order that the

amount of the arbitrators' fees and expenses shall be considered and adjusted by such means and upon such terms as it may direct.

(3) If the application is made after any amount has been paid to the arbitrators by way of fees or expenses, the court may order the repayment of such amount (if any) as is shown to be excessive, but shall not do so unless it is shown that it is reasonable in the circumstances to order repayment.

(4) The above provisions have effect subject to any order of the court under section 24(4) or 25(3)(b) (order as to entitlement to fees or expenses in case of removal or resignation of arbitrator).

(5) Nothing in this section affects any liability of a party to any other party to pay all or any of the costs of the arbitration (see sections 59 to 65) or any contractual right of an arbitrator to payment of his fees and expenses.

(6) In this section references to arbitrators include an arbitrator who has ceased to act and an umpire who has not replaced the other arbitrators.

29 Immunity of arbitrator

(1) An arbitrator is not liable for anything done or omitted in the discharge or purported discharge of his functions as arbitrator unless the act or omission is shown to have been in bad faith.

(2) Subsection (1) applies to an employee or agent of an arbitrator as it applies to the arbitrator himself.

(3) This section does not affect any liability incurred by an arbitrator by reason of his resigning (but see section 25).

Jurisdiction of the arbitral tribunal
30 Competence of tribunal to rule on its own jurisdiction

(1) Unless otherwise agreed by the parties, the arbitral tribunal may rule on its own substantive jurisdiction, that is, as to:
(a)   whether there is a valid arbitration agreement,
(b)   whether the tribunal is properly constituted, and
(c)   what matters have been submitted to arbitration in accordance with the arbitration agreement.

(2) Any such ruling may be challenged by any available arbitral process of appeal or review or in accordance with the provisions of this Part.

31 Objection to substantive jurisdiction of tribunal

(1) An objection that the arbitral tribunal lacks substantive jurisdiction at the outset of the proceedings must be raised by a party not later than the time he takes the first step in the proceedings to contest the merits of any matter in relation to which he challenges the tribunal's jurisdiction.

A party is not precluded from raising such an objection by the fact that he has appointed or participated in the appointment of an arbitrator.

(2) Any objection during the course of the arbitral proceedings that the arbitral tribunal is exceeding its substantive jurisdiction must be made as soon as possible after the matter alleged to be beyond its jurisdiction is raised.

(3) The arbitral tribunal may admit an objection later than the time specified in subsection (1) or (2) if it considers the delay justified.

(4) Where an objection is duly taken to the tribunal's substantive jurisdiction and the tribunal has power to rule on its own jurisdiction, it may:
(a)   rule on the matter in an award as to jurisdiction, or
(b)   deal with the objection in its award on the merits.

If the parties agree which of these courses the tribunal should take, the tribunal shall proceed accordingly.

(5) The tribunal may in any case, and shall if the parties so agree, stay proceedings whilst an application is made to the court under section 32 (determination of preliminary point of jurisdiction).

32 Determination of preliminary point of jurisdiction

(1) The court may, on the application of a party to arbitral proceedings (upon notice to the other parties), determine any question as to the substantive jurisdiction of the tribunal.

A party may lose the right to object (see section 73).

(2) An application under this section shall not be considered unless:

(a)   it is made with the agreement in writing of all the other parties to the proceedings, or

(b)   it is made with the permission of the tribunal and the court is satisfied:

    (i)   that the determination of the question is likely to produce substantial savings in costs,

    (ii)   that the application was made without delay, and

    (iii)   that there is good reason why the matter should be decided by the court.

(3) An application under this section, unless made with the agreement of all the other parties to the proceedings, shall state the grounds on which it is said that the matter should be decided by the court.

(4) Unless otherwise agreed by the parties, the arbitral tribunal may continue the arbitral proceedings and make an award while an application to the court under this section is pending.

(5) Unless the court gives leave, no appeal lies from a decision of the court whether the conditions specified in subsection (2) are met.

(6) The decision of the court on the question of jurisdiction shall be treated as a judgment of the court for the purposes of an appeal.

But no appeal lies without the leave of the court which shall not be given unless the court considers that the question involves a point of law which is one of general importance or is one which for some other special reason should be considered by the Court of Appeal.

The arbitral proceedings
33 General duty of the tribunal

(1) The tribunal shall:

(a)   act fairly and impartially as between the parties, giving each party a reasonable opportunity of putting his case and dealing with that of his opponent, and

(b)   adopt procedures suitable to the circumstances of the particular case, avoiding unnecessary delay or expense, so as to provide a fair means for the resolution of the matters falling to be determined.

(2) The tribunal shall comply with that general duty in conducting the arbitral proceedings, in its decisions on matters of procedure and evidence and in the exercise of all other powers conferred on it.

34 Procedural and evidential matters

(1) It shall be for the tribunal to decide all procedural and evidential matters, subject to the right of the parties to agree any matter.

(2) Procedural and evidential matters include:
(a)   when and where any part of the proceedings is to be held;
(b)   the language or languages to be used in the proceedings and whether translations of any relevant documents are to be supplied;
(c)   whether any and if so what form of written statements of claim and defence are to be used, when these should be supplied and the extent to which such statements can be later amended;
(d)   whether any and if so which documents or classes of documents should be disclosed between and produced by the parties and at what stage;
(e)   whether any and if so what questions should be put to and answered by the respective parties and when and in what form this should be done;
(f)   whether to apply strict rules of evidence (or any other rules) as to the admissibility, relevance or weight of any material (oral, written or other) sought to be tendered on any matters of fact or opinion, and the time, manner and form in which such material should be exchanged and presented;
(g)   whether and to what extent the tribunal should itself take the initiative in ascertaining the facts and the law;
(h)   whether and to what extent there should be oral or written evidence or submissions.

(3) The tribunal may fix the time within which any directions given by it are to be complied with, and may if it thinks fit extend the time so fixed (whether or not it has expired).

35 Consolidation of proceedings and concurrent hearings

(1) The parties are free to agree:

(a)   that the arbitral proceedings shall be consolidated with other arbitral proceedings, or

(b)   that concurrent hearings shall be held,

on such terms as may be agreed.

(2) Unless the parties agree to confer such power on the tribunal, the tribunal has no power to order consolidation of proceedings or concurrent hearings.

36 Legal or other representation

Unless otherwise agreed by the parties, a party to arbitral proceedings may be represented in the proceedings by a lawyer or other person chosen by him.

37 Power to appoint experts, legal advisers or assessors

(1) Unless otherwise agreed by the parties:
(a)   the tribunal may:
    (i)   appoint experts or legal advisers to report to it and the parties, or
    (ii)   appoint assessors to assist it on technical matters, and may allow any such expert, legal adviser or assessor to attend the proceedings; and
(b)   the parties shall be given a reasonable opportunity to comment on any information, opinion or advice offered by any such person.

(2) The fees and expenses of an expert, legal adviser or assessor appointed by the tribunal for which the arbitrators are liable are expenses of the arbitrators for the purposes of this Part.

38 General powers exercisable by the tribunal

(1) The parties are free to agree on the powers exercisable by the arbitral tribunal for the purposes of and in relation to the proceedings.

(2) Unless otherwise agreed by the parties the tribunal has the following powers.

(3) The tribunal may order a claimant to provide security for the costs of the arbitration.

This power shall not be exercised on the ground that the claimant is:

(a)   an individual ordinarily resident outside the United Kingdom, or

(b)   a corporation or association incorporated or formed under the law of a country outside the United Kingdom, or whose central management and control is exercised outside the United Kingdom.

(4) The tribunal may give directions in relation to any property which is the subject of the proceedings or as to which any question arises in the proceedings, and which is owned by or is in the possession of a party to the proceedings:

(a)   for the inspection, photographing, preservation, custody or detention of the property by the tribunal, an expert or a party, or

(b)   ordering that samples be taken from, or any observation be made of or experiment conducted upon, the property.

(5) The tribunal may direct that a party or witness shall be examined on oath or affirmation, and may for that purpose administer any necessary oath or take any necessary affirmation.

(6) The tribunal may give directions to a party for the preservation for the purposes of the proceedings of any evidence in his custody or control.

39 Power to make provisional awards

(1) The parties are free to agree that the tribunal shall have power to order on a provisional basis any relief which it would have power to grant in a final award.

(2) This includes, for instance, making:

(a)   a provisional order for the payment of money or the disposition of property as between the parties, or

(b)   an order to make an interim payment on account of the costs of the arbitration.

(3) Any such order shall be subject to the tribunal's final adjudication; and the tribunal's final award, on the merits or as to costs, shall take account of any such order.

(4) Unless the parties agree to confer such power on the tribunal, the tribunal has no such power.

This does not affect its powers under section 47 (awards on different issues, &c.).

40 General duty of parties

(1) The parties shall do all things necessary for the proper and expeditious conduct of the arbitral proceedings.

(2) This includes:
(a)   complying without delay with any determination of the tribunal as to procedural or evidential matters, or with any order or directions of the tribunal, and
(b)   where appropriate, taking without delay any necessary steps to obtain a decision of the court on a preliminary question of jurisdiction or law (see sections 32 and 45).

41 Powers of tribunal in case of party's default

(1) The parties are free to agree on the powers of the tribunal in case of a party's failure to do something necessary for the proper and expeditious conduct of the arbitration.

(2) Unless otherwise agreed by the parties, the following provisions apply.

(3) If the tribunal is satisfied that there has been inordinate and inexcusable delay on the part of the claimant in pursuing his claim and that the delay:
(a)   gives rise, or is likely to give rise, to a substantial risk that it is not possible to have a fair resolution of the issues in that claim, or
(b)   has caused, or is likely to cause, serious prejudice to the respondent,

the tribunal may make an award dismissing the claim.

(4) If without showing sufficient cause a party:
(a)   fails to attend or be represented at an oral hearing of which due notice was given, or
(b)   where matters are to be dealt with in writing, fails after due notice to submit written evidence or make written submissions,

the tribunal may continue the proceedings in the absence of that party or, as the case may be, without any written evidence or submissions on his behalf, and may make an award on the basis of the evidence before it.

(5) If without showing sufficient cause a party fails to comply with any order or directions of the tribunal, the tribunal may make a peremptory order to the same effect, prescribing such time for compliance with it as the tribunal considers appropriate.

(6) If a claimant fails to comply with a peremptory order of the tribunal to provide security for costs, the tribunal may make an award dismissing his claim.

(7) If a party fails to comply with any other kind of peremptory order, then, without prejudice to section 42 (enforcement by court of tribunal's peremptory orders), the tribunal may do any of the following:
(a)   direct that the party in default shall not be entitled to rely upon any allegation or material which was the subject matter of the order;
(b)   draw such adverse inferences from the act of non-compliance as the circumstances justify;
(c)   proceed to an award on the basis of such materials as have been properly provided to it;
(d)   make such order as it thinks fit as to the payment of costs of the arbitration incurred in consequence of the non-compliance.

Powers of court in relation to arbitral proceedings

42 Enforcement of peremptory orders of tribunal

(1) Unless otherwise agreed by the parties, the court may make an order requiring a party to comply with a peremptory order made by the tribunal.

(2) An application for an order under this section may be made:
(a)   by the tribunal (upon notice to the parties),
(b)   by a party to the arbitral proceedings with the permission of the tribunal (and upon notice to the other parties), or
(c)   where the parties have agreed that the powers of the court under this section shall be available.

(3) The court shall not act unless it is satisfied that the applicant has exhausted any available arbitral process in respect of failure to comply with the tribunal's order.

(4) No order shall be made under this section unless the court is satisfied that the person to whom the tribunal's order was directed has failed to comply with it within the time prescribed in the order or, if no time was prescribed, within a reasonable time.

(5) The leave of the court is required for any appeal from a decision of the court under this section.

43 Securing the attendance of witnesses

(1) A party to arbitral proceedings may use the same court procedures as are available in relation to legal proceedings to secure the attendance before the tribunal of a witness in order to give oral testimony or to produce documents or other material evidence.

(2) This may only be done with the permission of the tribunal or the agreement of the other parties.

(3) The court procedures may only be used if:
(a)   the witness is in the United Kingdom, and
(b)   the arbitral proceedings are being conducted in England and Wales or, as the case may be, Northern Ireland.

(4) A person shall not be compelled by virtue of this section to produce any document or other material evidence which he could not be compelled to produce in legal proceedings.

44 Court powers exercisable in support of arbitral proceedings

(1) Unless otherwise agreed by the parties, the court has for the purposes of and in relation to arbitral proceedings the same power of making orders about the matters listed below as it has for the purposes of and in relation to legal proceedings.

(2) Those matters are:
(a)   the taking of the evidence of witnesses;
(b)   the preservation of evidence;

(c)   making orders relating to property which is the subject of the proceedings or as to which any question arises in the proceedings:
    (i)   for the inspection, photographing, preservation, custody or detention of the property, or
    (ii)   ordering that samples be taken from, or any observation be made of or experiment conducted upon, the property;
and for that purpose authorising any person to enter any premises in the possession or control of a party to the arbitration;
(d)   the sale of any goods the subject of the proceedings;
(e)   the granting of an interim injunction or the appointment of a receiver.

(3) If the case is one of urgency, the court may, on the application of a party or proposed party to the arbitral proceedings, make such orders as it thinks necessary for the purpose of preserving evidence or assets.

(4) If the case is not one of urgency, the court shall act only on the application of a party to the arbitral proceedings (upon notice to the other parties and to the tribunal) made with the permission of the tribunal or the agreement in writing of the other parties.

(5) In any case the court shall act only if or to the extent that the arbitral tribunal, and any arbitral or other institution or person vested by the parties with power in that regard, has no power or is unable for the time being to act effectively.

(6) If the court so orders, an order made by it under this section shall cease to have effect in whole or in part on the order of the tribunal or of any such arbitral or other institution or person having power to act in relation to the subject-matter of the order.

(7) The leave of the court is required for any appeal from a decision of the court under this section.

45 Determination of preliminary point of law

(1) Unless otherwise agreed by the parties, the court may on the application of a party to arbitral proceedings (upon notice to the other parties) determine any question of law arising in the

course of the proceedings which the court is satisfied substantially affects the rights of one or more of the parties.

An agreement to dispense with reasons for the tribunal's award shall be considered an agreement to exclude the court's jurisdiction under this section.

(2) An application under this section shall not be considered unless:
(a)   it is made with the agreement of all the other parties to the proceedings, or
(b)   it is made with the permission of the tribunal and the court is satisfied:
    (i)   that the determination of the question is likely to produce substantial savings in costs, and
    (ii)   that the application was made without delay.

(3) The application shall identify the question of law to be determined and, unless made with the agreement of all the other parties to the proceedings, shall state the grounds on which it is said that the question should be decided by the court.

(4) Unless otherwise agreed by the parties, the arbitral tribunal may continue the arbitral proceedings and make an award while an application to the court under this section is pending.

(5) Unless the court gives leave, no appeal lies from a decision of the court whether the conditions specified in subsection (2) are met.

(6) The decision of the court on the question of law shall be treated as a judgment of the court for the purposes of an appeal.

But no appeal lies without the leave of the court which shall not be given unless the court considers that the question is one of general importance, or is one which for some other special reason should be considered by the Court of Appeal.

The award
46 Rules applicable to substance of dispute

(1) The arbitral tribunal shall decide the dispute:
(a)   in accordance with the law chosen by the parties as applicable to the substance of the dispute, or

(b)   if the parties so agree, in accordance with such other considerations as are agreed by them or determined by the tribunal.

(2) For this purpose the choice of the laws of a country shall be understood to refer to the substantive laws of that country and not its conflict of laws rules.

(3) If or to the extent that there is no such choice or agreement, the tribunal shall apply the law determined by the conflict of laws rules which it considers applicable.

47 Awards on different issues, &c

(1) Unless otherwise agreed by the parties, the tribunal may make more than one award at different times on different aspects of the matters to be determined.

(2) The tribunal may, in particular, make an award relating:
(a)   to an issue affecting the whole claim, or
(b)   to a part only of the claims or cross-claims submitted to it for decision.

(3) If the tribunal does so, it shall specify in its award the issue, or the claim or part of a claim, which is the subject matter of the award.

48 Remedies

(1) The parties are free to agree on the powers exercisable by the arbitral tribunal as regards remedies.

(2) Unless otherwise agreed by the parties, the tribunal has the following powers.

(3) The tribunal may make a declaration as to any matter to be determined in the proceedings.

(4) The tribunal may order the payment of a sum of money, in any currency.

(5) The tribunal has the same powers as the court:
(a)   to order a party to do or refrain from doing anything;
(b)   to order specific performance of a contract (other than a contract relating to land);

(c)   to order the rectification, setting aside or cancellation of a deed or other document.

49 Interest

(1) The parties are free to agree on the powers of the tribunal as regards the award of interest.

(2) Unless otherwise agreed by the parties the following provisions apply.

(3) The tribunal may award simple or compound interest from such dates, at such rates and with such rests as it considers meets the justice of the case:
(a)   on the whole or part of any amount awarded by the tribunal, in respect of any period up to the date of the award;
(b)   on the whole or part of any amount claimed in the arbitration and outstanding at the commencement of the arbitral proceedings but paid before the award was made, in respect of any period up to the date of payment.

(4) The tribunal may award simple or compound interest from the date of the award (or any later date) until payment, at such rates and with such rests as it considers meets the justice of the case, on the outstanding amount of any award (including any award of interest under subsection (3) and any award as to costs).

(5) References in this section to an amount awarded by the tribunal include an amount payable in consequence of a declaratory award by the tribunal.

(6) The above provisions do not affect any other power of the tribunal to award interest.

50 Extension of time for making award

(1) Where the time for making an award is limited by or in pursuance of the arbitration agreement, then, unless otherwise agreed by the parties, the court may in accordance with the following provisions by order extend that time.

(2) An application for an order under this section may be made:
(a)   by the tribunal (upon notice to the parties), or

(b)   by any party to the proceedings (upon notice to the tribunal and the other parties),

but only after exhausting any available arbitral process for obtaining an extension of time.

(3) The court shall only make an order if satisfied that a substantial injustice would otherwise be done.

(4) The court may extend the time for such period and on such terms as it thinks fit, and may do so whether or not the time previously fixed (by or under the agreement or by a previous order) has expired.

(5) The leave of the court is required for any appeal from a decision of the court under this section.

51 Settlement

(1) If during arbitral proceedings the parties settle the dispute, the following provisions apply unless otherwise agreed by the parties.

(2) The tribunal shall terminate the substantive proceedings and, if so requested by the parties and not objected to by the tribunal, shall record the settlement in the form of an agreed award.

(3) An agreed award shall state that it is an award of the tribunal and shall have the same status and effect as any other award on the merits of the case.

(4) The following provisions of this Part relating to awards (sections 52 to 58) apply to an agreed award.

(5) Unless the parties have also settled the matter of the payment of the costs of the arbitration, the provisions of this Part relating to costs (sections 59 to 65) continue to apply.

52 Form of award

(1) The parties are free to agree on the form of an award.

(2) If or to the extent that there is no such agreement, the following provisions apply.

(3) The award shall be in writing signed by all the arbitrators or all those assenting to the award.

(4) The award shall contain the reasons for the award unless it is an agreed award or the parties have agreed to dispense with reasons.

(5) The award shall state the seat of the arbitration and the date when the award is made.

53 Place where award treated as made

Unless otherwise agreed by the parties, where the seat of the arbitration is in England and Wales or Northern Ireland, any award in the proceedings shall be treated as made there, regardless of where it was signed, despatched or delivered to any of the parties.

54 Date of award

(1) Unless otherwise agreed by the parties, the tribunal may decide what is to be taken to be the date on which the award was made.

(2) In the absence of any such decision, the date of the award shall be taken to be the date on which it is signed by the arbitrator or, where more than one arbitrator signs the award, by the last of them.

55 Notification of award

(1) The parties are free to agree on the requirements as to notification of the award to the parties.

(2) If there is no such agreement, the award shall be notified to the parties by service on them of copies of the award, which shall be done without delay after the award is made.

(3) Nothing in this section affects section 56 (power to withhold award in case of non-payment).

56 Power to withhold award in case of non-payment

(1) The tribunal may refuse to deliver an award to the parties except upon full payment of the fees and expenses of the arbitrators.

(2) If the tribunal refuses on that ground to deliver an award, a party to the arbitral proceedings may (upon notice to the other parties and the tribunal) apply to the court, which may order that:

(a)　the tribunal shall deliver the award on the payment into court by the applicant of the fees and expenses demanded, or such lesser amount as the court may specify,

(b)　the amount of the fees and expenses properly payable shall be determined by such means and upon such terms as the court may direct, and

(c)　out of the money paid into court there shall be paid out such fees and expenses as may be found to be properly payable and the balance of the money (if any) shall be paid out to the applicant.

(3) For this purpose the amount of fees and expenses properly payable is the amount the applicant is liable to pay under section 28 or any agreement relating to the payment of the arbitrators.

(4) No application to the court may be made where there is any available arbitral process for appeal or review of the amount of the fees or expenses demanded.

(5) References in this section to arbitrators include an arbitrator who has ceased to act and an umpire who has not replaced the other arbitrators.

(6) The above provisions of this section also apply in relation to any arbitral or other institution or person vested by the parties with powers in relation to the delivery of the tribunal's award.

As they so apply, the references to the fees and expenses of the arbitrators shall be construed as including the fees and expenses of that institution or person.

(7) The leave of the court is required for any appeal from a decision of the court under this section.

(8) Nothing in this section shall be construed as excluding an application under section 28 where payment has been made to the arbitrators in order to obtain the award.

57 Correction of award or additional award

(1) The parties are free to agree on the powers of the tribunal to correct an award or make an additional award.

(2) If or to the extent there is no such agreement, the following provisions apply.

(3) The tribunal may on its own initiative or on the application of a party:

(a)   correct an award so as to remove any clerical mistake or error arising from an accidental slip or omission or clarify or remove any ambiguity in the award, or

(b)   make an additional award in respect of any claim (including a claim for interest or costs) which was presented to the tribunal but was not dealt with in the award.

These powers shall not be exercised without first affording the other parties a reasonable opportunity to make representations to the tribunal.

(4) Any application for the exercise of those powers must be made within 28 days of the date of the award or such longer period as the parties may agree.

(5) Any correction of an award shall be made within 28 days of the date the application was received by the tribunal or, where the correction is made by the tribunal on its own initiative, within 28 days of the date of the award or, in either case, such longer period as the parties may agree.

(6) Any additional award shall be made within 56 days of the date of the original award or such longer period as the parties may agree.

(7) Any correction of an award shall form part of the award.

58 Effect of award

(1) Unless otherwise agreed by the parties, an award made by the tribunal pursuant to an arbitration agreement is final and binding both on the parties and on any persons claiming through or under them.

(2) This does not affect the right of a person to challenge the award by any available arbitral process of appeal or review or in accordance with the provisions of this Part.

Costs of the arbitration
59 Costs of the arbitration

(1) References in this Part to the costs of the arbitration are to:
(a)   the arbitrators' fees and expenses,
(b)   the fees and expenses of any arbitral institution concerned, and
(c)   the legal or other costs of the parties.

(2) Any such reference includes the costs of or incidental to any proceedings to determine the amount of the recoverable costs of the arbitration (see section 63).

60 Agreement to pay costs in any event

An agreement which has the effect that a party is to pay the whole or part of the costs of the arbitration in any event is only valid if made after the dispute in question has arisen.

61 Award of costs

(1) The tribunal may make an award allocating the costs of the arbitration as between the parties, subject to any agreement of the parties.

(2) Unless the parties otherwise agree, the tribunal shall award costs on the general principle that costs should follow the event except where it appears to the tribunal that in the circumstances this is not appropriate in relation to the whole or part of the costs.

62 Effect of agreement or award about costs

Unless the parties otherwise agree, any obligation under an agreement between them as to how the costs of the arbitration are to be borne, or under an award allocating the costs of the arbitration, extends only to such costs as are recoverable.

63 The recoverable costs of the arbitration

(1) The parties are free to agree what costs of the arbitration are recoverable.

(2) If or to the extent there is no such agreement, the following provisions apply.

(3) The tribunal may determine by award the recoverable costs of the arbitration on such basis as it thinks fit.

If it does so, it shall specify:
(a)   the basis on which it has acted, and
(b)   the items of recoverable costs and the amount referable to each.

(4) If the tribunal does not determine the recoverable costs of the arbitration, any party to the arbitral proceedings may apply to the court (upon notice to the other parties) which may:
(a)   determine the recoverable costs of the arbitration on such basis as it thinks fit, or
(b)   order that they shall be determined by such means and upon such terms as it may specify.

(5) Unless the tribunal or the court determines otherwise:
(a)   the recoverable costs of the arbitration shall be determined on the basis that there shall be allowed a reasonable amount in respect of all costs reasonably incurred, and
(b)   any doubt as to whether costs were reasonably incurred or were reasonable in amount shall be resolved in favour of the paying party.

(6) The above provisions have effect subject to section 64 (recoverable fees and expenses of arbitrators).

(7) Nothing in this section affects any right of the arbitrators, any expert, legal adviser or assessor appointed by the tribunal, or any arbitral institution, to payment of their fees and expenses.

64 Recoverable fees and expenses of arbitrators

(1) Unless otherwise agreed by the parties, the recoverable costs of the arbitration shall include in respect of the fees and expenses of the arbitrators only such reasonable fees and expenses as are appropriate in the circumstances.

(2) If there is any question as to what reasonable fees and expenses are appropriate in the circumstances, and the matter is not already before the court on an application under section 63(4), the court may on the application of any party (upon notice to the other parties):
(a)   determine the matter, or

(b)   order that it be determined by such means and upon such terms as the court may specify.

(3) Subsection (1) has effect subject to any order of the court under section 24(4) or 25(3)(b) (order as to entitlement to fees or expenses in case of removal or resignation of arbitrator).

(4) Nothing in this section affects any right of the arbitrator to payment of his fees and expenses.

65 Power to limit recoverable costs

(1) Unless otherwise agreed by the parties, the tribunal may direct that the recoverable costs of the arbitration, or of any part of the arbitral proceedings, shall be limited to a specified amount.

(2) Any direction may be made or varied at any stage, but this must be done sufficiently in advance of the incurring of costs to which it relates, or the taking of any steps in the proceedings which may be affected by it, for the limit to be taken into account.

Powers of the court in relation to award
66 Enforcement of the award

(1) An award made by the tribunal pursuant to an arbitration agreement may, by leave of the court, be enforced in the same manner as a judgment or order of the court to the same effect.

(2) Where leave is so given, judgment may be entered in terms of the award.

(3) Leave to enforce an award shall not be given where, or to the extent that, the person against whom it is sought to be enforced shows that the tribunal lacked substantive jurisdiction to make the award.

The right to raise such an objection may have been lost (see section 73).

(4) Nothing in this section affects the recognition or enforcement of an award under any other enactment or rule of law, in particular under Part II of the [1950 c. 27.] *Arbitration Act* 1950 (enforcement of awards under Geneva Convention) or

the provisions of Part III of this Act relating to the recognition and enforcement of awards under the New York Convention or by an action on the award.

67 Challenging the award: substantive jurisdiction

(1) A party to arbitral proceedings may (upon notice to the other parties and to the tribunal) apply to the court:
(a)   challenging any award of the arbitral tribunal as to its substantive jurisdiction; or
(b)   for an order declaring an award made by the tribunal on the merits to be of no effect, in whole or in part, because the tribunal did not have substantive jurisdiction.

A party may lose the right to object (see section 73) and the right to apply is subject to the restrictions in section 70(2) and (3).

(2) The arbitral tribunal may continue the arbitral proceedings and make a further award while an application to the court under this section is pending in relation to an award as to jurisdiction.

(3) On an application under this section challenging an award of the arbitral tribunal as to its substantive jurisdiction, the court may by order:
(a)   confirm the award,
(b)   vary the award, or
(c)   set aside the award in whole or in part.

(4) The leave of the court is required for any appeal from a decision of the court under this section.

68 Challenging the award: serious irregularity

(1) A party to arbitral proceedings may (upon notice to the other parties and to the tribunal) apply to the court challenging an award in the proceedings on the ground of serious irregularity affecting the tribunal, the proceedings or the award.

A party may lose the right to object (see section 73) and the right to apply is subject to the restrictions in section 70(2) and (3).

(2) Serious irregularity means an irregularity of one or more of the following kinds which the court considers has caused or will cause substantial injustice to the applicant:

(a)   failure by the tribunal to comply with section 33 (general duty of tribunal);

(b)   the tribunal exceeding its powers (otherwise than by exceeding its substantive jurisdiction: see section 67);

(c)   failure by the tribunal to conduct the proceedings in accordance with the procedure agreed by the parties;

(d)   failure by the tribunal to deal with all the issues that were put to it;

(e)   any arbitral or other institution or person vested by the parties with powers in relation to the proceedings or the award exceeding its powers;

(f)   uncertainty or ambiguity as to the effect of the award;

(g)   the award being obtained by fraud or the award or the way in which it was procured being contrary to public policy;

(h)   failure to comply with the requirements as to the form of the award; or

(i)   any irregularity in the conduct of the proceedings or in the award which is admitted by the tribunal or by any arbitral or other institution or person vested by the parties with powers in relation to the proceedings or the award.

(3) If there is shown to be serious irregularity affecting the tribunal, the proceedings or the award, the court may:

(a)   remit the award to the tribunal, in whole or in part, for reconsideration,

(b)   set the award aside in whole or in part, or

(c)   declare the award to be of no effect, in whole or in part.

The court shall not exercise its power to set aside or to declare an award to be of no effect, in whole or in part, unless it is satisfied that it would be inappropriate to remit the matters in question to the tribunal for reconsideration.

(4) The leave of the court is required for any appeal from a decision of the court under this section.

69 Appeal on point of law

(1) Unless otherwise agreed by the parties, a party to arbitral proceedings may (upon notice to the other parties and to the

tribunal) appeal to the court on a question of law arising out of an award made in the proceedings.

An agreement to dispense with reasons for the tribunal's award shall be considered an agreement to exclude the court's jurisdiction under this section.

(2) An appeal shall not be brought under this section except:
(a)   with the agreement of all the other parties to the proceedings, or
(b)   with the leave of the court.

The right to appeal is also subject to the restrictions in section 70(2) and (3).

(3) Leave to appeal shall be given only if the court is satisfied:
(a)   that the determination of the question will substantially affect the rights of one or more of the parties,
(b)   that the question is one which the tribunal was asked to determine,
(c)   that, on the basis of the findings of fact in the award:
       (i)   the decision of the tribunal on the question is obviously wrong, or
       (ii)   the question is one of general public importance and the decision of the tribunal is at least open to serious doubt, and
(d)   that, despite the agreement of the parties to resolve the matter by arbitration, it is just and proper in all the circumstances for the court to determine the question.

(4) An application for leave to appeal under this section shall identify the question of law to be determined and state the grounds on which it is alleged that leave to appeal should be granted.

(5) The court shall determine an application for leave to appeal under this section without a hearing unless it appears to the court that a hearing is required.

(6) The leave of the court is required for any appeal from a decision of the court under this section to grant or refuse leave to appeal.

(7) On an appeal under this section the court may by order:
(a)   confirm the award,
(b)   vary the award,

(c)   remit the award to the tribunal, in whole or in part, for reconsideration in the light of the court's determination, or

(d)   set aside the award in whole or in part.

The court shall not exercise its power to set aside an award, in whole or in part, unless it is satisfied that it would be inappropriate to remit the matters in question to the tribunal for reconsideration.

(8) The decision of the court on an appeal under this section shall be treated as a judgment of the court for the purposes of a further appeal.

But no such appeal lies without the leave of the court which shall not be given unless the court considers that the question is one of general importance or is one which for some other special reason should be considered by the Court of Appeal.

70 Challenge or appeal: supplementary provisions

(1) The following provisions apply to an application or appeal under section 67, 68 or 69.

(2) An application or appeal may not be brought if the applicant or appellant has not first exhausted:

(a)   any available arbitral process of appeal or review, and

(b)   any available recourse under section 57 (correction of award or additional award).

(3) Any application or appeal must be brought within 28 days of the date of the award or, if there has been any arbitral process of appeal or review, of the date when the applicant or appellant was notified of the result of that process.

(4) If on an application or appeal it appears to the court that the award:

(a)   does not contain the tribunal's reasons, or

(b)   does not set out the tribunal's reasons in sufficient detail to enable the court properly to consider the application or appeal,

the court may order the tribunal to state the reasons for its award in sufficient detail for that purpose.

(5) Where the court makes an order under subsection (4), it may make such further order as it thinks fit with respect to any additional costs of the arbitration resulting from its order.

(6) The court may order the applicant or appellant to provide security for the costs of the application or appeal, and may direct that the application or appeal be dismissed if the order is not complied with.

The power to order security for costs shall not be exercised on the ground that the applicant or appellant is:
(a)   an individual ordinarily resident outside the United Kingdom, or
(b)   a corporation or association incorporated or formed under the law of a country outside the United Kingdom, or whose central management and control is exercised outside the United Kingdom.

(7) The court may order that any money payable under the award shall be brought into court or otherwise secured pending the determination of the application or appeal, and may direct that the application or appeal be dismissed if the order is not complied with.

(8) The court may grant leave to appeal subject to conditions to the same or similar effect as an order under subsection (6) or (7).

This does not affect the general discretion of the court to grant leave subject to conditions.

71 Challenge or appeal: effect of order of court

(1) The following provisions have effect where the court makes an order under section 67, 68 or 69 with respect to an award.

(2) Where the award is varied, the variation has effect as part of the tribunal's award.

(3) Where the award is remitted to the tribunal, in whole or in part, for reconsideration, the tribunal shall make a fresh award in respect of the matters remitted within three months of the date of the order for remission or such longer or shorter period as the court may direct.

(4) Where the award is set aside or declared to be of no effect, in whole or in part, the court may also order that any provision that an award is a condition precedent to the bringing of legal proceedings in respect of a matter to which the arbitration agreement applies, is of no effect as regards the subject matter of the award or, as the case may be, the relevant part of the award.

Miscellaneous
72 Saving for rights of person who takes no part in proceedings

(1) A person alleged to be a party to arbitral proceedings but who takes no part in the proceedings may question:
(a)   whether there is a valid arbitration agreement,
(b)   whether the tribunal is properly constituted, or
(c)   what matters have been submitted to arbitration in accordance with the arbitration agreement,

by proceedings in the court for a declaration or injunction or other appropriate relief.

(2) He also has the same right as a party to the arbitral proceedings to challenge an award:
(a)   by an application under section 67 on the ground of lack of substantive jurisdiction in relation to him, or
(b)   by an application under section 68 on the ground of serious irregularity (within the meaning of that section) affecting him;

and section 70(2) (duty to exhaust arbitral procedures) does not apply in his case.

73 Loss of right to object

(1) If a party to arbitral proceedings takes part, or continues to take part, in the proceedings without making, either forthwith or within such time as is allowed by the arbitration agreement or the tribunal or by any provision of this Part, any objection:
(a)   that the tribunal lacks substantive jurisdiction,
(b)   that the proceedings have been improperly conducted,
(c)   that there has been a failure to comply with the arbitration agreement or with any provision of this Part, or
(d)   that there has been any other irregularity affecting the tribunal or the proceedings,

he may not raise that objection later, before the tribunal or the court, unless he shows that, at the time he took part or continued to take part in the proceedings, he did not know and could not with reasonable diligence have discovered the grounds for the objection.

(2) Where the arbitral tribunal rules that it has substantive jurisdiction and a party to arbitral proceedings who could have questioned that ruling:
(a)   by any available arbitral process of appeal or review, or
(b)   by challenging the award,

does not do so, or does not do so within the time allowed by the arbitration agreement or any provision of this Part, he may not object later to the tribunal's substantive jurisdiction on any ground which was the subject of that ruling.

74 Immunity of arbitral institutions, &c

(1) An arbitral or other institution or person designated or requested by the parties to appoint or nominate an arbitrator is not liable for anything done or omitted in the discharge or purported discharge of that function unless the act or omission is shown to have been in bad faith.

(2) An arbitral or other institution or person by whom an arbitrator is appointed or nominated is not liable, by reason of having appointed or nominated him, for anything done or omitted by the arbitrator (or his employees or agents) in the discharge or purported discharge of his functions as arbitrator.

(3) The above provisions apply to an employee or agent of an arbitral or other institution or person as they apply to the institution or person himself.

75 Charge to secure payment of solicitors' costs

The powers of the court to make declarations and orders under section 73 of the [1974 c. 47.] *Solicitors Act* 1974 or Article 71H of the [S.I. 1976/582 (N.I. 12).] *Solicitors (Northern Ireland) Order* 1976 (power to charge property recovered in the proceedings with the payment of solicitors' costs) may be exercised in relation to arbitral proceedings as if those proceedings were proceedings in the court.

Supplementary

76 Service of notices, &c

(1) The parties are free to agree on the manner of service of any notice or other document required or authorised to be given or served in pursuance of the arbitration agreement or for the purposes of the arbitral proceedings.

(2) If or to the extent that there is no such agreement the following provisions apply.

(3) A notice or other document may be served on a person by any effective means.

(4) If a notice or other document is addressed, pre-paid and delivered by post:
(a)   to the addressee's last known principal residence or, if he is or has been carrying on a trade, profession or business, his last known principal business address, or
(b)   where the addressee is a body corporate, to the body's registered or principal office,

it shall be treated as effectively served.

(5) This section does not apply to the service of documents for the purposes of legal proceedings, for which provision is made by rules of court.

(6) References in this Part to a notice or other document include any form of communication in writing and references to giving or serving a notice or other document shall be construed accordingly.

77 Powers of court in relation to service of documents

(1) This section applies where service of a document on a person in the manner agreed by the parties, or in accordance with provisions of section 76 having effect in default of agreement, is not reasonably practicable.

(2) Unless otherwise agreed by the parties, the court may make such order as it thinks fit:
(a)   for service in such manner as the court may direct, or
(b)   dispensing with service of the document.

(3) Any party to the arbitration agreement may apply for an order, but only after exhausting any available arbitral process for resolving the matter.

(4) The leave of the court is required for any appeal from a decision of the court under this section.

78 Reckoning periods of time

(1) The parties are free to agree on the method of reckoning periods of time for the purposes of any provision agreed by them or any provision of this Part having effect in default of such agreement.

(2) If or to the extent there is no such agreement, periods of time shall be reckoned in accordance with the following provisions.

(3) Where the act is required to be done within a specified period after or from a specified date, the period begins immediately after that date.

(4) Where the act is required to be done a specified number of clear days after a specified date, at least that number of days must intervene between the day on which the act is done and that date.

(5) Where the period is a period of seven days or less which would include a Saturday, Sunday or a public holiday in the place where anything which has to be done within the period falls to be done, that day shall be excluded.

In relation to England and Wales or Northern Ireland, a "public holiday" means Christmas Day, Good Friday or a day which under the [1971 c. 80.] *Banking and Financial Dealings Act 1971* is a bank holiday.

79 Power of court to extend time limits relating to arbitral proceedings

(1) Unless the parties otherwise agree, the court may by order extend any time limit agreed by them in relation to any matter relating to the arbitral proceedings or specified in any provision of this Part having effect in default of such agreement.

This section does not apply to a time limit to which section 12 applies (power of court to extend time for beginning arbitral proceedings, &c.).

(2) An application for an order may be made:
(a)　by any party to the arbitral proceedings (upon notice to the other parties and to the tribunal), or
(b)　by the arbitral tribunal (upon notice to the parties).

(3) The court shall not exercise its power to extend a time limit unless it is satisfied:
(a)　that any available recourse to the tribunal, or to any arbitral or other institution or person vested by the parties with power in that regard, has first been exhausted, and
(b)　that a substantial injustice would otherwise be done.

(4) The court's power under this section may be exercised whether or not the time has already expired.

(5) An order under this section may be made on such terms as the court thinks fit.

(6) The leave of the court is required for any appeal from a decision of the court under this section.

80 Notice and other requirements in connection with legal proceedings

(1) References in this Part to an application, appeal or other step in relation to legal proceedings being taken "upon notice" to the other parties to the arbitral proceedings, or to the tribunal, are to such notice of the originating process as is required by rules of court and do not impose any separate requirement.

(2) Rules of court shall be made:
(a)　requiring such notice to be given as indicated by any provision of this Part, and
(b)　as to the manner, form and content of any such notice.

(3) Subject to any provision made by rules of court, a requirement to give notice to the tribunal of legal proceedings shall be construed:
(a)　if there is more than one arbitrator, as a requirement to give notice to each of them; and

(b)   if the tribunal is not fully constituted, as a requirement to give notice to any arbitrator who has been appointed.

(4) References in this Part to making an application or appeal to the court within a specified period are to the issue within that period of the appropriate originating process in accordance with rules of court.

(5) Where any provision of this Part requires an application or appeal to be made to the court within a specified time, the rules of court relating to the reckoning of periods, the extending or abridging of periods, and the consequences of not taking a step within the period prescribed by the rules, apply in relation to that requirement.

(6) Provision may be made by rules of court amending the provisions of this Part:
(a)   with respect to the time within which any application or appeal to the court must be made,
(b)   so as to keep any provision made by this Part in relation to arbitral proceedings in step with the corresponding provision of rules of court applying in relation to proceedings in the court, or
(c)   so as to keep any provision made by this Part in relation to legal proceedings in step with the corresponding provision of rules of court applying generally in relation to proceedings in the court.

(7) Nothing in this section affects the generality of the power to make rules of court.

81 Saving for certain matters governed by common law

(1) Nothing in this Part shall be construed as excluding the operation of any rule of law consistent with the provisions of this Part, in particular, any rule of law as to:
(a)   matters which are not capable of settlement by arbitration;
(b)   the effect of an oral arbitration agreement; or
(c)   the refusal of recognition or enforcement of an arbitral award on grounds of public policy.

(2) Nothing in this Act shall be construed as reviving any jurisdiction of the court to set aside or remit an award on the ground of errors of fact or law on the face of the award.

82 Minor definitions

(1) In this Part:

"arbitrator", unless the context otherwise requires, includes an umpire;

"available arbitral process", in relation to any matter, includes any process of appeal to or review by an arbitral or other institution or person vested by the parties with powers in relation to that matter;

"claimant", unless the context otherwise requires, includes a counterclaimant, and related expressions shall be construed accordingly;

"dispute" includes any difference;

"enactment" includes an enactment contained in Northern Ireland legislation;

"legal proceedings" means civil proceedings in the High Court or a county court;

"peremptory order" means an order made under section 41(5) or made in exercise of any corresponding power conferred by the parties;

"premises" includes land, buildings, moveable structures, vehicles, vessels, aircraft and hovercraft;

"question of law" means:

(a) for a court in England and Wales, a question of the law of England and Wales, and

(b) for a court in Northern Ireland, a question of the law of Northern Ireland;

"substantive jurisdiction", in relation to an arbitral tribunal, refers to the matters specified in section 30(1)(a) to (c), and references to the tribunal exceeding its substantive jurisdiction shall be construed accordingly.

(2) References in this Part to a party to an arbitration agreement include any person claiming under or through a party to the agreement.

83 Index of defined expressions: Part I

In this Part the expressions listed below are defined or otherwise explained by the provisions indicated:

agreement, agree and agreed	section 5(1)
agreement in writing	section 5(2) to (5)
arbitration agreement	sections 6 and 5(1)

arbitrator	section 82(1)
available arbitral process	section 82(1)
claimant	section 82(1)
commencement (in relation to arbitral proceedings)	section 14
costs of the arbitration	section 59
the court	section 105
dispute	section 82(1)
enactment	section 82(1)
legal proceedings	section 82(1)
Limitation Acts	section 13(4)
notice (or other document)	section 76(6)
party –	
– in relation to an arbitration agreement	section 82(2)
– where section 106(2) or (3) applies	section 106(4)
peremptory order	section 82(1) (and see section 41(5))
premises	section 82(1)
question of law	section 82(1)
recoverable costs	sections 63 and 64
seat of the arbitration	section 3
serve and service (of notice or other document)	section 76(6)
substantive jurisdiction (in relation to an arbitral tribunal)	section 82(1) (and see section 30(1)(a) to (c))
upon notice (to the parties or the tribunal)	section 80
written and in writing	section 5(6)

84 Transitional provisions

(1) The provisions of this Part do not apply to arbitral proceedings commenced before the date on which this Part comes into force.

(2) They apply to arbitral proceedings commenced on or after that date under an arbitration agreement whenever made.

(3) The above provisions have effect subject to any transitional provision made by an order under section 109(2) (power to include transitional provisions in commencement order).

Part II: OTHER PROVISIONS RELATING TO ARBITRATION

Domestic arbitration agreements

85 Modification of Part I in relation to domestic arbitration agreement

(1) In the case of a domestic arbitration agreement the provisions of Part I are modified in accordance with the following sections.

(2) For this purpose a "domestic arbitration agreement" means an arbitration agreement to which none of the parties is:

(a)   an individual who is a national of, or habitually resident in, a state other than the United Kingdom, or

(b)   a body corporate which is incorporated in, or whose central control and management is exercised in, a state other than the United Kingdom,

and under which the seat of the arbitration (if the seat has been designated or determined) is in the United Kingdom.

(3) In subsection (2) "arbitration agreement" and "seat of the arbitration" have the same meaning as in Part I (see sections 3, 5(1) and 6).

86 Staying of legal proceedings

(1) In section 9 (stay of legal proceedings), subsection (4) (stay unless the arbitration agreement is null and void, inoperative, or incapable of being performed) does not apply to a domestic arbitration agreement.

(2) On an application under that section in relation to a domestic arbitration agreement the court shall grant a stay unless satisfied:

(a)   that the arbitration agreement is null and void, inoperative, or incapable of being performed, or

(b)   that there are other sufficient grounds for not requiring the parties to abide by the arbitration agreement.

(3) The court may treat as a sufficient ground under subsection (2)(b) the fact that the applicant is or was at any material time not ready and willing to do all things necessary for the proper

conduct of the arbitration or of any other dispute resolution procedures required to be exhausted before resorting to arbitration.

(4) For the purposes of this section the question whether an arbitration agreement is a domestic arbitration agreement shall be determined by reference to the facts at the time the legal proceedings are commenced.

87 Effectiveness of agreement to exclude court's jurisdiction

(1) In the case of a domestic arbitration agreement any agreement to exclude the jurisdiction of the court under:
(a)   section 45 (determination of preliminary point of law), or
(b)   section 69 (challenging the award: appeal on point of law),

is not effective unless entered into after the commencement of the arbitral proceedings in which the question arises or the award is made.

(2) For this purpose the commencement of the arbitral proceedings has the same meaning as in Part I (see section 14).

(3) For the purposes of this section the question whether an arbitration agreement is a domestic arbitration agreement shall be determined by reference to the facts at the time the agreement is entered into.

88 Power to repeal or amend sections 85 to 87

(1) The Secretary of State may by order repeal or amend the provisions of sections 85 to 87.

(2) An order under this section may contain such supplementary, incidental and transitional provisions as appear to the Secretary of State to be appropriate.

(3) An order under this section shall be made by statutory instrument and no such order shall be made unless a draft of it has been laid before and approved by a resolution of each House of Parliament.

Consumer arbitration agreements

89 Application of unfair terms regulations to consumer arbitration agreements

(1) The following sections extend the application of the [S.I. 1994/3159] *Unfair Terms in Consumer Contracts Regulations 1994* in relation to a term which constitutes an arbitration agreement.

For this purpose "arbitration agreement" means an agreement to submit to arbitration present or future disputes or differences (whether or not contractual).

(2) In those sections "the Regulations" means those regulations and includes any regulations amending or replacing those regulations.

(3) Those sections apply whatever the law applicable to the arbitration agreement.

90 Regulations apply where consumer is a legal person

The Regulations apply where the consumer is a legal person as they apply where the consumer is a natural person.

91 Arbitration agreement unfair where modest amount sought

(1) A term which constitutes an arbitration agreement is unfair for the purposes of the Regulations so far as it relates to a claim for a pecuniary remedy which does not exceed the amount specified by order for the purposes of this section.

(2) Orders under this section may make different provision for different cases and for different purposes.

(3) The power to make orders under this section is exercisable:
(a)   for England and Wales, by the Secretary of State with the concurrence of the Lord Chancellor,
(b)   for Scotland, by the Secretary of State with the concurrence of the Lord Advocate, and
(c)   for Northern Ireland, by the Department of Economic Development for Northern Ireland with the concurrence of the Lord Chancellor.

(4) Any such order for England and Wales or Scotland shall be made by statutory instrument which shall be subject to annulment in pursuance of a resolution of either House of Parliament.

(5) Any such order for Northern Ireland shall be a statutory rule for the purposes of the [S.I. 1979/1573 (N.I. 12).] *Statutory Rules (Northern Ireland) Order* 1979 and shall be subject to negative resolution, within the meaning of section 41(6) of the [1954 c. 33 (N.I.).] *Interpretation Act (Northern Ireland)* 1954.

Small claims arbitration in the county court

92 Exclusion of Part I in relation to small claims arbitration in the county court

Nothing in Part I of this Act applies to arbitration under section 64 of the [1984 c. 28.] *County Courts Act* 1984.

Appointment of judges as arbitrators

93 Appointment of judges as arbitrators

(1) A judge of the Commercial Court or an official referee may, if in all the circumstances he thinks fit, accept appointment as a sole arbitrator or as umpire by or by virtue of an arbitration agreement.

(2) A judge of the Commercial Court shall not do so unless the Lord Chief Justice has informed him that, having regard to the state of business in the High Court and the Crown Court, he can be made available.

(3) An official referee shall not do so unless the Lord Chief Justice has informed him that, having regard to the state of official referees' business, he can be made available.

(4) The fees payable for the services of a judge of the Commercial Court or official referee as arbitrator or umpire shall be taken in the High Court.

(5) In this section:

"arbitration agreement" has the same meaning as in Part I; and "official referee" means a person nominated under section 68(1)(a) of the [1981 c. 54.] *Supreme Court Act* 1981 to deal with official referees' business.

(6) The provisions of Part I of this Act apply to arbitration before a person appointed under this section with the modifications specified in Schedule 2.

Statutory arbitrations
94 Application of Part I to statutory arbitrations

(1) The provisions of Part I apply to every arbitration under an enactment (a "statutory arbitration"), whether the enactment was passed or made before or after the commencement of this Act, subject to the adaptations and exclusions specified in sections 95 to 98.

(2) The provisions of Part I do not apply to a statutory arbitration if or to the extent that their application:
(a)   is inconsistent with the provisions of the enactment concerned, with any rules or procedure authorised or recognised by it, or
(b)   is excluded by any other enactment.

(3) In this section and the following provisions of this Part "enactment":
(a)   in England and Wales, includes an enactment contained in subordinate legislation within the meaning of the [1978 c. 30.] *Interpretation Act* 1978;
(b)   in Northern Ireland, means a statutory provision within the meaning of section 1(f) of the [1954 c. 33 (N.I.).] *Interpretation Act (Northern Ireland)* 1954.

95 General adaptation of provisions in relation to statutory arbitrations

(1) The provisions of Part I apply to a statutory arbitration:
(a)   as if the arbitration were pursuant to an arbitration agreement and as if the enactment were that agreement, and
(b)   as if the persons by and against whom a claim subject to arbitration in pursuance of the enactment may be or has been made were parties to that agreement.

(2) Every statutory arbitration shall be taken to have its seat in England and Wales or, as the case may be, in Northern Ireland.

96 Specific adaptations of provisions in relation to statutory arbitrations

(1) The following provisions of Part I apply to a statutory arbitration with the following adaptations.

(2) In section 30(1) (competence of tribunal to rule on its own jurisdiction), the reference in paragraph (a) to whether there is a valid arbitration agreement shall be construed as a reference to whether the enactment applies to the dispute or difference in question.

(3) Section 35 (consolidation of proceedings and concurrent hearings) applies only so as to authorise the consolidation of proceedings, or concurrent hearings in proceedings, under the same enactment.

(4) Section 46 (rules applicable to substance of dispute) applies with the omission of subsection (1)(b) (determination in accordance with considerations agreed by parties).

97 Provisions excluded from applying to statutory arbitrations

The following provisions of Part I do not apply in relation to a statutory arbitration:
(a)   section 8 (whether agreement discharged by death of a party);
(b)   section 12 (power of court to extend agreed time limits);
(c)   sections 9(5), 10(2) and 71(4) (restrictions on effect of provision that award condition precedent to right to bring legal proceedings).

98 Power to make further provision by regulations

(1) The Secretary of State may make provision by regulations for adapting or excluding any provision of Part I in relation to statutory arbitrations in general or statutory arbitrations of any particular description.

(2) The power is exercisable whether the enactment concerned is passed or made before or after the commencement of this Act.

(3) Regulations under this section shall be made by statutory instrument which shall be subject to annulment in pursuance of a resolution of either House of Parliament.

Part III: RECOGNITION AND ENFORCEMENT OF CERTAIN FOREIGN AWARDS

Enforcement of Geneva Convention awards

99 Continuation of Part II of the Arbitration Act 1950

Part II of the [1950 c. 27.] *Arbitration Act* 1950 (enforcement of certain foreign awards) continues to apply in relation to foreign awards within the meaning of that Part which are not also New York Convention awards.

Recognition and enforcement of New York Convention awards

100 New York Convention awards

(1) In this Part a "New York Convention award" means an award made, in pursuance of an arbitration agreement, in the territory of a state (other than the United Kingdom) which is a party to the New York Convention.

(2) For the purposes of subsection (1) and of the provisions of this Part relating to such awards:
(a)   "arbitration agreement" means an arbitration agreement in writing, and
(b)   an award shall be treated as made at the seat of the arbitration, regardless of where it was signed, despatched or delivered to any of the parties.

In this subsection "agreement in writing" and "seat of the arbitration" have the same meaning as in Part I.

(3) If Her Majesty by Order in Council declares that a state specified in the Order is a party to the New York Convention, or is a party in respect of any territory so specified, the Order shall, while in force, be conclusive evidence of that fact.

(4) In this section "the New York Convention" means the Convention on the Recognition and Enforcement of Foreign Arbitral Awards adopted by the United Nations Conference on International Commercial Arbitration on 10th June 1958.

101 Recognition and enforcement of awards

(1) A New York Convention award shall be recognised as binding on the persons as between whom it was made, and may accordingly be relied on by those persons by way of defence, set-off or otherwise in any legal proceedings in England and Wales or Northern Ireland.

(2) A New York Convention award may, by leave of the court, be enforced in the same manner as a judgment or order of the court to the same effect.

As to the meaning of "the court" see section 105.

(3) Where leave is so given, judgment may be entered in terms of the award.

102 Evidence to be produced by party seeking recognition or enforcement

(1) A party seeking the recognition or enforcement of a New York Convention award must produce:
(a)   the duly authenticated original award or a duly certified copy of it, and
(b)   the original arbitration agreement or a duly certified copy of it.

(2) If the award or agreement is in a foreign language, the party must also produce a translation of it certified by an official or sworn translator or by a diplomatic or consular agent.

103 Refusal of recognition or enforcement

(1) Recognition or enforcement of a New York Convention award shall not be refused except in the following cases.

(2) Recognition or enforcement of the award may be refused if the person against whom it is invoked proves:
(a)   that a party to the arbitration agreement was (under the law applicable to him) under some incapacity;
(b)   that the arbitration agreement was not valid under the law to which the parties subjected it or, failing any indication thereon, under the law of the country where the award was made;

(c)   that he was not given proper notice of the appointment of the arbitrator or of the arbitration proceedings or was otherwise unable to present his case;

(d)   that the award deals with a difference not contemplated by or not falling within the terms of the submission to arbitration or contains decisions on matters beyond the scope of the submission to arbitration (but see subsection (4));

(e)   that the composition of the arbitral tribunal or the arbitral procedure was not in accordance with the agreement of the parties or, failing such agreement, with the law of the country in which the arbitration took place;

(f)   that the award has not yet become binding on the parties, or has been set aside or suspended by a competent authority of the country in which, or under the law of which, it was made.

(3) Recognition or enforcement of the award may also be refused if the award is in respect of a matter which is not capable of settlement by arbitration, or if it would be contrary to public policy to recognise or enforce the award.

(4) An award which contains decisions on matters not submitted to arbitration may be recognised or enforced to the extent that it contains decisions on matters submitted to arbitration which can be separated from those on matters not so submitted.

(5) Where an application for the setting aside or suspension of the award has been made to such a competent authority as is mentioned in subsection (2)(f), the court before which the award is sought to be relied upon may, if it considers it proper, adjourn the decision on the recognition or enforcement of the award.

It may also on the application of the party claiming recognition or enforcement of the award order the other party to give suitable security.

104 Saving for other bases of recognition or enforcement

Nothing in the preceding provisions of this Part affects any right to rely upon or enforce a New York Convention award at common law or under section 66.

Part IV: GENERAL PROVISIONS

105 Meaning of "the court": jurisdiction of High Court and county court

(1) In this Act "the court" means the High Court or a county court, subject to the following provisions.

(2) The Lord Chancellor may by order make provision:
(a)   allocating proceedings under this Act to the High Court or to county courts; or
(b)   specifying proceedings under this Act which may be commenced or taken only in the High Court or in a county court.

(3) The Lord Chancellor may by order make provision requiring proceedings of any specified description under this Act in relation to which a county court has jurisdiction to be commenced or taken in one or more specified county courts.

Any jurisdiction so exercisable by a specified county court is exercisable throughout England and Wales or, as the case may be, Northern Ireland.

(4) An order under this section:
(a)   may differentiate between categories of proceedings by reference to such criteria as the Lord Chancellor sees fit to specify, and
(b)   may make such incidental or transitional provision as the Lord Chancellor considers necessary or expedient.

(5) An order under this section for England and Wales shall be made by statutory instrument which shall be subject to annulment in pursuance of a resolution of either House of Parliament.

(6) An order under this section for Northern Ireland shall be a statutory rule for the purposes of the [S.I. 1979/1573 (N.I. 12).] *Statutory Rules (Northern Ireland) Order* 1979 which shall be subject to annulment in pursuance of a resolution of either House of Parliament in like manner as a statutory instrument and section 5 of the [1946 c. 36.] *Statutory Instruments Act* 1946 shall apply accordingly.

106 Crown application

(1) Part I of this Act applies to any arbitration agreement to which Her Majesty, either in right of the Crown or of the Duchy of Lancaster or otherwise, or the Duke of Cornwall, is a party.

(2) Where Her Majesty is party to an arbitration agreement otherwise than in right of the Crown, Her Majesty shall be represented for the purposes of any arbitral proceedings:
(a) where the agreement was entered into by Her Majesty in right of the Duchy of Lancaster, by the Chancellor of the Duchy or such person as he may appoint, and
(b) in any other case, by such person as Her Majesty may appoint in writing under the Royal Sign Manual.

(3) Where the Duke of Cornwall is party to an arbitration agreement, he shall be represented for the purposes of any arbitral proceedings by such person as he may appoint.

(4) References in Part I to a party or the parties to the arbitration agreement or to arbitral proceedings shall be construed, where subsection (2) or (3) applies, as references to the person representing Her Majesty or the Duke of Cornwall.

107 Consequential amendments and repeals

(1) The enactments specified in Schedule 3 are amended in accordance with that Schedule, the amendments being consequential on the provisions of this Act.

(2) The enactments specified in Schedule 4 are repealed to the extent specified.

108 Extent

(1) The provisions of this Act extend to England and Wales and, except as mentioned below, to Northern Ireland.

(2) The following provisions of Part II do not extend to Northern Ireland:
• section 92 (exclusion of Part I in relation to small claims arbitration in the county court), and
• section 93 and Schedule 2 (appointment of judges as arbitrators).

(3) Sections 89, 90 and 91 (consumer arbitration agreements) extend to Scotland and the provisions of Schedules 3 and 4 (consequential amendments and repeals) extend to Scotland so far as they relate to enactments which so extend, subject as follows.

(4) The repeal of the [1975 c. 3.] *Arbitration Act* 1975 extends only to England and Wales and Northern Ireland.

109 Commencement

(1) The provisions of this Act come into force on such day as the Secretary of State may appoint by order made by statutory instrument, and different days may be appointed for different purposes.

(2) An order under subsection (1) may contain such transitional provisions as appear to the Secretary of State to be appropriate.

110 Short title

This Act may be cited as the *Arbitration Act* 1996.

SCHEDULES

Section 4(1).

SCHEDULE 1: MANDATORY PROVISIONS OF PART I
sections 9 to 11 (stay of legal proceedings);
section 12 (power of court to extend agreed time limits);
section 13 (application of Limitation Acts);
section 24 (power of court to remove arbitrator);
section 26(1) (effect of death of arbitrator);
section 28 (liability of parties for fees and expenses of arbitrators);
section 29 (immunity of arbitrator);
section 31 (objection to substantive jurisdiction of tribunal);
section 32 (determination of preliminary point of jurisdiction);
section 33 (general duty of tribunal);
section 37(2) (items to be treated as expenses of arbitrators);
section 40 (general duty of parties);
section 43 (securing the attendance of witnesses);

section 56 (power to withhold award in case of non-payment);

section 60 (effectiveness of agreement for payment of costs in any event);

section 66 (enforcement of award);

sections 67 and 68 (challenging the award: substantive jurisdiction and serious irregularity), and sections 70 and 71 (supplementary provisions; effect of order of court) so far as relating to those sections;

section 72 (saving for rights of person who takes no part in proceedings);

section 73 (loss of right to object);

section 74 (immunity of arbitral institutions, &c.);

section 75 (charge to secure payment of solicitors' costs).

Section 93(6).

SCHEDULE 2: MODIFICATIONS OF PART I IN RELATION TO JUDGE-ARBITRATORS*

SCHEDULE 3: CONSEQUENTIAL AMENDMENTS*

Section 107(2).

SCHEDULE 4: REPEALS*

* See www.opsi.gov.uk/acts/acts1996/Ukpga_19960023_en_1

Appendix 3A: RICS PS and GN: Surveyors acting as expert witnesses

The text of the 3rd edition of the RICS practice statement and guidance note: *Surveyors acting as expert witnesses* is reproduced below. This edition comes into effect on 1 January 2009.

Surveyors acting as expert witnesses: RICS practice statement and guidance note (3rd edition)

Acknowledgments

An extract from *The Surveyor in Court* is reproduced in this document with permission from P. H. Clarke FRICS.

Crown copyright material is reproduced with the permission of the Controller of HMSO and the Queen's Printer for Scotland.

Contents

Surveyors acting as expert witnesses: guidance note

Copyright notice

An acknowledgment of RICS copyright ownership should appear on any extract from, or copy of, the PS and GN that is reproduced, save when the Statement of Truth (PS 5.1(i)) or other declarations (PS 5.1(j)) are being used in expert reports, or when reproducing *Appendix A: Sample Terms of Engagement*.

Appendix A: Sample Terms of Engagement may be reproduced without the need for prior consent from RICS. Where it is adapted and integrated into personalised terms of engagement, no copyright acknowledgment is required; however any other usage by way of reproduction requires an acknowledgment of copyright.

Reproduction (other than as specified above) or republishing in any format requires express written permission from RICS. A request for such permission, or any other enquiry related to copyright, may be addressed to:

RICS Publishing and Content Services
Surveyor Court
Westwood Way
Coventry
CV4 8JE
United Kingdom

Surveyors acting as expert witnesses: RICS practice statements

This is a practice statement (PS). There may be disciplinary consequences for RICS members for a failure to comply with a PS.

RICS members should also note that when an allegation of professional negligence is made against them, the court is likely to take account of any relevant PS published by RICS in deciding whether or not they acted with reasonable competence. Failure to comply with practice statements may, accordingly, lead to a finding of negligence against an RICS member.

In the opinion of RICS, if RICS members conform to the requirements of this PS they should have at least a partial defence to an allegation of negligence by virtue of having followed those practices.

Where RICS members depart from the practice required by this PS, they should do so only for good reason and the client must be informed in writing of the fact of and the reasons for the departure. In the event of litigation, the court may require you to explain why you decided to act as you did. Also, an RICS member who has not followed this PS and whose actions are called into question in an RICS disciplinary case, may be asked to justify the steps he or she took.

Investigation of alleged breaches of a practice statement

In the interest of maintaining the highest professional standards, breaches of any aspect of a practice statement that are reported to RICS will be reviewed, and may be investigated, by RICS Regulation, normally when the underlying dispute has been resolved. Reports of this nature should be made in writing and can be made confidentially to:

RICS Regulation
PO Box 2291
Coventry
CV4 8ZJ
United Kingdom
T: + 44 (0)20 7695 1670
E: regulation@rics.org

Any RICS member adjudged to merit referral by RICS investigative staff may be referred for disciplinary action. If the relevant disciplinary body considers it justified, an RICS member may be publicly reprimanded, fined and/or expelled from RICS, depending on the severity of the breach.

Comments on this publication

Although RICS cannot undertake to respond personally to each such communication, if you have any comments or feedback on any aspect of this publication, please feel free to write to:

RICS Dispute Resolution Faculty
12 Great George Street
London
SW1P 3AD
United Kingdom
E: dr.faculty@rics.org

Surveyors acting as expert witnesses: practice statement: Preamble

Whilst in general this text is gender neutral, on occasions where masculine terms only are used (such as in legislation quotes) these should be taken as also referring to the feminine (e.g. 'she', 'her'), and to 'they' or 'it' (in the case of a corporate body), as the context so requires.

References to the singular also include the plural and vice versa where the context so requires. Unless otherwise specified, references to 'you', 'member', 'surveyor' or to 'expert witness surveyor' are to members of RICS of any class of membership, save for Honorary Members. References to 'PS' denote 'practice statement'.

Where you are acting as an Assessor, Valuation Officer, Listing Officer, District Valuer or Commissioner of Valuation (or as an authorised representative thereof) in local taxation matters and are acting in pursuit of a statutory duty, you will not usually be operating in a client/adviser framework and will generally not have a direct client.

There are variations in terminology, legislation and case law references pertinent to expert witness practice across the different legal jurisdictions within the UK. Not all of these are exhaustively referenced below but where it is felt appropriate some are highlighted.

For the purposes of this PS, the generic expression 'tribunal' means any body whose function it is to determine disputes. This therefore includes:
- **courts and tribunals (including Lands Tribunals and Agricultural Land Tribunals; Leasehold Valuation Tribunals; Residential Property Tribunals; Valuation Tribunals);**
- **arbitrators/arbiters or arbitral panels/tribunals;**
- **adjudicators (including those operating under the *Housing Grants, Construction and Regeneration Act 1996*);**
- **committees (including Rent Assessment Committees, Valuation Appeal Committees);**
- **inspectors, commissioners and reporters (e.g. in planning proceedings, including Inquiries, Hearings, Examinations in Public – independent panels; Independent Examination and proceedings of the**

Infrastructure Planning Commission, and Planning and Water Appeals Commissions); and
- **independent experts.**

Note: It is expected that once provisions of the *Tribunals, Courts and Enforcement Act* 2007 are implemented, some of the tribunals listed above will take on a different designation, but at the time of publication this is not in place.

Principal message

As a surveyor actively involved in a dispute that may come before a tribunal, you may find yourself carrying out one or more roles, including that of an expert witness. Your primary duty as an expert witness (sometimes referred to as a 'skilled witness' in Scotland) is not to a client but to the tribunal. You will need to follow the requirements of *Surveyors acting as expert witnesses*: RICS practice statement. Your primary duty to the tribunal is to ensure that the expert evidence provided by you:
- **must be, and must be seen to be, your independent and unbiased product, and fall within your expertise, experience and knowledge;**
- **must state the main facts and assumptions it is based upon, and not omit material facts that might be relevant to your conclusions; and**
- **must be impartial and uninfluenced by those instructing or paying you to give the evidence.**

It is imperative that you do not stray from the duties of an expert witness by acting in a partial, misleading or untruthful manner. In those instances when you may adopt a dual role of surveyor-advocate and expert witness, it is also imperative that you differentiate at all times clearly between the two roles (see PS 9).

PS 1 Application of practice statement

1.1　　The start date of application of this PS is 1 January 2009. This PS applies to any RICS member (usually described hereafter as 'the expert witness surveyor' or 'you') who provides expert evidence, whether oral or written, to the proceedings of any tribunal in the United Kingdom, except for criminal proceedings.

1.2   This PS does not apply to you when acting in any capacity other than as an expert witness (for example, in the capacity of a witness of fact). In cases where you are using your professional experience, knowledge and expertise in the role of surveyor-advocate, *Surveyors acting as advocates*: RICS practice statement will apply.

1.3   You give expert evidence when you draw upon your professional experience, knowledge and expertise to provide evidence to a tribunal, such evidence being distinct from:
(a)   advice not given for the purpose of a tribunal's proceedings;
(b)   evidence of fact; and
(c)   advocacy of a case.

1.4   Since this PS only applies to the provision of expert evidence by you when appointed as an expert witness, it does not apply for the purpose of assisting your client to decide whether to initiate or defend proceedings to be heard by a tribunal. However, where you are giving advice in writing to your client and consider that you may be required to give expert evidence in such proceedings, you must advise your client in writing if your advice or investigations would fall short of that necessary to enable expert evidence complying with this PS to be provided.

1.5   Where you act as an expert witness and consider that there are special circumstances which render it inappropriate or impractical for the assignment to be undertaken wholly in accordance with this PS, the fact of, and reasons for, the departure must as soon as reasonably practical be given in writing to your client, and must also be contained in any expert report prepared; alternatively you may wish to decline instructions or withdraw from a case. Where you depart from the PS you may be required to justify to RICS the reasons for the departure. RICS is entitled to take disciplinary measures if it is not satisfied with the reasons given and/or the manner in which the departure has been notified or evidenced. In the event of litigation, a court may require you to explain why you decided to act as you did.

1.6 The *Civil Procedure Rules* (CPR), together with associated Practice Directions, Forms, Protocols, and court guides, all apply to the procedure of the Supreme Court and the County Court in England and Wales; other rules and procedures may apply elsewhere. Surveyors proposing to act as expert witnesses are, as a matter of professional conduct, expected to make themselves aware of the need to comply with the CPR, or other rules and procedures, and to comply with these in those circumstances when they apply.

PS 2 Duty in providing expert evidence

2.1 Your overriding duty as an expert witness surveyor is to the tribunal to whom the expert evidence is given. This duty overrides the contractual duty to your client. The duty to the tribunal is to set out the facts fully and give truthful, impartial and independent opinions, covering all relevant matters, whether or not they favour your client. This applies irrespective of whether or not the evidence is given either on oath or affirmation. Special care must be taken to ensure that expert evidence is not biased towards those who are responsible for instructing or paying you. The duty endures for the whole assignment. Opinions should not be exaggerated or seek to obscure alternative views or other schools of thought, but should instead recognise and, where appropriate, address them.

2.2 Where, for any reason, you are unable to comply with any order or direction of the tribunal you must as soon as practicable:
(a) prepare a written record of the reason for such non-compliance; and
(b) give copies of that record to your client and to the tribunal.

2.3 The duty to the tribunal set out at PS 2.1 applies whether your expert evidence is given orally or in writing.

2.4 As an expert witness surveyor you must be able to show that you have full knowledge of the duties relating to the role of an expert witness when giving evidence.

2.5 You are entitled to accept instructions from your employer to give expert evidence on behalf of that employer. Prior to accepting such instructions, you must satisfy yourself that your employer understands that your primary duty in giving evidence is to the tribunal and that this may mean that your evidence will conflict with your employer's view of the matter or the way in which your employer would prefer to see matters put.

2.6 Where you are acting – or have previously acted – for a party on a matter (in the course of, for instance, negotiations) and the matter requires, or may in the future require, the giving of expert evidence, you must throughout consider, and then decide, whether you can fully satisfy the overriding duty to the tribunal to provide evidence that is truthful, independent, impartial, and complete as to coverage of relevant matters.

2.7 As an expert witness surveyor you must not malign the professional competence of another expert witness. If you feel that expressing doubts about the competence of another expert witness is both justified and necessary in order for you to present a full picture to the tribunal, you may bring to its attention where you consider the experience, knowledge and expertise of another expert witness is lacking, inappropriate or exaggerated, or where you consider evidence is biased, explaining why. Comments should be focused on the facts, interpretation of data and analysis of opinion.

PS 3 Acting as an expert witness, and instructions

3.1 You must only act as an expert witness and give expert evidence where you have:
  (a) the ability to act impartially in the assignment;
  (b) the experience, knowledge and expertise appropriate for the assignment; and
  (c) the resources to complete the assignment within the required timescales and to the required standard.

3.2 If you have any doubt as to whether you should accept instructions to act as an expert witness, you must advise your prospective client accordingly. If you consider that the tribunal might attach less or no weight to your evidence as a result of particular circumstances, you have a duty to advise your prospective client accordingly.

3.3   Prior to accepting instructions to act as an expert witness, you must:

(a)   advise your prospective client in writing that this PS and, where appropriate, the CPR, or other rules, will apply;

(b)   make a written offer to your prospective client to supply a copy of the PS; and notify your prospective client that your firm's Complaints Handling Procedure (CHP) (if the firm is an RICS-regulated firm) will not apply to your engagement as expert witness;

(c)   ensure without delay that you advise your prospective client in writing of the nature and scope of your obligations under the CPR, or other rules that might apply, and of your general obligations, in particular that the overriding duty of the expert witness in giving evidence is to the tribunal;

(d)   ensure that there is a written record, held by you and sent to (or received from) your prospective client, as to the matters on which expert evidence is required, whether such record is upon the initiative of yourself or those instructing you, and confirm in writing if you propose that any part of the assignment is likely to be undertaken by a person other than yourself;

(e)   carry out a check to satisfy yourself that no conflict of interest arises (see also PS 2.5–2.6). If you have any doubt whatsoever in this respect, any potential or actual conflict must be reported to those offering instructions as soon as it becomes apparent. If you consider that the tribunal might attach less or no weight to your evidence as a result of such circumstances, you must advise your prospective client accordingly.

3.4   (a)   Courts of law will only in exceptional circumstances accept evidence from an expert witness acting under a conditional fee arrangement. There are a number of court protocols and practice directions, and case law, which make the impermissibility of such a fee arrangement clear. Even where such evidence is admitted, the courts may well give it little weight.

(b) Where the fee arrangement for your instructions is intended to be a conditional fee, you must, prior to accepting instructions to act as an expert witness, advise your prospective client in writing of the risk that the tribunal may view evidence given under a conditional fee arrangement as being tainted by bias, and may attach less weight to it; it may even refuse to admit it at all, or find the whole conditional fee arrangement void. You must only proceed to act on a conditional fee arrangement where the client has so consented expressly in writing. You are required by PS 5.1(j)(iii) to make a declaration to the tribunal in respect of conditional fee arrangements.

3.5 You must confirm to your prospective client in writing and in good time whether or not you accept the prospective client's instructions. Your acceptance should cover your terms of engagement (including the basis upon which your fees will be charged) and any specific mandates given as to important or contentious matters. You must then ensure that all such documents, together with communications from your client, are kept by you as a proper record of your instructions. Any change or supplement to the terms that may be made from time to time should be added to your records.

3.6 Any potential or actual conflict arising after instructions have been accepted must be notified immediately to your client. In such circumstances the same reporting procedures and considerations as per PS 3.3(e) above should apply. This paragraph (PS 3.6) does not apply to Single Joint Experts (see instead PS 8.7).

PS 4 Inspections

4.1 Where any inspection of any property/facility is, in your view, required, it must always, where reasonably possible, be carried out to the extent necessary to produce an opinion that is professionally competent. This should have regard to its purpose and the circumstances of the case.

PS 5 Reports and oral evidence

Note: In certain tribunals or circumstances, terminology other than 'reports' may be used; for example, in planning appeals. If produced as evidence for planning inquiries, they would be called 'proofs of evidence' in England and Wales, and Northern Ireland, and 'precognitions' in Scotland; and if produced for hearings or exchanges of written representations they would be called 'statements'.

5.1 In providing a written report to be lodged before a tribunal, you must comply with any rules, orders or directions of the tribunal to which the report is to be presented. You must:

(a) Give details of your qualifications, and relevant experience, knowledge and expertise (commensurate in detail with the nature and complexity of the case).

(b) State the substance of all material instructions (whether written or oral). The statement should summarise the facts and instructions given to you that are material to the opinions expressed in the report or upon which those opinions are based. The omission of 'off-the-record' oral instructions is not permitted.

(c) Give details of any literature or other material which you have relied upon in making the report, including the opinions of others.

(d) State who carried out any test, experiment or survey which you have used for the report, the methodology and nature thereof, and whether or not the test, experiment or survey has been carried out under your supervision.

(e) Give the qualifications and relevant experience, knowledge and expertise of the person who carried out any such test, experiment or survey.

(f) Consider all matters material to the instruction. You must state clearly all assumptions and facts upon which your opinion and reasoning is based, distinguishing between those facts that you believe to be true and those you have assumed (specifying those you have been instructed to assume). Where facts are known to be in dispute you must state separate opinions on each hypothesis put forward. A view in favour of one or other disputed set of facts should not be expressed unless, solely due to your particular experience, knowledge and expertise, you consider one set of facts to be improbable or less probable, in which case a view can be expressed with appropriate reasons. You must indicate where, in what way and why, an opinion is provisional, if you consider that further information is required or if, for whatever reason, you believe a final and unqualified opinion cannot be expressed.

(g) Where there are ranges of opinion on the matters dealt with in the report:

    (i) summarise the ranges of opinion and their sources; and

    (ii) give reasons for your own opinion.

(h) Include a summary of the conclusions reached.

(i) Verify the report with a Statement of Truth. In cases where the CPR apply, the wording stipulated by the CPR for the Statement of Truth must always be used – see CPR Practice Direction 35 and the *Protocol for the Instruction of Experts to give Evidence in Civil Claims*. The form of wording to be used in relation to non-CPR cases must follow the rules or requirements of the particular tribunal concerned. Where no specific wording for a Statement of Truth is specified by a tribunal's rules or requirements, the following default wording (that of the CPR's Statement of Truth) must be used:

> 'I confirm that insofar as the facts stated in my report are within my own knowledge I have made clear which they are and I believe them to be true, and that the opinions I have expressed represent my true and complete professional opinion.'

> *Crown copyright material is reproduced with the permission of the Controller of HMSO and the Queen's Printer for Scotland.*

(j) Include all the following declarations at the end of the report:

    (i) 'I confirm that my report includes all facts which I regard as being relevant to the opinions which I have expressed and that attention has been drawn to any matter which would affect the validity of those opinions.'

(ii) **A** – 'I confirm that my duty to [*specify the tribunal**] as an expert witness overrides any duty to those instructing or paying me, that I have understood this duty and complied with it in giving my evidence impartially and objectively, and that I will continue to comply with that duty as required.' (*The reference used may vary, as appropriate to the particular forum.)

This declaration (PS 5.1(j)(ii)A) should be used in relation to the proceedings of all tribunals **except those in Scotland**, for which the declaration immediately below (PS 5.1(j)(ii)B) should be adopted instead:

B – 'I confirm that in preparing this report I have assumed the same duty which would apply to me when giving my expert opinions in a court of law under oath or affirmation. I confirm that this duty overrides any duty to those instructing or paying me, that I have understood this duty and complied with it in giving my opinions impartially and objectively, and that I will continue to comply with that duty as required.'

(iii) 'I confirm that I am not instructed under any conditional fee arrangement.'

Where however you are instructed under a conditional fee arrangement, PS 10.1 mandates that you must disclose that fact by making this declaration to the tribunal: 'I confirm that I am instructed under a conditional fee arrangement.'

(iv) 'I confirm that I have no conflicts of interest of any kind other than those already disclosed in my report.'

(v) 'I confirm that my report complies with the requirements of the Royal Institution of Chartered Surveyors (RICS), as set down in *Surveyors acting as expert witnesses*: RICS practice statement.'

(k) Personally sign and date the report.

5.2 The scope of PS 5.1 covers written reports. In relation to expert evidence to be given orally where no written report has been lodged or submitted to the tribunal, you must at the outset declare to the tribunal that the expert evidence you give complies with the requirements of the Royal Institution of Chartered Surveyors (RICS), as set down in *Surveyors acting as expert witnesses*: RICS practice statement; or, in the event, any departure from the requirements of the PS should be outlined to the tribunal. You must also declare to the tribunal whether you are instructed under a conditional fee arrangement.

PS 6 Amendment of the contents of written reports

6.1   If after disclosure of your report you identify a material inaccuracy or omission, or have a change of opinion on any matter, you must without delay and in writing notify any intention to make changes, and the reasons for such changes, to:
(a)   those instructing you;
(b)   other parties to the dispute (through legal representatives, if any); and
(c)   where appropriate, the tribunal.

6.2   You may be invited to amend or expand a report to ensure accuracy, consistency, completeness, relevance and clarity. You must disregard any suggestions or alterations that do not accord with your true opinions, or distort them.

PS 7 Agreeing facts and resolving differences

7.1   As an expert witness, you may be instructed by your client to communicate with the other party in an attempt to agree facts, and to clarify, narrow and resolve the differences between parties. You may in any event be ordered to do this by the tribunal; you must follow any lawful order or direction of the tribunal, notwithstanding any directive by a client to the contrary.

7.2   Where, for any reason, you are unable to comply with any order or direction of the tribunal concerning the matters set out in PS 7.1, you must as soon as practicable:
(a)   prepare a written record of the reason for such non-compliance; and
(b)   give copies of that record to your client and to the tribunal.

7.3 Even where you have not been instructed by your client to communicate with the other party or so ordered by the tribunal, or where the tribunal does not specify any requirements in regard to the manner or scope of such communications, you must raise with your client the possible advantages, disadvantages and appropriateness of:

(a) making such communications at as early a stage as possible;

(b) identifying with counterpart experts the issues in dispute, the reasons for any differences of opinion and the actions that might be taken to resolve outstanding issues between parties;

(c) preparing a statement for the tribunal showing:

(i) those facts and issues which are agreed;

(ii) those facts and issues which have not been agreed and the reasons for any disagreement on any issue.

PS 8 Single Joint Expert (SJE)

8.1 As an SJE you are appointed pursuant to an order by a court of law (CPR 35.7) and then treated by the court as being appointed jointly by parties to the dispute. You should be clear as to the following points, and if necessary, you should require the parties to clarify them:

(a) the subject matter of your instructions;

(b) the need for expert evidence;

(c) the issues to be addressed;

(d) the method of presentation of the evidence (written or oral);

(e) the release of the expert evidence to the parties; and

(f) the need to limit your opinions to your core fields of expertise.

8.2 As an SJE you must recognise that you will owe equal duties to all parties to the dispute and must remain independent and transparent in your dealings. You should keep the parties informed of material steps you are taking.

8.3 If you have previously given advice to a party you must only accept an appointment as an SJE (whether in the same case or otherwise) where all parties have been fully informed of all relevant information about your prior involvement.

8.4   As an SJE, if you have not received instructions from your clients, you must give notice to them of a deadline for the receipt by you of instructions. If you do not receive those instructions, you should apply to the court for directions under CPR 35.14.

8.5   Irrespective of whether you have received instructions containing conflicting facts and/or allegations, you should provide a single report.

8.6   Where a difficulty arises that appears to lead to incompatibility with your duties as an SJE, you must carefully consider whether to resign the appointment. You should first discuss with those instructing you the particular difficulties experienced and request that they attempt to resolve the matter where possible. You should, as a last resort, consider whether it would be more appropriate to make a written request to the court for directions. In the event of resignation of your appointment, you should notify those instructing you in writing, serving a statement of your reasons.

8.7   Where a potential or actual conflict of interest arises after acceptance of instructions as an SJE, it must be notified immediately to those instructing you. If you consider that the tribunal might attach less or no weight to your evidence as a result of such circumstances, you must advise those instructing you accordingly.

PS 9 Advocacy and expert witness roles

9.1   In certain circumstances surveyors can act in the same case (but not at the same time) both as surveyor-advocate and as expert witness (see also *Surveyors acting as advocates*: RICS practice statement). This is known as acting 'in a dual role'. You should only act in a dual role where:
   (a)   neither the rules nor the customs of the particular tribunal prohibit you from so acting; and
   (b)   other relevant factors make it appropriate (e.g. the disproportionality of retaining two persons in separate roles).

9.2   Where however you intend, or are invited, to act in a dual role as surveyor-advocate and as expert witness you must:

    (a)   having regard to 9.1 above, consider both whether it is permissible to do so (see also PS 3.1) and also whether it is appropriate; and

    (b)   promptly communicate to your client the results of such considerations, setting out in writing the likely advantages and disadvantages, as you see them, of acting in a dual role in the particular circumstances of the case, so as to enable the client to decide whether you should indeed act in such a dual role. In such communication you must detail:

        (i)   the possible impact on your impartiality as expert witness, and any possible impact in terms of the perception of that impartiality by others; and any possible impact on your advocacy submissions;

        (ii)   whether or not you will be able to fulfill both roles properly at all times; and

        (iii)   whether or not it would be disproportionate in all the circumstances, or otherwise in the client's best interests, for a separate person to be retained to undertake one of the roles.

9.3   Having complied with PS 9.2 above, you may only act in both roles if the client instructs you so to act.

9.4   Where you confirm instructions to act in such a dual role, you must clearly distinguish between those two roles at all times, whether in oral hearings or in written presentations.

PS 10 Conditional fees

10.1   Where you are instructed to give expert evidence under a conditional fee arrangement (see also PS 3.4), you must declare the existence of such a conditional fee arrangement to the tribunal (see PS 5.1(j)(iii)), so that its effect can be taken into account. For the avoidance of doubt, PS 10.1 also applies to your expert witness role where you are to act in the same case in a dual role (i.e. both as expert witness and surveyor-advocate – see also *Surveyors acting as advocates*: PS 3.6).

Surveyors acting as expert witnesses: RICS guidance notes

This is a guidance note (GN). It provides advice to members of RICS on aspects of the profession. Where procedures are recommended for specific professional tasks, these are intended to embody 'best practice', that is, procedures which in the opinion of RICS meet a high standard of professional competence.

RICS members are not required to follow the advice and recommendations contained in the GN. They should however note the following points.

When an allegation of professional negligence is made against an RICS member, the court is likely to take account of the contents of any relevant GN published by RICS in deciding whether or not the member had acted with reasonable competence.

In the opinion of RICS, if RICS members conform to the practices recommended in this GN they should have at least a partial defence to an allegation of negligence by virtue of having followed those practices. However, RICS members have the responsibility of deciding when it is inappropriate to follow the guidance.

On the other hand, it does not follow that RICS members will be adjudged negligent if they have not followed the practices recommended in this GN. It is for each surveyor to decide on the appropriate procedure to follow in any professional task. However, where RICS members depart from the good practice recommended in this GN, they should do so only for good reason. In the event of litigation, a court may require an RICS member to explain why he or she decided not to adopt the recommended practice. Also, an RICS member who has not followed this GN, and whose actions are called into question in a RICS disciplinary case, may be asked to justify the steps he or she took and this may be taken into account.

In addition, guidance notes are relevant to professional competence in that every RICS member should be up to date and should have informed him or herself of guidance notes within a reasonable time of their promulgation.

Surveyors acting as expert witnesses: guidance note: Preamble

Whilst in general this text is gender neutral, on occasions where masculine terms only are used (such as in legislation quotes), these should be taken as also referring to the feminine (e.g. 'she', 'her'), and to 'they' or 'it' (in the case of a corporate body), as the context so requires.

References to the singular also include the plural and vice versa where the context so requires. Unless otherwise specified, references to 'you', 'member', 'surveyor' or to 'expert witness surveyor' are to members of RICS of any class of membership, save for Honorary Members. References to 'PS' denote 'practice statement', and those to 'GN' denote 'guidance note'.

Where you are acting as an Assessor, Valuation Officer, Listing Officer, District Valuer or Commissioner of Valuation (or as an authorised representative thereof) in local taxation-related matters and are acting in pursuit of a statutory duty, you are unlikely to be operating in a client/adviser framework and will generally not have a direct client.

There are variations in terminology, legislation and case law references pertinent to expert witness practice that can be found across the different legal jurisdictions within the UK. These are not exhaustively referenced below, but where felt appropriate are suitably highlighted.

For the purposes of this GN, the generic expression 'tribunal' means any body whose function it is to determine disputes. This therefore includes:
- **courts and tribunals (including Lands Tribunals and Agricultural Land Tribunals; Leasehold Valuation Tribunals; Residential Property Tribunals; Valuation Tribunals);**
- **arbitrators/arbiters or arbitral panels/tribunals;**
- **adjudicators (including those operating under the *Housing Grants, Construction and Regeneration Act 1996*);**
- **Committees (including Rent Assessment Committees, Valuation Appeal Committees);**
- **inspectors, commissioners and reporters (e.g. in planning proceedings, including Inquiries, Hearings, Examinations in Public – independent panels; Independent Examination and proceedings of the**

Infrastructure Planning Commission, and Planning and Water Appeals Commissions);
- **independent experts.**

Note: It is expected that once provisions of the *Tribunals, Courts and Enforcement Act* 2007 are implemented, some of the tribunals listed above will take on a different designation, but at the time of publication this is not yet in place.

GN 1 Application of guidance note and introduction

1.1   (a)   The start date of application of this guidance note is 1 January 2009. This guidance note (GN) applies where any RICS member (usually described hereafter as 'the expert witness surveyor' or 'you') provides expert evidence, whether oral or written, to the proceedings of any tribunal in the United Kingdom, except for criminal proceedings. It is recommended the GN be considered in conjunction with the foregoing practice statement (PS).

      (b)   The GN provides information on good practice considered to be appropriate where you are required to give expert evidence (including acting as a Single Joint Expert under the *Civil Procedure Rules* (CPR)). The CPR do not apply in Scotland or Northern Ireland. Some tribunals have their own specific rules, which make provisions for expert evidence (for example – not an exhaustive list – Valuation Tribunals, Lands Tribunals; in Northern Ireland, see the Commercial List Practice Directions). Furthermore, the main provisions of CPR do not specifically apply to arbitration proceedings under the *Arbitration Act* 1996 (which have party autonomy as a key characteristic) or to any other proceedings outside the County Court or the Supreme Court of England and Wales.

1.2   As a surveyor actively involved in a dispute that may come before a tribunal, you may find yourself carrying out one (or more) of the roles identified below.

      (a)   **Surveyor-advocate** – in this capacity you will act to put a party's case and interests to a tribunal. You will need to follow the requirements of, and have regard to, *Surveyors acting as advocates*: RICS practice statement and guidance note. Your primary duty will be to your client, but it is also subject to some important duties to the tribunal that place limits on what it is proper to do in pursuit of your client's interests.

(b)   **Adviser** – in this capacity, you will be retained to give advice to a client. Frequently this will be by a report or assessment of the merits of a case. In this capacity it is not contemplated that a tribunal will be asked to place reliance on such advice. Your advice is not for the purpose of a tribunal's proceedings (see also GN 3.1 and GN 22.4).

(c)   **Expert witness (and as a Single Joint Expert (SJE), see PS 8 and GN 17)** – your primary duty as an expert witness, including as an SJE, will be not to those instructing or paying you but to the tribunal. In this instance you will need to follow the requirements of, and have regard to *Surveyors acting as expert witnesses*: RICS practice statement and guidance note.

(d)   **Negotiator** – in this capacity you will be acting to negotiate a resolution to certain matters as best you may, in the interests of a party. In such a role you will have no involvement with a tribunal, except insofar as you or others may perceive a possibility that a failed negotiation may then necessitate a reference to a tribunal; at which point you or another professional person may be engaged to act as an advocate or provide expert evidence as an expert witness. It is possible that some negotiators may not find it possible to act as an expert witness as their impartiality may be damaged, or may be perceived to be damaged, by the prior or continuing role of negotiator. It is recommended that you be alert to this.

(e)   **Case manager** – in this capacity you will be acting on behalf of a party and will be responsible for the general conduct, management and administration of its case, marshalling and coordinating that party's team of representatives/ advisers (if any) and liaising, as appropriate, with the tribunal and the opposing party.

(f)   **Witness of fact** – in this capacity you will normally have been asked to provide testimony on oath or on affirmation as to something you saw, heard, experienced, said or did (i.e. evidence of fact). This includes the evidence which surveyors sometimes give, in addition to their opinion evidence, as to measurements they have made or examinations which they have carried out.

See also PS 1.2.

1.3 The PS emphasises and distinguishes the roles that a surveyor can adopt, in particular as an advocate or expert witness (or in a dual role in the same case, albeit at different times). The PS will apply whenever you express an opinion in your role as expert witness. The need for you to act as an expert witness and follow all the requirements of the PS will be determined by the rules of the relevant tribunal, by prevailing custom and the nature of the dispute: you, your client and any agreement or contract with the opposing party can influence whether you are obliged to comply with the requirements of the PS or not. A common misunderstanding is that it is always mandatory to act as an expert witness in proceedings before an independent expert (in an expert determination process). Whether the role of expert witness or surveyor-advocate is adopted will depend on the powers conferred upon the independent expert under a lease or other instrument, on the relationship between the parties' surveyors and upon any agreement between them and the independent expert. Nothing in the PS or this GN should be construed as suggesting that an independent expert has powers to mandate that presentations made to him or her **must** be in the form of expert evidence, as opposed to advocacy submissions. However, if, in the light of all circumstances, a surveyor **agrees** to present expert evidence rather than advocacy submissions, conformity with the expert witness PS is required.

1.4 The GN has been prepared against the background of comment emanating primarily from UK courts regarding the duties and responsibilities of expert witnesses (sometimes called 'skilled witnesses' in Scotland). Those duties and responsibilities are now referenced in, for example, the CPR, including their Practice Directions, Protocols, Forms, and court guides. It should be noted that in cases to which the CPR apply there may be additional and/or different requirements for surveyors acting as expert witnesses over and above those which apply in non-CPR cases and vice versa (e.g. an arbitrator might impose requirements over and above those required by the CPR).

1.5 (a) All surveyors are, as a matter of professional conduct, expected to comply with the applicable rules of tribunals, including the CPR, in those circumstances in which they apply, and to make themselves aware of the need to comply. The requirements of the CPR relating to expert witnesses are currently principally set out in the following:

- CPR Part 35 and its Practice Direction *Experts and Assessors*, including the *Protocol for the Instruction of Experts to give Evidence in Civil Claims*, produced by the Civil Justice Council (CJC);
- CPR Part 22 and its Practice Direction (Statements of Truth);
- any relevant Pre-Action Protocols.

Various court guides contain commentary on expert witness matters (e.g. *The Admiralty and Commercial Courts Guide*, section H2 and Appendix 11; the *Chancery Guide*, Chapter 4; the *Queen's Bench Guide*, section 7.9; the *Technology and Construction Court* (TCC) *Guide*, section 13).

(b) This GN is not intended to provide a commentary on the CPR in particular, though it may serve as an aid to the interpretation of some of its provisions. The CPR, the Practice Directions, Forms, Protocols and the various court guides are subject to amendment, and to interpretation by the courts. Amendments are generally published from time to time online.

(c) If you are acting as an expert witness in a case, you are advised to make yourself aware of the existence and effect of changes to the rules of the relevant tribunal.

1.6 (a) Impartiality of expert witnesses is of the utmost importance. By emphasising the expert witness's overriding and primary duty to the tribunal when acting as an expert witness (see the **Principal message** in the *Preamble* of the PS, PS 2.1 and PS 2.3), the PS aims to assist in ensuring the independence and impartiality of the evidence given by the expert witness.

(b)   As regards the position of the expert witness in Scotland, although the characteristic of impartiality is not always expressed judicially in as strong terms as it is in other jurisdictions, any expert report prepared for the purpose of Scottish proceedings is required to be impartial, independent, truthful and complete as to coverage of relevant matters. An expert report lodged in a court, and assuming its content is not agreed, will not become the evidence in chief of the witness or otherwise serve as a substitute for oral testimony. Tribunals that do not follow the strict rules of evidence adopted by the higher Scottish courts may adopt a different approach. If you are acting in Scottish proceedings and are unfamiliar with Scottish practice and the approach to evidence in that jurisdiction, you are advised to seek further guidance from any client (or its legal adviser) and/or the tribunal in question, including as to applicable procedural requirements.

1.7   The obligation imposed upon you to make the existence of the practice statement known to the client when accepting instructions to act as expert witness (PS 3.3(b)) is intended to help reduce misunderstandings and remove pressures upon you as an expert witness to support your client's case irrespective of your honest professional opinions. The obligation imposed on you by PS 5.1(i) to make a Statement of Truth, and the specified declarations of PS 5.1(j), are intended to assist in this respect.

1.8   A leading case setting out the duties and responsibilities of expert witnesses is *National Justice Compania Naviera SA v Prudential Assurance Co. Ltd* (The Ikarian Reefer) (1993) 2 Lloyd's Rep 68. Though a case from the jurisdiction of England and Wales, the principles enunciated have, within the appropriate context, been followed or broadly endorsed in other UK jurisdictions (including Scotland). In the case Cresswell J said:

'The duties and responsibilities of expert witnesses in civil cases include the following:

a) Expert evidence presented to the court should be, and should be seen to be, the independent product of the expert uninfluenced as to form or content by the exigencies of litigation (*Whitehouse v Jordan* [1981] 1 WLR 246 at p 256 per Lord Wilberforce).

b) An expert witness should provide independent assistance to the court by way of objective unbiased opinion in relation to matters within his expertise (see *Polivitte Ltd v Commercial Union Assurance Co. Plc* [1987] 1 Lloyd's Rep 379 at p 386 per Garland J and *Re J* [1990] FCR 193 per Cazalet J). An expert witness in the High Court should never assume the role of an advocate.

c) An expert witness should state the facts or assumptions upon which his opinion is based. He should not omit to consider material facts which could detract from his concluded opinion (*Re J* sup.).

d) An expert witness should make it clear when a particular question or issue falls outside his expertise.

e) If an expert's opinion is not properly researched because he considers that insufficient data is available, then this must be stated with an indication that his opinion is no more than a provisional one (*Re J* sup.). In cases where an expert witness who has prepared a report could not assert that the report contained the truth, the whole truth and nothing but the truth, without some qualification, the qualification should be stated within the report (*Derby & Co. Ltd and Others v Weldon and Others*, (No. 9) *Times*, 9 November 1990 per Staughton LJ).

f) If, after exchange of reports an expert witness changes his view on a material matter having read the other side's expert's report or for any other reason, such change of view should be communicated (through legal representatives) to the other side without delay and, when appropriate, to the court.

g) Where expert evidence refers to photographs, plans, calculations, analysis, measurements, survey reports or other similar documents, these must be provided to the opposite party at the same time as the exchange of reports (see 15.5 of the *Guide to Commercial Court Practice*).'

1.9 The PS and this GN apply the above principles and also much of the approach to expert evidence which underlies the relevant parts of the CPR. Those acting as expert witnesses in Scotland are recommended also to acquaint themselves with a number of Scottish court cases:

- *Davie v Magistrates of Edinburgh* [1953] SC 34
- *Elf Caledonia Ltd v London Bridge Engineering Ltd* [1997] ScotCS 1
- *Dingley v Chief Constable Strathclyde Police* [1998] SC 548
- *Karling v Purdue* [2004] ScotCS 221
- *McTear v Imperial Tobacco* [2005] 2 SC 1 (see paras 5.1–5.19 of opinion)
- *Amy Whitehead's Legal Representative v Graeme John Douglas & Anor* [2006] ScotCS CSOH 178.

1.10 Where relevant, surveyors would be expected to take proper account of other practice statements, guidance notes and codes produced by RICS when giving expert evidence in relation to any matter. For example, surveyors involved in dilapidations disputes are recommended to be familiar with the guidance note *Dilapidations*; surveyors involved in boundary disputes are advised to have regard to the forthcoming second edition of the guidance note *Boundaries: Guide to Procedure for Boundary Identification, Demarcation and Disputes in England and Wales*, once it is published; and surveyors involved in rating matters are advised to have regard to the *Rating Consultancy Code of Practice* and *Rating Appeals* guidance note.

GN 2 General duties

2.1 The various tasks that may be undertaken as an expert are to:

(a) assist a party to establish the facts and to assess the merits of a case and help with its preparation;

(b) define and agree issues between the parties;

(c)   help quantify or assess the amount of any sum in dispute and identify an appropriate basis on which a case might be settled;

(d)   give expert (opinion) evidence to the tribunal (which may be based upon and incorporate evidence of fact), where opinion evidence apart from that of an expert witness would not be admissible; and

(e)   conduct enquiries on behalf of the tribunal and report to that body as to findings (this would not normally apply in Scotland where an expert is normally instructed by one of the parties to an action).

2.2   Upon accepting an instruction to act as an expert witness, you assume a responsibility to the tribunal and to RICS to provide truthful, impartial and independent opinions, complete as to coverage of relevant matters. To that end it is recommended that you be satisfied, prior to accepting the instruction, that you have the experience, knowledge, expertise and resources to fulfill the task specified within any allocated time span.

2.3   If you cannot fulfill the criteria in PS 3.1, PS 3 makes it clear the instruction should be declined. Where appropriate, it is recommended that you advise the client of the possible need to employ additional expertise and make the client aware of the advantages and disadvantages of acting in such circumstances.

2.4   It is imperative that you fully understand and accept that, while an instruction to provide expert evidence may originate from a particular client, your duty to the tribunal overrides any duty to the client. PS 3.3(c) makes it obligatory to bring this to the client's attention.

2.5   You are entitled to give expert evidence on behalf of your employer (see PS 2.5). The difficulty that you can face is that it may be said that less weight should be attached to your evidence because you have a conflict of interest arising out of your employment. In order to address this risk, if you wish to act as an expert witness in these circumstances, it is recommended that you are in a position to satisfy the tribunal that you have a proper understanding of the requirements imposed upon an expert witness giving evidence, and that your employer understands that your overriding duty is to the tribunal. How this is done is a matter for you and your employer. It is recommended that the nature of the employee's duty when acting as an expert witness is recorded in writing by you and acknowledged in writing by the employer. Nothing in this paragraph, or the PS, should be construed as implying that an employed surveyor giving expert evidence on the instructions of his or her employer is not capable of giving unbiased, truthful expert evidence.

2.6 Where you are acting, or have previously acted, on a matter (e.g. in the course of negotiations, and/or as advocate), the implications of your duties to the tribunal as an expert witness may not be acceptable to the client and in such instances it would be advisable to consider declining instructions.

2.7 Failure to comply with the directions or orders of a tribunal, or applicable rules, or any excessive delay attributable to the expert witness, may result in your client being penalised in costs or being prevented from putting the expert evidence before the tribunal. Some courts have made orders for costs directly against expert witnesses who cause significant expense to be incurred, if doing so in reckless and blatant disregard of their duties to the court. See also GN 22.5.

2.8 In a construction dispute that proceeds to a reference to a tribunal, you may provide as evidence an interim valuation or final account or other documentation that you have prepared as a part of a previous negotiation. That evidence may include your own opinion as to rates and prices or other matters. For the avoidance of doubt, you are subject to the requirements of the PS where such evidence of opinion is placed before the tribunal.

2.9 PS 3.3(b) requires you to make a written offer to supply a copy of the practice statement to a prospective client. For this purpose a stand-alone version of the practice statement is available to members to download from www.rics.org.

GN 3 Advice and disclosure

3.1 Surveyors, as experts in their field, may be asked to provide initial advice (e.g. to assist in the identification and scoping of, or limitation to, any claim) to a client prior to being instructed to provide evidence as an expert witness for presentation to a tribunal. A variety of situations exists where a party may seek advice from you before a dispute has arisen or before litigation is contemplated, or even during litigation. Generally, where a party has engaged you for purposes other than the giving or preparation of expert evidence and it is not intended that you may later be instructed to do so, you may be referred to as an 'adviser' rather than an 'expert witness'. Generally, all such initial advice is given within the normal client/professional adviser relationship, rather than within the markedly different relationship that exists if you are acting as an expert witness.

3.2 If such initial advice is in relation to a dispute that might have to be resolved by a tribunal, then you need to be aware that the advice may be liable to disclosure in proceedings and might prejudice the interests of the client. Simply copying or delivering the advice to the client's solicitor or lawyer advocate (where it has one) is unlikely of itself to be sufficient to prevent such disclosure. If in doubt, it is recommended that legal advice be sought on the question of disclosure. Before accepting instructions to act as an expert witness, it is recommended that you advise the client (where that party is not an instructing lawyer) that communications generated between the client and yourself as surveyor may not be protected by litigation privilege and subsequently may have to be disclosed to the opposing party. Disclosure *per se* does not exist in Scotland, however, in some cases rules do allow for a party to apply for 'commission and diligence' (i.e. disclosure) of documents that are deemed to be relevant to the dispute. Therefore, care should also be taken in such instances when generating communications between you as surveyor and the client (where the latter is not an instructing lawyer acting in a professional capacity).

3.3 In cases to which the CPR apply, there is a specific rule that the duty of each expert witness is to help the court on the matters within his or her expertise, such duty overriding any obligation to the person from whom they have received instructions or by whom they are paid (CPR 35.3). The PS contains a similar requirement (PS 2.1) (which also applies in non-CPR cases); expert witnesses may therefore be obliged to make statements to a tribunal, or even in 'without prejudice' meetings of expert witnesses, which might be prejudicial to a client's case.

GN 4 Duties to the tribunal

4.1   If you are not entirely confident that any of the duties referred to in PS 2 can, for whatever reason, be properly fulfilled (or, having been instructed, that any such duty can continue to be properly fulfilled) you would normally be advised to decline instructions to act as an expert witness, or cease acting, having first discussed the matter with your client.

GN 5 Instructions and inspections

5.1   (a)   When you initially receive instructions, or at any later stage, it is recommended that you notify those instructing you as soon as possible where:

　　　　(i)   instructions may not be acceptable (e.g. where deadlines are unrealistic or instructions are unclear);

　　　　(ii)   instructions are, or become, insufficient for the completion of your task;

　　　　(iii)   you become aware you may not be able to fulfill one or more of the terms of your engagement; or

　　　　(iv)   you consider that your instructions and/or work are likely to have placed you in conflict with your duties as an expert witness.

It is advisable that you seek appropriate variations, additional resources and information in these circumstances, wherever possible.

　　(b)   Prior to acceptance of instructions, you are recommended to:

　　　　(i)   check that the instructions contain basic relevant information (e.g. names, contact details, dates of incidents, etc.), including the identity of the parties to the dispute;

　　　　(ii)   ascertain the name of the party you are to be instructed by;

(iii)   ascertain the identity of the tribunal;

(iv)   identify the type and purpose of evidence likely to be required and be satisfied that you have the necessary experience, knowledge and expertise to carry out the task;

(v)   check that a reasonable attempt has been made to identify the significant issues in the case and whether dates of any hearings/conferences are set out; and

(vi)   consider and decide whether any conflicts of interest would arise, or might be perceived to arise, if you were to be instructed.

5.2   A conflict of interest may arise, or be perceived to arise, out of a previous or current involvement with, for example, any party, dispute, or property, such that it would cause you to be unable – or be seen by a reasonable and disinterested observer to be unable – to fulfill your responsibility to be independent and to be able to act impartially.

A conflict of interest could be of any kind, including:
- a financial interest (e.g. other management fees or financial benefits that you or your firm gain from contracts in place);
- a personal connection; an obligation (e.g. as a member or officer of some other organisation);
- links to a business in competition with one of the parties to the dispute.

It is not possible to prescribe in advance a list of all such circumstances. Particular care should be taken where you have an established business, social or personal relationship with someone who might be affected by, or otherwise involved in, the dispute.

Where a conflict or potential conflict of interest arises, PS 3.3(e), PS 3.6 and – in the case of an SJE – PS 8.7 specify actions that are to be taken.

5.3   For details of the requirements to establish clear instructions and for terms of engagement, see PS 3. If standard terms of engagement are used, it is recommended they are attached to the acceptance of instructions. If in a particular case your standard terms are varied, it is advisable such variations be explained at the time. *Appendix A: Sample Terms of Engagement* serves as a guide and may be adapted for personal use (see also the copyright notice on page 1).

5.4 Circumstances may exist or arise where you may consider that part of your instruction may require, or necessitate assistance from, another person. In such circumstances it is recommended that you notify the client in a timely manner and give the name of the individual recommended to be engaged, together with information as to that person's experience, qualifications and expertise (see PS 3.3(d)).

5.5 In cases to which the CPR apply, you may file a written request to the court for directions to assist you in carrying out your function as an expert witness (CPR 35.14). You are recommended to give due consideration to making reference in your terms of engagement to the possibility of such an application and, when contemplating making an application to the court for directions, to any costs implications/possible judicial penalties. It is normally advisable for such a request to the court to be discussed with the client in advance. Care is advised to be taken to ensure that privileged or 'without prejudice' material is not disclosed during such an application (see Chancery Guide para 4.19; and Queen's Bench Guide at para 7.9.10). Unless the court orders otherwise, a request for directions will be copied to the client at least seven days before filing any request and to all other parties at least four days before filing it. The court, when it gives directions, may direct that a party be served with a copy of the directions (see CPR 35.14(3)). It is recommended that the client be made aware, before instructions are accepted, of the expert witness's rights under such provisions.

5.6 In cases to which the CPR apply, an expert witness instructed by one party may have written questions about the expert's report put to him or her by another party (see GN 9). It is recommended that the client be informed, before instructions are accepted, of the effect of this part of the CPR, and that you make it clear that you would be under a professional duty to reply to such questions unless it is not reasonable for you to do so.

5.7   You are recommended to indicate a likely reporting programme to the client. This programme will vary according to the assignment, but might follow three phases:

(a)   Initial report: you may provide a report setting out relevant opinions relating to the assignment. If your opinions are not accepted, assuming that the report is competent and researched, you may wish to consider withdrawing from the assignment.

(b)   Proof of evidence: this may also involve supplemental proofs or counter-proofs together with joint meetings of experts. This is often likely to take the form of an additional or extended report(s) in Scotland where witness statements are not normally lodged with the tribunal or exchanged with other parties to the proceedings.

(c)   Giving evidence orally to a tribunal.

All three phases may involve conferences with advocates or meetings with solicitors; advice given by you, whilst ancillary to the expert witness role, may not be given as an expert witness. For example, the person appointed may be asked by the advocate to advise on questions for a matching expert witness's cross-examination or to comment upon matters raised in matching evidence. In such circumstances you are not giving evidence, nor acting as a surveyor-advocate yourself, but instead giving professional advice to help another in advocacy.

5.8   PS 5.1(b) mandates that your report states the substance of all material instructions, whether written or oral. In cases to which CPR apply, those instructions are not privileged against disclosure. However, the court will not, in relation to those instructions, order disclosure of any specific document or permit any questioning in court other than by the party who instructed the expert, unless it is satisfied there are reasonable grounds to consider the statement of instructions given to be inaccurate or incomplete, or unless the party who gave the instructions consents to it. If this is the case, the court will allow cross-examination where it appears to be in the interests of justice to do so (see generally CPR 35.10 and the Practice Direction to Part 35). Subject to CPR 35.10(4), a party may apply for an order for inspection of any document mentioned in an expert's report which has not already been disclosed in the proceedings (CPR 31.14(2)). Such a right does not exist in that form in Scottish court proceedings where inspection will instead turn on the extent to which the document is founded upon in the pleadings, or otherwise is established as being relevant to the matters in dispute. You are advised to inform those instructing you of these matters, should they arise, in a timely manner.

5.9 Where your instructions are, or may be perceived to be, in conflict with your duties (e.g. because of a conflict or perceived conflict with your duty to the tribunal, through incompleteness of instructions or information being supplied), it is recommended that you consider withdrawing from the case. If proceedings have already been commenced, you may first wish to consider whether it would be more appropriate to make a written request for directions regarding the matter from the tribunal.

5.10 PS 4 concerns any inspection of property/facility related to the subject of the dispute. However nothing in PS 4 precludes you from providing an appropriately qualified opinion in the event that access to the property is impractical, or severely limited, after all reasonable efforts have been made by you (or on your behalf) to secure such access. It is recommended that you state the date or dates upon which a property was inspected and clearly state the extent of such access as was obtained.

GN 6 Purpose of expert evidence

6.1 The purpose of expert evidence is to assist or enable the tribunal to form its own independent judgment in respect of a particular matter. Therefore, the expert evidence given must provide all necessary detail from which your opinions and conclusions have been drawn in order to enable the tribunal to judge the appropriateness of those conclusions based upon the facts submitted.

GN 7 Evidence of fact

7.1 You may be required to assist the tribunal in establishing, clarifying and ordering logically, relevant facts. Insofar as you provide such assistance you are acting in the role of witness of fact, and this role does not include the expression of opinion, which is the domain of the expert witness. You should fully understand this fundamental distinction and are advised to ensure you recognise each role's distinctiveness. In addressing questions of fact and opinion, you should keep the two separate and discrete.

7.2   The duty to the tribunal (that is most emphatically spelt out in the CPR in England and Wales) takes precedence over any contractual, professional or other duty and this may, on occasions, conflict with confidentiality agreements. Evidence subject to confidentiality agreements cannot be ignored simply by virtue of the existence or assumed existence of such an agreement; advice should be sought before disclosing confidential information.

7.3   It is usual for those instructing expert witnesses to provide them with facts, literature or other material, which the expert witness may adopt if relevant to the matters with which he or she is dealing. As the PS indicates, these, and any other facts, literature or material which you establish for yourself and to which you have regard in forming any opinion, are to be set out in the report either fully, or by cross-reference to other documents which will be made available to the tribunal. Accordingly, it is advisable that any written report to be lodged before a tribunal includes a full schedule of the documents upon which you have relied and, where necessary, copies of such documents or the relevant portions thereof. The originals of all documents relied upon need to be available for inspection by other parties to the dispute and, unless agreed by the parties, by the tribunal. It is recommended therefore that you be sufficiently aware of the holders of all such documents. As indicated previously, reference to such documentation in any report prepared in relation to court proceedings in Scotland will not alter the normal rules relating to the recovery or disclosure of such material. There is no automatic requirement in such court proceedings for such material to be made available for inspection by other parties to the dispute or by the tribunal. Within the report you should give the source of factual information relied upon (see PS 5.1(c) and (d)).

7.4   Expert witnesses would be expected to carry out such factual research as they consider necessary to fully discharge their obligation to the tribunal including, where appropriate, inspection of any property/facility involved.

7.5 It is recommended that you give sufficient explanation of what you have done in ascertaining and checking facts to enable the tribunal to be satisfied that you have fully discharged your obligations.

7.6 (a) Where ordered by a tribunal to communicate with the other expert in order to attempt to agree facts and clarify, narrow or resolve the issues in dispute (see PS 7.1), you are recommended to request from your client a copy of any order or direction relating to such requirements (see also CPR Practice Direction 35 *Experts and Assessors*, para. 6A).

(b) The purpose of PS 7.3 is to encourage you – particularly in the absence of specific instructions from your client – to raise the issues specified in PS 7.3 with your client, with a view to facilitating a speedier resolution of the dispute. Factors you may wish to take into account when fulfilling PS 7.3's mandate may include (but might not be limited to):

(i) the commercial interests of your client in advancing or retarding the outcome of the dispute;

(ii) the likely costs of taking the steps in question at an early stage, compared to the costs at a later stage when the matter may have become more (or less) contentious;

(iii) the tactical advantage of being seen to have a well prepared case; and

(iv) the role that early discussions may have to play in prompting a settlement with the other party.

7.7 If you are in doubt about the admissibility (e.g. possibly because it is privileged) of any fact or statement upon which you are relying, it is recommended that you seek legal advice. Hearsay evidence is admissible in civil proceedings, provided that certain rules are followed (see *Appendix B: Hearsay evidence*). If you are in any doubt about use of hearsay evidence it may prove valuable to seek legal advice.

GN 8 Expert (opinion) evidence

8.1   Where an opinion has been formed based on incomplete knowledge of facts, then PS 5.1(f) expects such limitations to be stated fully in the evidence.

8.2   Differences of opinion between expert witnesses often occur due to the detail of facts and to the assumptions upon which they are relying being different; such differences need to be set out for the tribunal (see PS 5.1(f) and (g)).

8.3   It is recommended that you do not express, as your own opinion, an interpretation of statute or case law unless qualified to do so. You may, however, state an understanding of the point of law as a basis on which your conclusions on other questions are provided.

GN 9 Questions to expert witnesses and answers

9.1   In cases to which the CPR apply, a party may put written questions to an expert witness instructed by another party, or to a Single Joint Expert (see also GN 17). Unless the court gives permission, or the other party agrees, such questions:
(a)   may be put once only;
(b)   must be put within 28 days of service of the expert's report; and
(c)   must be for the purpose only of clarification of the report.

(See CPR 35.6; Practice Direction 35, paras 5.1 and 5.2.)

9.2   An expert witness's answers to the questions will be treated as part of the expert witness's evidence, and the PS and GN will continue to apply to such work by the expert witness. It is recommended that you copy your answers to your own client and be aware that your general duties will apply to your provision of answers.

9.3   Your client must pay any fees charged by you for answering the questions. However, this does not affect any decision of the tribunal as to the party who is ultimately to bear your costs.

9.4   (a)   It is recommended that you send any questions you receive from the other party to your client and, if appropriate, ask for further instructions. Where you are of the view that a question put to you is not aimed at clarification of your report, is disproportionate or has been put out of time, it is recommended that you refer to your client, giving reasons for not answering the question(s). If the client fails to resolve the problem or fails to approach the court for directions, you can consider the option to make a written request to the court for directions (see CPR 35.14 and para. 16.4 of the *Protocol for the Instruction of Experts to give Evidence in Civil Claims*).

(b) Where you do not answer the questions put to you without good cause, you should be aware that the tribunal may order either that the party who instructed you may not rely on your evidence, or that the party may not recover your fees and expenses from any other party, or it may make both orders.

9.5 It is recommended that the possibility of requesting directions from the tribunal (see also PS 8.4 and 8.6, and GN 5.5 and 17.5) ought only to be exercised where the tribunal's involvement is strictly necessary. A party's expert witness may not agree to more than one exchange of questions and answers, unless believed to be absolutely necessary, since a tribunal may subsequently consider whether such further exchanges and the party's conduct (and that of its expert witness) were justified, and may exercise its discretion on costs accordingly.

9.6 A request to the tribunal for directions by letter would normally, for CPR cases, be on written notice of at least seven days to the client and at least four days to the other party. The request would normally contain:
(a) the title of the claim;
(b) the reference of the claim (claim no.);
(c) the full name of the expert witness;
(d) details of why directions are being sought; and
(e) copies of any relevant documents.

GN 10 Documents

10.1 Any evidence given by you will, almost invariably, be based upon documents either provided to, or held by, you. If when acting as an expert witness you are passed papers or materials expressed to be 'privileged' and it is not clearly indicated that the client has decided that privilege has been waived therein, it is recommended that you either (whichever is more appropriate) immediately verify the status of the materials without reading the papers, or return the papers unread with an explanation for their return. The position is somewhat different in Scotland where the provision of such documentation will not alter the normal rules relating to the recovery or disclosure of such material; it is therefore suggested that you discuss the status of such materials with the client and any legal adviser rather than simply returning them, as expert witnesses will often receive copies of precognition statements which, although privileged, are provided so as to enable the expert witness to understand the factual basis upon which they are being asked to opine.

10.2 When accepting instructions, it is recommended that you request details of all relevant documents and, if you consider it necessary, ask to inspect the client's files to satisfy yourself that these have been supplied.

10.3 Documents from your own resources often provide useful factual information upon which to rely. Such documents might include text, published material, photographs, plans, the opinion of others, codes of practice; and RICS practice statements, guidance notes, codes and information papers.

10.4 During the course of your enquiries you may be made aware that other documents exist which might be of relevance but not be available. In such circumstances, where applicable, it may be necessary for you to consider taking advantage of the provisions of CPR 35.14 and CPR 35.9, and/or to seek legal advice regarding the procurement of such documents.

GN 11 Oral evidence

11.1 In many instances where you are required to give oral evidence, such evidence will be given under oath or affirmation but, whether or not such oath or affirmation is required, oral evidence must always be impartial, independent and your truthful and honest opinion (PS 2.1). If you do not know the answer to a particular question, it is recommended that you say so rather than endeavour to give an answer that might prove to be incorrect or misleading.

11.2 Preparation is important and it is recommended that you:
   (a)   ensure that appropriate arrangements have been made so that all documents necessary for proving your evidence are available;
   (b)   remind yourself of the detail of any written evidence which you have previously presented, and also of the detail of the contents of files, as specific points may need to be addressed before and during the hearing, including while giving evidence.

11.3 You should bear in mind that if you refer to documents or notes whilst giving evidence, the advocate or the tribunal can request sight of those documents or notes. This includes annotations on such documents or notes.

11.4 Where you have to refer to bulky material in your evidence, or to video, film or other screen-based material, it is your responsibility to ensure that appropriate arrangements have been made in a timely manner to enable such material to be communicated to the tribunal.

11.5 When giving evidence, you will be questioned by advocates. However, all answers are expected to be addressed to the tribunal. Concise answers are preferable, but you should not let advocates prevent a full answer being given.

11.6 Adjournments of the hearing (whether for lunch, overnight or longer periods) can sometimes occur. While you are under oath or affirmation you are not permitted to discuss the case with anyone during those adjournments, i.e. the expert is in seclusion. This restriction includes your client and client's advisers, advocates, fellow experts and colleagues. Adjournments between hearing dates can be lengthy, and in such instances you are advised to be alert to requesting that you be released from the restriction immediately before the hearing is so adjourned.

GN 12 Advising advocates

12.1 As an expert, you may be required to advise advocates.

12.2 Immediately prior to any hearing it is not uncommon for advocates of opposing parties to discuss between themselves aspects of the case, including possible compromise solutions. Expert advice is often needed during such negotiations and you therefore need to ensure that you are available well before the hearing is due to begin. Such advice is not expert evidence.

12.3 During the hearing the advocate may wish to consult with you, the expert witness, while other witnesses are giving evidence, especially during cross-examination. It is important that you establish whether the advocate wishes you to be available for such consultation. The expert is often asked to sit immediately behind the advocate in order that he or she can be consulted directly during the proceedings.

12.4 Expert witnesses not under oath or affirmation are commonly required to discuss other matters relating to the case with advocates during adjournments. An expert witness should not expect to have free time during adjournments (except to another day).

GN 13 Expert witnesses' written reports

13.1 It is recommended that your report be addressed to the tribunal and not the party from whom your instructions originate. Your written report as an expert witness surveyor should ideally be presented in an organised, concise and referenced way, distinguishing (where possible) between matters of plain fact, observations upon those facts, and inferences drawn from them. It is recommended that you use plain language and, wherever use of technical terms is necessary, explain such terms to aid the understanding of the tribunal. It is advisable not to use words, terms, and/or a form of presentation with the deliberate intention of limiting the ability of readers from checking the correctness of any statement, calculation or opinion given. As regards your summary of conclusions, there may be circumstances where it would be beneficial to the tribunal to place a short summary at the start of the report while giving full conclusions at its end. The tribunal may find it easier to understand the flow of the report's logic if an executive summary of the report has been provided at the outset.

13.2 In PS 5.1 the Statement of Truth (PS 5.1(i)) and declaration that the expert witness understands his or her duty to the tribunal (PS 5.1(j)(ii)) can follow each other or be combined into a sole declaration if desired.

13.3 The requirement in PS 5.1(g) is directed primarily to issues of practice or principle on which there exists a known and acknowledged range of opinion between experts in the field, or different schools of thought (e.g. in the valuation arena, on the use of All Risks Yield valuation methodology compared with Discounted Cash Flow methodology). It does not mean that on every occasion on which you think that another expert witness might disagree with you, you are specifically required to say so and go on to say what view another expert witness might hold and why the expert witness takes the view he or she does. Nonetheless, your duty to the tribunal requires you to put forward a fair and balanced assessment. This includes identifying any points that can fairly be made against the expert witness and saying why they do not cause you to change views.

13.4 It should be noted that the requirements in PS 5.1 may be varied or supplemented by, for example, various court guides or the rules or directions of a particular tribunal.

13.5 It is recommended that you keep matters of fact and opinion separate and discrete.

13.6 If you have relied upon extensive documents, it is recommended that a chronological schedule of these, incorporating a summary of their content, be placed in an appendix to assist readers. It is advisable that copies of key documents are cross-referenced to relevant parts in the report and annexed to the report if practicable or required.

13.7 If after disclosure of your report you identify a material inaccuracy, omission or have a change of opinion on any matter, it is recommended that (where possible) you consult your client before taking further action. Where you have changed your opinions and are to amend your report, a simple signed memorandum/addendum to that effect will usually suffice.

GN 14 Form and content of an expert witness's written report

14.1 This section gives guidance on the structure and scope of the content of a typical report by an expert witness. It is usually helpful to tribunals if paragraphs and pages within the report are numbered. It is recommended that any documents or supporting materials on which you rely be listed in any report you prepare and adequate reference should be given to enable them to be identified. Where appropriate, regard should be had to any specific report requirements of particular tribunals. Some variations to this structure will be appropriate on occasion, to take account of:

(a) any prior agreement between the parties as to the order in which the various issues are to be addressed (and possibly determined);

(b) any direction of the tribunal as to the procedure or as to the order in which the issues are to be considered; and

(c) any statutory material or official guidance as to the procedure applicable in particular types of proceedings.

14.2 It is advisable that the front sheet reveal, not obscure, the name of the expert witness, and reference the proceedings and tribunal; the nature of the evidence; the instructing party and client; the subject/title of the report; and the date of the report. It would usually be entitled 'Report', or where appropriate 'Supplemental Report', 'Amended Report', or 'Further Amended Report'.

14.3 Thereafter, the report often takes the following form:

(a) **Introductory material**

(i) a brief résumé of the experience, qualifications and expertise of the expert witness (commensurate in detail with the nature and complexity of the case). A fuller description/CV can be attached as an appendix;

(ii)   the names of the persons to be referred to in the report, together with a short description of their respective roles;

(iii)   a brief outline of the nature of the dispute;

(iv)   all material instructions;

(v)   chronology as to the expert's involvement in the case and a chronology of relevant events, where such a history exists; and

(vi)   the issues that the expert proposes to address in the report (you may wish to number them) and an executive summary of the main report.

No opinions are expressed in this section. As regards the statement/description of experience and qualifications (including by way of any CV attached), it is important you check that all such description and text is accurate and up to date.

(b)   **Enquiries made by the expert witness and the facts upon which the expert witness's opinion is based**

For example, this section (which is factual only) might include a description of inspections or surveys carried out, a note of those present, and the findings reached. The description is usually given in itemised subparagraphs, with subheadings as appropriate.

This section of the report would also:

(i)   distinguish between facts which the expert witness has been told to assume, those provided which the expert witness has chosen to assume, and those the expert witness has established for him or herself (or those others acting on his or her behalf have established);

(ii)   identify the various sources of facts and material provided to and derived by the expert witness; and

(iii)   list the documents upon which the expert witness relies in the report, and provide references to enable their identification.

Where the parties have also agreed a statement of facts, the opportunity may be taken to highlight those facts which could not be agreed, but which are important enough to be mentioned.

Where asked to make an assumption, it is advisable to indicate your belief that it is unreasonable or improbable (i.e. qualify the point as necessary) as the case may be.

(c) **Opinions and conclusions**

This would give the expert witness's opinion on each issue (in particular the expert's response to any specific questions asked by the client) and the reasons in full on each of them in turn. It may be helpful on occasion to place a short summary of conclusions at the beginning of the report, with full conclusions at the end.

(d) **Statement of Truth, declarations, and signature**

The Statement of Truth and declarations must be included as per the stipulations in the practice statement (see PS 5.1(i) and (j)), along with the signature of the writer and the date (PS 5.1(k)).

(e) **Appendices**

Appendices may include, for example, CVs, plans, photographs and other materials. It is recommended that you do not annex more than is reasonably necessary to support the opinions given in your report.

GN 15 Meetings between the expert witness and the lawyer

15.1 The bringing together of the lawyer and the expert witness as early as possible is to be encouraged. This enables the strengths and weaknesses of your report, and the client's case, to be evaluated. It may result in you wishing to make changes to the report, and/or the client wishing to settle the matter.

15.2 You must remember the duty in providing expert evidence is that it is your truthful, independent and impartial opinion being put forth, and not the views of the client, lawyer or a collegiate approach of those involved in preparing the case.

GN 16 Narrowing differences and meetings between experts

16.1 (a)   PS 7 aims to facilitate earlier settlement and reduction of costs by mandating a proactive and cooperative approach amongst opposing surveyor expert witnesses. An obvious way to achieve this is to hold a meeting with your counterpart, in order to achieve a greater understanding, and resolution, of issues in dispute. Such meetings offer the opportunity to pool relevant technical information, to identify areas of disagreement, and to see how those areas may be narrowed or eliminated altogether. Points of disagreement may usefully be presented by means of a *Scott Schedule* (see *Appendix D: Definitions*). Even if this process does not result in a settlement of the dispute, it may well lead to shorter, clearer reports, and save time, thereby reducing costs. It can also be useful for combined meetings to take place that include expert witnesses for each side from various disciplines.

(b)　It is generally best if such meetings occur before reports intended for disclosure are written, as expert witnesses can tend to be slow to alter opinions thereafter and time can be wasted. An exchange of skeletal reports before such meetings may assist the process. It is recommended that you approach experts' meetings with a willingness to listen, and be cooperative and constructive, otherwise the worth of such meetings can be devalued. In a court context, it is generally expected that the claimant's expert witness is the convenor of such meetings (or of the first such meeting at least). Neutral territory (or 'on-site') may be preferred venues. It is useful to pre-agree a broad agenda – identifying any relevant material you intend to introduce or rely on in discussions – and to agree and jointly sign minutes after the meeting, to avoid misunderstandings later. You are reminded of the obligation upon you under PS 2.7 to avoid maligning the professional competence of your opposite number.

16.2　In some circumstances, such experts' discussions and meetings may be required by the tribunal (and indeed the CPR expressly provide for this). An expert witness in the courts in England and Wales is expected to be aware of the overriding objective that courts deal with cases justly, taking into account proportionality, expeditiousness and fairness (CPR 1.1) and it is advisable to bear this in mind in terms of the arrangements for experts' meetings. In the field of town and country planning, there is a statutory requirement (by virtue of the appropriate *Inquiries Procedure Rules*) for the opposing parties to prepare and agree a *Statement of Common Ground* on a statutory timetable ahead of any public inquiry, such statement containing agreed factual information about the proposal which is the subject of the inquiry.

16.3 In cases to which the CPR apply, parties' lawyers will not usually be present at such meetings unless all parties agree, or the court so directs (see para. 18.8 of the *Protocol for the Instruction of Experts to give Evidence in Civil Claims*, and, for example, the TCC guide, para. 13.5.2).

16.4 The discussions between the experts at such meetings will ordinarily be 'without prejudice' (although it is advisable to confirm this beforehand), and may not therefore be referred to subsequently in the absence of agreement. In the context of court proceedings in England and Wales, such agreement between experts does not bind the parties unless they expressly agree to be bound by it (see CPR 35.12(4)). It should be noted that such provisions may be varied or supplemented by the rules and directions of a tribunal. It is recommended that, in advance of any such discussion or meeting taking place, the expert witness discuss with the client and any legal adviser the purpose of the discussion or meeting, having regard to the terms of any order or direction by a tribunal, where available.

16.5 It is usually desirable that at the end of any 'without prejudice' meeting between expert witnesses, irrespective of whether a tribunal has so ordered, a statement be prepared setting out those issues agreed and those not, and the underlying reasons, as well as a list of new issues arising or further actions to be taken or recommended.

16.6 With the consent of your client, you may step outside the expert witness remit to conduct 'without prejudice' meetings to explore and possibly settle differences as to facts and opinions.

GN 17 Single Joint Expert

17.1 In cases to which the CPR apply, where parties wish to submit expert evidence on a particular issue the court may direct that evidence on that issue is to be given by a Single Joint Expert (SJE). In general terms, the matter is one for the court's discretion having regard to all circumstances. The duties and responsibilities to the tribunal of a surveyor acting as a Single Joint Expert (SJE) are, in general, largely the same as for any other surveyor acting as an expert witness. Where the instructing parties cannot agree who should be the SJE, the court may either select the SJE from a list prepared or identified by those parties, or specify that the SJE be selected in such other manner as the court may direct. Each party may give instructions to the SJE but should, at the same time, send a copy of the instructions to the other instructing parties (see also CPR 35.8). Court rules in Scotland do not provide for the appointment of SJEs as such. However, a court can appoint its own expert witness to examine reports or other evidence, and in such circumstances, the expert's primary duty will be to the court. That expert's duties otherwise will be similar to those of the SJE as detailed in PS 8.

17.2 The court may give directions about the payment of the SJE's fees and expenses, and any inspection, examination or experiments which the SJE wishes to carry out. The court may, before the SJE is instructed, limit the amount that can be paid to the SJE by way of fees and expenses, and direct that the instructing parties pay that amount to the court. Unless the court otherwise directs, the instructing parties are jointly and severally liable for the SJE's fees and expenses.

17.3 There is no specific deadline by which an SJE must be appointed, but it is likely that any appointment, if made, will be fairly early on in the life of the proceedings, especially in less complex cases.

17.4 In order to give competent instructions to an SJE, and/or to put pertinent written questions to him or her (see GN 9.1), it will be necessary for the parties to have a clear idea of the case they wish to establish or defend. This may involve taking separate advice from their own expert witnesses prior to instructing, or putting questions to, the SJE.

17.5 As an SJE you are recommended to ensure that you are clear as to what you are instructed to do and the issues you are to address. You are recommended to ask the parties for a copy of any court order under which your appointment is being made. You are also recommended to act even-handedly in your dealings with the parties and to keep them all informed of material steps being taken by, for example, copying correspondence to the parties. It is prudent to minimise or avoid telephone contact with the parties and rely instead on written communications that can more easily be copied to all parties at the same time. If there is any uncertainty, or your instructions conflict in a material respect, it is advisable to seek clarification with the parties. If they are unable to agree, it is recommended that you consider an application to the court for directions. It is also recommended that you give due consideration to making reference in your terms of engagement to the possibility of such an application and, when contemplating making an application to the court for directions, to any costs implications/possible judicial penalties.

17.6 An SJE is an expert witness for the purposes of the provisions of the CPR relating to expert witnesses. It follows that, for example, your report must comply with the requirements of the CPR; the parties may put written questions to the SJE; and the SJE may ask the court for directions. Any meeting or conference attended would normally be a joint one with all instructing parties (unless the parties have agreed otherwise or the court has so directed).

17.7 An SJE's answers to questions put will be treated as part of the expert witness evidence, and are covered by the Statement of Truth.

17.8 Inasmuch as conflicting instructions may lead to different opinions, your report will need to contain multiple opinions on any issue, taking account of different assumptions of fact.

GN 18 Expert evidence, advocacy and 'a dual role'

18.1 Undertaking the two roles of expert witness and surveyor-advocate before many tribunals is prohibited as surveyors have no general right, by virtue of their status as surveyors, to appear as advocates in such cases (though an individual might be able to act by virtue of legal qualifications and of rights of audience gained under section 27 of the *Courts and Legal Services Act 1990* or similar provisions).

18.2 In certain tribunals some surveyors do adopt a dual role, i.e. act in the same case (but not at the same time) as surveyor-advocate and expert witness. PS 9 obliges you to consider the permissibility and appropriateness of undertaking a dual role in the same case.

The principal advantages and disadvantages of the dual role may be summarised as follows:
(a) The dual role may avoid or limit expense and delay, and therefore be a proportionate response to the circumstances of a case and the needs of the client.
(b) The weight to be attached to the evidence given by you as an expert witness, and to the submissions you make as surveyor-advocate, may be adversely affected if the dual role of surveyor-advocate and expert witness is undertaken.

It is always imperative to understand the distinction between the two roles and that it is impossible for both roles to be carried out at the same time. The PS obliges you to distinguish at all times which role you are undertaking. On occasions where surveyors undertake the dual role and fall below the necessary standards required of each role, the effect can be adverse, leading to the case being much weakened and often to criticism of the surveyor by the tribunal (which may also then be available to the client by any written decision of the tribunal). For example, if you give expert evidence unsupported by proper reasons, or omit material facts, the tribunal may form the view that it is in effect little more than advocacy of your client's case, and thus give it little or no weight. Advocacy that mixes expert (opinion) evidence in its submissions is not allowed under *Surveyors acting as advocates*: RICS practice statement.

A tribunal will do its best to assess the merits of each party's case: the weight of the opinion evidence and the nature and power of the advocacy submissions are important factors in the formation of any decisions by the tribunal.

18.3 PS 9.1 and 9.2 make reference to proportionality as a factor influencing any decision to adopt a dual role. Proportionality considerations encompass the following (which is not necessarily exhaustive):

(a)   whether it is more cost effective to split or to combine the roles from the point of view of your client (whether or not full or partial recovery of costs from any other party may be available);

(b)   whether it is more expedient to split or combine the roles;

(c)   whether the general conduct of the case, from the point of view of the tribunal, would be assisted by splitting or combining the roles; and

(d)   whether it would be prejudicial to the integrity of the tribunal's process to act in both roles.

18.4 The presence of one or more of the following factors may be grounds for you to decide not to adopt the dual role:

(a)   the case includes difficult points of law which are material to the decision;

(b)   one or both of the parties regard the initial hearing as the first step to a decision by a higher tribunal;

(c)   the other party will be legally represented;

(d)   the issues of fact and/or opinion are numerous, requiring evidence from several witnesses on each side; or

(e)   the amount at stake is high.

18.5 The dangers and difficulties of acting in a dual role were emphasised in the case of *Multi-Media Productions Ltd v Secretary of State for the Environment and Another* (1988) EGCS 83 (also reported at [1989] JPL 96), following an inspector's dismissal of a planning appeal. The court warned that:

- combining the roles of expert and advocate before a public local enquiry was an undesirable practice; and
- an expert witness had to give a true and unbiased opinion, the advocate had to do the best for his or her client.

An expert who has also undertaken the role of advocate runs the risk that his or her evidence is later treated with some caution by a tribunal. In another instance, a compensation case before the Lands Tribunal of England and Wales, the expert witness for the claimants was allowed to 'manage' their cases because they were not legally represented. As P. H. Clarke FRICS (formerly of the Lands Tribunal of England and Wales) reports in his book *The Surveyor in Court*, at page 156:

> 'The tribunal said, after giving a list of his errors (both as advocate and expert) that "this is a classic example, if ever one was needed, of the undesirability of having a valuer attempting to double his role of expert witness with that of advocate." In rating appeals before the Lands Tribunal the valuation officer frequently appears on behalf of himself, as a litigant in person. This has sometimes produced unfavourable comment from the tribunal. In *W. & R. R. Adam Ltd v Hockin* (VO) (1966) 13 RRC 1, the member said (p.4):
>
>> "... the position of an expert is quite distinct from and not always compatible with that of an advocate. It goes without saying that the duty of the advocate is to present his client's case as best he may on the evidence available whereas the expert witness is there to give the court the benefit of his special training and/or experience in order to help the court come to the right decision. It is important therefore that the expert witness should be consistent in his opinions and should not be, nor appear to be, partisan for his opinions then become of less weight. ...".'

The extract above is reproduced with the permission of P. H. Clarke FRICS.

18.6 You are under a duty in the PS to make it clear to the tribunal which role you are fulfilling at all times. The following is worth emphasising:
   (a)   As elaborated in *Surveyors acting as advocates*: RICS practice statement and guidance note: when acting as a surveyor-advocate, you have a duty in your role to promote the client's case; an advocate is someone who speaks on behalf of a party and

puts the party's best case to a tribunal with the purpose of persuading that body of the correctness of the party's argument. As surveyor-advocate you retain a duty to assist the tribunal and you must not mislead it. You must not make an advocacy submission unless properly arguable, must not mis-state facts and must draw a tribunal's attention to all relevant legal authority of which you are aware, whether supportive of your client's case or not. However, and critically, unlike an expert witness, you must not express—expert opinion evidence, unless permitted to do so by the tribunal. Your task is simply to advance the argument that you consider best promotes your client's case. A fuller statement on advocacy, the surveyor-advocate's role and the principles underlying conduct of that role, can be found in *Surveyors acting as advocates*.

(b) When acting as an expert witness, the PS makes clear your primary and overriding duty is to the tribunal to which evidence is to be given. The duty is to be truthful as to fact, honest and impartial as to opinion, and complete as to coverage of relevant matters. The PS specifies that special care must be taken to ensure it is not biased towards the party who is responsible for instructing or paying for the evidence. It follows therefore that (unlike an advocate) an expert witness cannot advance a view in which he or she does not believe.

(c) Expert witness reports would not generally be expected to include reference to questions of admissibility; reference to questions of interpretation of a contract (see GN 8.3) and comments that are in the nature of advocacy submissions about an opposing expert's evidence. You may find yourself at greater risk of slipping into 'advocacy mode' at the rebuttal stage of presentation of evidence, when the focus of your evidence shifts from explanation of your own opinion to a more critical role in dealing with the matching expert witness surveyor's report.

18.7 It is advisable to decide and agree with those appointing you, at the outset of any reference to a tribunal, what role or roles you are to adopt, and to make clear the distinctions between, and the limitations of, the roles.

Surveyors acting as advocates makes it clear that as a surveyor-advocate you are not able, when conducting that role, at any stage to present expert opinion evidence, unless permitted to do so by the tribunal.

18.8 PS 9.4 makes it clear that you are required to distinguish the distinct roles of surveyor-advocate and expert witness at all times. In oral hearings it is sometimes convenient for the roles to be distinguished by standing when in one role and sitting when in the other, or giving evidence from a witness stand at the side of the room and making submissions as advocate from a position in front of the tribunal. Where, however, factual evidence is most conveniently interspersed with advocacy, moving from one position to another is disruptive, and standing or sitting may be the most convenient way of distinguishing the roles. It is not expected by the PS that you interrupt the flow of giving evidence at every turn to announce which role you are conducting, but only that you act prudently to avoid any possibility of confusing or misleading the tribunal. If you are acting as surveyor-advocate and expert witness, you should always ensure that you are familiar with the procedures of the relevant tribunal and that the means adopted for distinguishing advocacy from expert evidence are appropriate to those procedures. In the alternative, it should be perfectly possible for you to announce the order of your presentation initially (it is recommended that you do this in any case) and undertake to inform the tribunal when your expert evidence begins, so that it is clear which material can be tested by cross-examination.

18.9 The two roles are even more difficult to distinguish where a matter is conducted by written representations. If the distinction is not obvious, it is advisable to place submissions by way of advocacy in one document and expert opinion evidence in another document or, at least, in separate, clearly distinguishable parts of the same document. See GN 3.5 of *Surveyors acting as advocates*.

18.10 If undertaking the two roles, you and your client ought to be aware of the severe disadvantage that might arise where, in a hearing, you are giving evidence under oath or affirmation in your capacity as expert witness and an adjournment occurs. Under such circumstances, you would be unable to discuss any aspect of the case with your client during that adjournment, unless leave is granted by the tribunal; leave may be sought.

18.11 It is permissible for the expert witness to act as case manager, a role that concerns the procedural aspects of any particular case. However, great care should be taken that your impartiality as an expert witness is not compromised in undertaking such a role.

GN 19 Basis of charging fees

19.1 The basis of charging may vary depending upon the nature of your appointment.

19.2 When appointed by a party to a dispute, PS 3.5 requires you to set out clearly in writing the scope and the basis of your fees. For example, this might be by reference to the work to be undertaken, and daily or hourly rates or a fixed fee. Provision may also be made for additional payments in respect of:
(a)   travelling time;
(b)   expenses and disbursements;
(c)   attendance at hearings; and
(d)   late notice, cancellation fees or settlement after you have been booked to attend a hearing.

19.3 Levels of fees and expenses payable may be determined by the rules of particular bodies, by summary or other cost assessment and/or statutory provisions. You are recommended to establish or satisfy yourself of the fee basis and amounts payable prior to accepting instructions; you should be aware of the fact that some tribunals, in determining costs or expenses, may treat any advocacy work undertaken as work done by a lay representative.

19.4 Regard should be had to the possibility that the level of fee a successful client may recover from the other party might be subject to revision under the detailed or summary assessment of costs procedures (known as taxation in Scotland). It is considered important for both the basis of fee charging and for possible detailed or summary assessment purposes that careful and detailed time-sheets and records of tasks undertaken are kept. Some tribunals may require adoption of record-keeping broken down into specific units. It is recommended that you check with the tribunal in question.

GN 20 Conditional fees

20.1 The following provisions are worthy of general note in relation to *conditional fee* arrangements (see *Appendix D: Definitions*):

- The Code of Conduct applicable to solicitors in England and Wales states in Rule 11.07 'You must not make, or offer to make, payments to a witness dependent upon the nature of the evidence given or upon the outcome of the case'.

- Paragraph 7.6 of the Civil Justice Council *Protocol for the Instruction of Experts to give Evidence in Civil Claims* (annexed to the Practice Direction of Part 35 of the CPR in England and Wales) states that payments that are 'contingent upon the nature of the expert evidence given in legal proceedings, or upon the outcome of a case, must not be offered or accepted'. The Protocol states its aim is to give interpretative guidance upon the provisions of the CPR relating to expert evidence.

- In Northern Ireland, Practice Direction no. 6/2002 (*Commercial list practice direction – expert evidence*) states: '5. Payments of fees, charges or expenses to an expert witness contingent upon the nature of the expert evidence given in legal proceedings, or upon the outcome of a case, must not be offered or accepted. To do so would contravene the expert's overriding duty to the court. …'

- The joint *Code of Practice for Experts* issued by the Academy of Experts and the EWI (endorsed 22 June 2005 by the Master of the Rolls) states: '2. An Expert who is retained or employed in any contentious proceeding shall not enter into any arrangement which could compromise his impartiality nor make his fee dependent on the outcome of the case nor should he accept any benefits other than his fee and expenses.'

20.2 In relation to PS 10, both the *Principal message* of the PS and PS 2.1 emphasise the duty to set out the facts fully and give truthful, impartial and independent opinions, covering all relevant matters. The existence of a conditional fee arrangement is clearly relevant, even if you take the view that your opinion has not been influenced by it. The point is that the existence of the arrangement may contravene your overriding duty to the tribunal and compromise your impartiality. Accordingly, it is a matter that should be disclosed so that the evidence can be properly weighed by the tribunal. PS 10 does not require you to disclose the commercial and numerical details of your fee arrangement, only that you are operating on a conditional fee basis (see PS 5.1(j)(iii)). However it is possible that a tribunal – either of its own initiative or following a challenge by a party – may order fuller disclosure of details of your fee arrangement. Accordingly, it is also recommended that you cater for this eventuality and the consequential loss of commercial confidentiality in your standard terms of engagement with your client.

20.3 (a) Rather than adopting a conditional fee arrangement, it is strongly recommended that you consider making other fee arrangements with your prospective client wherever possible. As PS 3.4 indicates, you are required to advise your client in writing of the risk that a tribunal may view evidence given under a conditional fee arrangement as being tainted by bias, and may attach less weight to it; it may even refuse to admit it at all; or declare the whole conditional fee arrangement void (see GN 20.3(b)–(e) below). Whilst RICS recognises that conditional fee arrangements are adopted in some surveying specialisms, it would not expect any of its members to allow the quality of their evidence to be influenced detrimentally by the potential remuneration arising from a conditional fee arrangement.

(b) You should be aware of a longstanding rule (the rule against champerty) that outlaws conditional fee arrangements for certain types of cases undertaken before some tribunals in England, Wales and Northern Ireland (but not Scotland). (**Note**: Although the case law pertaining to the issue of champerty is drawn, for the purposes of this document, from decisions of the courts in England and Wales, it is believed these would be persuasive to tribunals in Northern Ireland.) Your concern should be to ensure that:

(i)   the rule does not apply to you; and

(ii)   the rule does not apply to the proceedings in which you are engaged as an expert witness or the tribunal before which you will be appearing.

In practice, there is very little guidance in the decided case law on these two subjects; this part of the guidance note is therefore conservative and cautionary.

(c)   As to GN 20.3(b)(i), historically, the rule has only been used so as to penalise lawyers. The rule has its roots in the perceived need to protect the integrity of public justice, and in particular to avoid *advocates* putting themselves in a position where their own interest may conflict with their duties to the court. The public policy behind the rule would appear to apply as readily to surveyors acting as expert witnesses as it does to advocates, although there is no recorded instance of a case in which a surveyor or his or her client has been penalised by the rule. In practice, it is unlikely (but not inconceivable) that the rule would now be extended to include expert witnesses.

(d)   As to GN 20.3(b)(ii) above, it is difficult to provide a conclusive list of the types of proceedings to which the rule applies. Disputes between parties that require resolution by tribunals (e.g. litigation, arbitration, adjudication, independent expert determination, and proceedings before the land(s) tribunals) are more likely to fall within the ambit of the rule than other proceedings involving the consideration of questions of an administrative or public nature (e.g. determination of planning permission, rating and fair rents). It should, however, be stressed that there is only one recorded instance in which the rule has been applied outside the sphere of litigation (in that case, to arbitration).

(e)   Where the rule does apply, the effect is to render the conditional fee arrangement unenforceable. The result will be not merely that the successful party will be unable to recover the conditional fee from the other party, but also that the expert witness will be unable to recover the conditional fee from his or her client. Accordingly, where you are thinking of entering into a conditional fee arrangement for a case in England, Wales and Northern Ireland (but not Scotland), a critical consideration will be whether, in the event of a challenge to a conditional fee arrangement, the tribunal you will appear before will regard the proceedings as of the type to which the rule would apply (using the criteria referred to in GN 20.3(d) above). If the proceedings are not likely to be so regarded, then you are likely to be within the law when entering into the arrangement. It is strongly recommended that you advise your client of the risk of unenforceability as set out in this paragraph GN 20.3, and decide whether you yourself wish to proceed in those circumstances.

20.4 It is also recommended that you carefully consider whether to pursue – or instead to avoid – conditional fee arrangements in any other instructions undertaken by you or your colleagues that are linked with your role as an expert witness. An obvious example might be other work involving the same property whether or not for the same client. Such fee arrangements may be perceived to endanger the duty of impartiality and independence required of you when acting as an expert witness.

20.5 PS 10.1 also applies where you are to act in the same case in a dual role, i.e. both as expert witness and advocate (see *Surveyors acting as advocates*: PS 3.6 and GN 4.6). Accordingly, even if your role is primarily to be that of an advocate, and your expert evidence in the case is to be very limited in nature, you are bound by PS 10.1.

GN 21 Responsibility for fees

21.1 The responsibility for payment of your fees would normally be clearly incorporated in the terms of engagement entered into. These may identify one party as being solely responsible for payment. Alternatively, consideration may be given to making more than one party (e.g. solicitors, claims consultants or similar) jointly and severally responsible for payment.

21.2 It is recommended that you should advise that liability will exist for all fees and disbursements properly incurred in accordance with your terms of engagement, even though those fees and disbursements may subsequently be reduced under the detailed or summary assessment of costs or, alternatively, to the extent that they are not fully recovered from another party to the dispute. Prior to confirmation of your terms of engagement, it is recommended that you clarify whether those appointing you are required to obtain any form of authority or approval to secure your fees and disbursements, or any portion thereof. It is also recommended that you clarify whether any order or direction has been made limiting the amount of your fees and disbursements.

21.3   In a case to which the CPR apply, if you do not answer written questions asked by the party who does not instruct you, the court may order that the party who instructed the expert cannot recover the fees or expenses of that expert from any other party (see also GN 9.3 and 9.4).

GN 22 Immunity of the expert witness

England and Wales

22.1   All witnesses, including expert witnesses, are immune from any civil court proceedings arising out of their evidence (*Dawkins v Lord Rokeby* (1873) LR 8 QB 255 at 264). The immunity covers oral testimony and expert witness reports and extends to:

    (a)   a statement or conduct which can fairly be said to be part of the process of investigating a crime or a possible crime with a view to prosecution in respect of the matter being investigated (*Evans v London Hospital Medical College* [1981] 1 WLR 184); and

    (b)   a statement or conduct which could fairly be said to be preliminary to the giving of expert evidence in civil proceedings – judged by the principal purpose for which the work was done (*Stanton v Callaghan* [2000] 1 QB 75).

22.2   The immunity only bars civil suits. The immunity does not protect a witness against a criminal prosecution for perjury, for perverting the course of justice or for contempt of court. There are a number of exemptions to the immunity, which can be found in *Appendix C: Immunity of the expert witness – exemptions.*

22.3 Following the recent England and Wales case of *General Medical Council v Professor Sir Roy Meadow* [2006] EWCA Civ 1390, it is now confirmed as good law that the immunity does not extend to proceedings brought by a professional body (such as RICS) against an expert witness in respect of forensic expert evidence. In other words, RICS has the power to investigate and bring disciplinary proceedings against RICS members for breaches of their duties as expert witnesses; it has instigated such proceedings in the past and will continue to do so as appropriate, in the public interest.

22.4 (a) It is difficult to give comprehensive guidance since the immunity does not draw distinct lines between work done by an expert which is within the forensic process and work which is outside of that process and outside of the immunity. This is especially the case in civil proceedings where, for example, a surveyor may advise a client as to where a boundary lies between two properties and later may be called to give expert evidence in a boundary dispute. The initial advice may not be immune: the later forensic expert evidence may be. As observed by Simon Tuckey QC in the case of *Palmer v Durnford Ford* [1992] 1 QB 483 each case will turn on its own facts:

'The immunity would only extend to what could fairly be said to be preliminary to his giving evidence in court judged perhaps by the principal purpose for which the work was done. So the production or approval of a report for the purposes of disclosure to the other side would be immune but work done for the principal purpose of advising the client would not. Each case would depend upon its own facts with the court concerned to protect the expert from liability for the evidence which he gave in court and the work principally and proximately leading to it.'

(b) The key question would be to ask what the principal purpose of the work undertaken was – to give evidence or to advise the client? There are many grey areas and many questions remain open and untested in the courts. The prudent course for a surveyor to adopt is probably that, unless proceedings have begun or are likely to begin and he or she is instructed to prepare an expert report with a view to giving evidence and thus participating in the tribunal's process, the surveyor should assume that, until that point has been reached, the principle of immunity from suit may well **not** apply to claims relating to his or her professional services provided at an earlier stage.

22.5 The immunity does not make the expert witnesses exempt from wasted costs orders in court proceedings in England and Wales (there is nothing to suppose that it would in Northern Ireland either) if the expert's evidence causes significant expense to be incurred and does so in flagrant disregard to his or her duties to a court. *See Phillips & Others v Symes & Others* [2004] EWHC 2330 Ch.

22.6 A surveyor who acts as an advocate will owe duties to his or her client and to the tribunal in a similar manner as a lawyer advocate would do so (see *Surveyors acting as advocates*: RICS practice statement and guidance note). There is now no (lawyer) advocate's immunity from civil proceedings (*Arthur J. S. Hall & Co. v Simons (A. P.)* [2002] 1 AC 615). Although there is no direct authority on the point, it is likely to be the case, similarly, that you will have no immunity as a **surveyor**-advocate either. You will therefore need to be careful to ensure that it is always clear when you are acting in the role of surveyor-advocate rather than another role (such as expert witness).

22.7 Some commentators argue that the immunity attaching to an expert witness applies logically, and as an extension of the public policy underlying it, to the giving of evidence to and before all the tribunals listed in the *PS Preamble*. There is no authority directly on the point.

22.8 At the time of publication, it is fair to say that there are many calls for experts to lose their immunity from civil court proceedings; especially following the ruling in *Meadow* and the lifting of the immunity to allow wasted costs orders. Members are advised to stay updated with developments in the law in this field, but are reminded once again, per GN 22.3, that the traditional immunity is not a shield against disciplinary proceedings being brought by RICS.

Scotland

22.9 The general principles of Scottish law relating to expert witness immunity are substantially the same as English law, although there is no direct equivalent of a 'wasted costs' order (see GN 22.5 above). The law was reviewed in the case of *Karling v Purdue* [2004] ScotCS 221. The real difficulty, both in England and Wales and in Scotland, is not only in defining the boundaries of immunity but in the application of any definition of those boundaries to a particular case. The position is summed up in two key passages in *Karling*:

'When an expert is engaged in the context of an existing litigation or a prospective litigation, he may perform a dual role. The first is advisory and the second is in his capacity as expert witness with all the responsibilities to the court as which that entails ... In one sense, all communications by an expert to his client constitute advice in one shape or form. He may advise him of his factual findings following on investigation; he may advise him of his conclusions based on those findings and/or other established or assumed facts. He may suggest a particular strategy or tactic. Part or all of this may be included in a report to be lodged as a production to which he may in due course speak. All of the foregoing may be intimately or closely connected with proceedings, actual, contemplated or possible. The difficulty of identifying whether the work of an expert or part of it falls within or outwith the protective circle of immunity is greater in the context of civil proceedings than criminal proceedings. The period between engagement and the giving of evidence or the settlement of the case may be several years. Initial engagement may occur where litigation is not in contemplation.

In civil proceedings, as the English authorities illustrate, the position will often not be clear-cut. Experts may be engaged before actions are raised; their role may initially be restricted, and subsequently broadened, e.g. as to topic to report on, and as to function. Some experts are particularly good at providing detailed background information which can be used in cross examination, but are not themselves skilled at giving evidence and explaining their position simply and persuasively to the court. In civil proceedings many permutations are possible where fine distinctions may have to be made.'

22.10 The difficulties were also illustrated in the discussion in *General Medical Council v Professor Sir Roy Meadow* [2006] EWCA Civ 1390. A key question would be to ask what the principal purpose of the work undertaken was – to give evidence or to advise the client? In particular, when engaged to prepare a report, consider whether an expert has been so instructed with a view, in due course, to giving evidence in civil proceedings. There are many grey areas and many questions remain open and untested. The prudent course for a surveyor to adopt is probably that, unless proceedings have begun or are likely to begin and he or she is instructed to prepare an expert report with a view to giving evidence and thus participating in the tribunal's process, the surveyor should assume that, until that point has been reached, the principle of immunity from suit may well **not** apply to claims relating to his or her professional services provided at an earlier stage.

22.11 For the avoidance of doubt, RICS considers that the positions as stated in GN 22.6–22.8, and the exemptions listed in Appendix C, apply equally in Scotland, subject to the following qualifications. The leading Scottish case on advocates' immunity is *Wright v Paton Farrell* [2006] SC 404 (IH), in which the Court, although concerned with criminal proceedings, indicated that *Hall* would be highly influential in relation to the question of an advocate's immunity from suit for the negligent conduct of civil proceedings. In relation to malicious prosecution, reference may be made to *McKie v Strathclyde Joint Police Board* [2004] SLT 982. In relation to disclosure of confidential material, reference may be made to *Watson v McEwan* [1905] 7 F (HL) 109, 13 SLT 340.

Northern Ireland

22.12 The position set out in the preceding England and Wales section of GN 22 is equally applicable to the situation in Northern Ireland; whilst tribunals in Northern Ireland are not bound to follow the decisions of other tribunals in the UK, the decisions cited are persuasive to Northern Irish tribunals and broadly reflect the procedure adopted in those tribunals.

Appendix A: Sample Terms of Engagement

Note: This appendix forms a part of *Surveyors acting as expert witnesses*: RICS guidance note. Its sample terms are not intended to be mandatory or prescriptive, and may be adapted as required. It is recognised that a variety of circumstances will prevail in the range of assignments surveyors may undertake and that clauses may not be appropriate in every circumstance. For example, where a Client appoints a surveyor directly, without using an Appointer, the terms would need to be amended accordingly. Other or additional terms of engagement may also be indicated, for example, by a protocol established under the CPR or in guides that supplement the CPR in certain courts.

Terms of Engagement

1 Recital of appointment

1.1   The Appointer has appointed the named surveyor (see 1.5) to provide the following services in respect of [*state identity of property/facility*] and in accordance with these Terms of Engagement.

[*state the nature and extent of the instructions, their purposes, the services which may be provided*]

1.2   The appointment is one which is subject to *Surveyors acting as expert witnesses*: RICS practice statement, a copy of which is available on request.

1.3   The Appointer is:

1.4   The Client is:

1.5   The Expert Surveyor is:

[*also state identity and qualifications of any assistant, and extent of their intended involvement*]

1.6   The Tribunal is:

[*state name of tribunal to which expert evidence is to be submitted*]

2 Definitions

Unless otherwise agreed by the parties:

2.1 'Appointer' means the person(s), organisation(s), or department(s) from whom instructions are received.

2.2 'Client' means the person(s), organisation(s), or department(s) on whose behalf the Expert Surveyor has been instructed to provide the services listed in 1.1 of these Terms of Engagement.

2.3 'Expert Surveyor' means the person named at 1.5, and appointed to provide the services described in 1.1 of these Terms of Engagement.

2.4 'Assignment' means the matter(s) referred to the Expert Surveyor by the Appointer, in respect of which the services are required, and to which these Terms of Engagement apply.

2.5 'Fees' means (in the absence of written agreement to the contrary) the reasonable charges of the Expert Surveyor based on the Expert Surveyor's agreed hourly/daily rate. [*Set out hourly/daily rates*] Time spent travelling and waiting may be charged at the full hourly/daily rate. Value Added Tax will be charged in addition (where applicable).

2.6 'Disbursements' means the cost, reasonably incurred, of (by way of non-exclusive example) all photography, reproduction of drawings, diagrams, etc., printing and duplicating, and all out-of-pocket expenses, including travel, subsistence and hotel accommodation. Value Added Tax will be charged in addition (where applicable).

3 The Appointer

3.1 The Appointer shall:
   (a) provide timely, full and clear instructions in writing supported by good quality copies of all relevant documents within his or her possession – including all court orders and directions which may affect the preparation of advice or reports – along with a timetable for provision of the Expert Surveyor's services; at such times as the timetable

is altered, such alterations shall be notified promptly to the Expert Surveyor;

(b) treat expeditiously every reasonable request by the Expert Surveyor for authority, information or materials, and for further instructions, as he or she may require;

(c) update and/or vary without delay the Expert Surveyor's instructions, as circumstances require;

(d) not alter or add to, nor permit others so to do, the content of an Expert Surveyor's report, or any text, document or materials supporting such report, before submission to the Tribunal, without the Expert Surveyor's permission;

(e) where possible, at the Expert Surveyor's request, arrange access to the property/facility relevant to the Assignment in order that the Expert Surveyor can inspect such and make relevant enquiries;

(f) ascertain the availability of the Expert Surveyor for hearings, meetings and appointments at which his or her presence is required;

(g) give adequate written notice to the Expert Surveyor of any attendance required at hearings, meetings and appointments;

(h) not use the Expert Surveyor's report or other works for any other purpose save that directly related to the Assignment.

4 The Expert Surveyor

4.1 The Expert Surveyor shall:

(a) undertake only those tasks in respect of which he or she considers that he or she has adequate experience, knowledge, expertise and resources;

(b) use reasonable skill and care in the performance of his or her instructions and duties;

(c) comply with appropriate codes, rules and guidelines, including those of RICS;

(d) notify the Appointer of any matter which could disqualify the Expert Surveyor or render it undesirable for the Appointer to continue with the appointment;

(e) answer questions or requests for information from the Appointer within a reasonable time;

(f) endeavour to make him or herself available for all hearings, meetings, etc. of which he or she has received adequate written notice;

(g)   treat all aspects of the Assignment as confidential;

(h)   provide all relevant information to allow the Appointer to defend the Expert Surveyor's Fees or Disbursements at any costs assessment;

(i)   respond promptly to any complaint by the Appointer within a reasonable time;

(j)   retain all intellectual property rights and ownership rights in his or her work and any other original works created by him or her in relation to or in connection with the Assignment on which he or she is instructed, unless otherwise agreed in writing.

5 Fees and Disbursements

5.1   The Expert Surveyor may present invoices at such intervals as he or she considers reasonable during the course of the Assignment, and payment of each invoice shall be due on presentation.

5.2   For the avoidance of doubt, the Expert Surveyor shall be entitled to charge for Fees and Disbursements where, due to settlement of the dispute, or for any other reason not being the fault of the Expert Surveyor:

(a)   the Expert Surveyor's time has been necessarily reserved for a specific hearing, meeting, appointment or other relevant engagement;

(b)   specific instructions have been given to the Expert Surveyor for an inspection and report; and

(c)   the reservation of time is not required because the engagement has been cancelled or postponed and/or the instructions have been terminated.

5.3   The Expert Surveyor shall also be entitled to charge for answering questions from a party relating to the Assignment or for the provision of any addendum reports.

5.4   The Appointer and [identify party] shall be jointly and severally responsible for payment of the Expert Surveyor's Fees and Disbursements.

5.5   Any restriction or cap by the Tribunal, or by another competent authority, of the recoverability of an Expert

Surveyor's Fees and Disbursements, shall not affect the liability of the Appointer to pay those Fees and Disbursements.

5.6 The Appointer shall pay to the Expert Surveyor, if applicable, interest under the *Late Payment of Commercial Debts (Interest) Act* 1998 on all unpaid invoices, or will pay to the Expert Surveyor, at the Expert Surveyor's sole discretion, simple interest at [...]% per month (or part thereof) on all invoices which are unpaid after 30 days from the date of issue of the invoice, calculated from the expiry of such 30-day period, together with the full amount of administrative, legal and other costs incurred in obtaining settlement of unpaid invoices.

6 Disputes over Fees and Disbursements

6.1 In the event of a dispute as to the amount of the Expert Surveyor's Fees and Disbursements, such sum as is not disputed shall be paid forthwith pending resolution of the dispute, irrespective of any set off or counter claim which may be alleged.

6.2 Any dispute relating to the amount of the Expert Surveyor's Fees and Disbursements shall, in the first instance, be referred to [*e.g.* the Expert Surveyor's firm].

6.3 Any dispute over Fees or Disbursements that cannot be resolved by [*e.g.* the Expert Surveyor's firm] shall be referred to [*e.g.* a mediator chosen by agreement of both parties]. Where agreement cannot be reached on the identity of [*e.g.* a mediator], the services of [*e.g.* the RICS Dispute Resolution Service (DRS)] shall be used to appoint [*e.g.* a mediator]. In the event that any dispute cannot be resolved by [*e.g.* mediation], the courts of [*state jurisdiction e.g.* England and Wales] shall have exclusive jurisdiction in relation to the dispute and its resolution.

6.4 The law of [*state law e.g.* England and Wales] shall govern these Terms of Engagement.

Appendix B: Hearsay evidence

This appendix forms a part of *Surveyors acting as expert witnesses*: RICS guidance note.

The *Civil Evidence Act* 1995 and the *Civil Evidence (Scotland) Act* 1988 contain provisions that alter the previous hearsay rules (that hearsay evidence was not admissible). The Acts abolish the rule against hearsay evidence in civil proceedings, set out guidance as to hearsay evidence and require a party who wishes to adduce hearsay evidence to serve notice on the other party.

The Acts therefore provide that in civil proceedings evidence otherwise admissible shall not be excluded solely on the grounds that it is hearsay. 'Civil proceedings' means civil proceedings before any courts and tribunals where the strict rules of evidence apply, whether as a matter of law or by agreement of the parties (in Scotland, this also includes any hearing by the Sheriff under the *Children (Scotland) Act* 1995).

It would appear therefore that the provisions of the Acts would apply to an arbitration where the arbitrator has ruled that the strict rules of evidence shall apply or the parties have agreed that this shall be the position.

A party wishing to rely on hearsay evidence must first serve notice on the other party, giving particulars of this evidence. Failure to comply with this requirement will not affect the admissibility of the evidence. However, it may be taken into account by the tribunal in the exercise of its powers in connection with the proceedings and costs, and by the tribunal as a matter adversely affecting the weight to be given to the hearsay evidence.

The change in the hearsay rule by the Acts is a change of emphasis from admissibility to weight.

Generally, a tribunal would have regard to any circumstances from which any inference can be drawn as to the reliability of the hearsay evidence.

Appendix C: Immunity of the expert witness – exemptions

This appendix forms a part of *Surveyors acting as expert witnesses*: RICS guidance note.

GN 22 considers the issue of the immunity of expert witnesses. GN 22.2 refers to a number of exemptions. The principal exemptions are:

(a)   statements or conduct that lies outside of the situations described at GN 22.1(a) and (b). Where the principal purpose of the statement or conduct is not part of the process of investigating or prosecuting crime or not preliminary to the giving of expert evidence in civil proceedings then it will be outside of the immunity;

(b)   claims for misfeasance in public office/conspiracy to injure for having fabricated evidence (*Darker v Chief Constable of West Midlands* [2001] 1 AC 435);

(c)   libelling the opposing party in a report for prepared for court proceedings (*Schneider v Leigh* [1955] 2 QB 195);

(d)   committing the tort of malicious prosecution where the expert witness by giving malicious evidence 'procured' the prosecution (*Martin v Watson* [1996] AC 74);

(e)   an expert witness can be sued for breach of confidence where he or she discloses an expert report to another without consent from the client (*De Taranto v Cornelius* (2002) 68 BMLR 62).

Appendix D: Definitions

This appendix forms a part of both the practice statement and guidance note of *Surveyors acting as expert witnesses*. The following are short definitions of some terms from the PS and the GN. In certain circumstances other terms may be used. Members are advised to refer to a legal dictionary (or legal textbooks), and/or to relevant rules, directions and procedures of the tribunal in question. Members may also find it useful to view *Appendix B: Definitions* in the publication *Surveyors acting as advocates*.

Surveyor-advocate: a person who presents to the tribunal a client's properly arguable case as best as he or she may on the evidence and facts available; a spokesperson for a client who, subject to any restrictions imposed by the surveyor's duty to the tribunal, must do for his or her client all that the client might properly do for him or herself if he or she could. Sometimes also referred to as party representative (although this term is occasionally loosely also used to refer to the surveyor as a negotiator). The advocacy role is markedly different from the role of an expert witness or a negotiator (see below).

Case manager: a person who, acting on behalf of a party, is responsible for the general conduct, management and administration of the case, marshalling and coordinating that party's team (if any) and liaising as appropriate with the tribunal and opposing party.

Conditional fee: this term refers to any arrangement where remuneration – however fixed or calculated – is to be made conditional upon the outcome of proceedings or upon the nature of evidence given. Other labels in common use are 'incentive-fee', 'speculative fee', 'success-fee', 'success-related fee', 'performance fee', 'no-win, no-fee' and 'contingency fee'.

CPR: The *Civil Procedure Rules* (known as CPR) can be found at www.justice.gov.uk/civil/procrules_fin/index.htm. This is the set of rules governing the procedure of the Supreme Court and County Court in England and Wales. These procedural rules are supplemented by Protocols, Pre-Action Protocols, Practice Directions and court guides. The objectives of the CPR are to make access to justice cheaper, quicker and fairer. Some of the CPR apply to action taken before proceedings are issued and so the scope of the CPR should be considered in respect of any matter likely to be litigious.

Direction: a requirement laid down by a tribunal.

Disclosure: the production and inspection of documents in accordance with applicable rules and/or directions of a tribunal. Different rules apply in the Scottish courts where documents can be recovered from another party (known as the 'haver') using 'commission and diligence'.

Evidence: this may be evidence of fact, expert (opinion) evidence or hearsay evidence. The weight to be attached to evidence by a tribunal will depend on various factors, the importance of which may vary from case to case.

Expert witness: a witness called by a tribunal to give expert opinion evidence by virtue of experience, knowledge and expertise of a particular area beyond that expected of a layperson. The overriding duty of the expert witness is to provide independent, impartial and unbiased evidence to the tribunal – covering all relevant matters, whether or not they favour the client – to assist the tribunal in reaching its determination.

Hearsay evidence: evidence by way of the oral statements of a person other than the witness who is testifying and/or by way of statements in documents, offered to prove the truth of what is stated. See also the *Civil Evidence (Scotland) Act* 1988 and the *Civil Evidence Act* 1995. In arbitral proceedings, subject to any agreement between the parties or prior direction given by the arbitrator, hearsay will be admissible, subject to notice being given to the other party.

Legal professional privilege (sometimes called 'legal advice privilege'): legal professional privilege attaches to, and protects:

- communications (whether written or oral) made confidentially;
- passing between a lawyer (acting in his or her professional legal capacity) and his or her client;
- solely for the purpose of giving or obtaining legal advice.

Licensed Access: RICS members are currently permitted by the General Council of the Bar of England and Wales to instruct a barrister direct, without the services of a solicitor for certain purposes. The surveyor should be experienced in the field to which the referral relates. The regime in England and Wales was formerly known as *Direct Professional Access* (DPA). The RICS guidance note *Direct Professional Access to Barristers* is currently under review. RICS members are also able to instruct counsel direct under the terms of the Scottish *Direct Access Rules* and, in Northern Ireland, under *Direct Professional Access*. The relevant Bar Councils (of England and Wales; and Northern Ireland) or the Faculty of Advocates in Scotland, can be consulted for further advice.

Litigation privilege: where litigation is in reasonable contemplation or in progress, this protects:

- written or oral communications made confidentially;
- between either a client and a lawyer, OR either of them and a third party;
- where the dominant purpose is for use in the proceedings;
- either for the purpose of giving or getting advice in relation to such proceedings, or for obtaining evidence to be used in such proceedings.

The privilege applies to proceedings in the High Court, County Court, employment tribunals and, where it is subject to English procedural law, arbitration. With regard to other tribunals, the position is less clear.

Negotiator: a person who negotiates a deal (of property or asset) or solution. Also, in dispute resolution, a person who seeks to negotiate the resolution of the dispute as best he or she may. A negotiator has no involvement in this role with a tribunal. A negotiator's role is markedly different to that of an advocate, expert witness, case manager or witness of fact.

Representation(s): this term may, depending on the circumstances and context, be used to refer to one or more of:
- a statement of case;
- an assertion of fact(s);
- expert opinion evidence; and
- an advocacy submission.

Representations may be made orally or in writing.

Scott Schedule: a document setting out, in tabular form, the items in dispute and containing (or allowing to be added) the contentions or agreement of each party. Named after a former Official Referee.

Single Joint Expert (SJE): an expert witness appointed pursuant to an order of a court, and instructed jointly by parties to a dispute. Though relatively rare in Scotland, courts in that jurisdiction can appoint their own expert.

Submission(s): the presentation by way of advocacy of a matter in dispute to the judgment of a tribunal. The term is occasionally used loosely in the surveying community to refer to evidence of fact or expert opinion evidence presented, or to a mix of such expert opinion evidence and advocacy; such usage is often misplaced.

Tribunal: see definition in *Preamble* to the PS.

'Without prejudice': the without prejudice rule will generally prevent statements made in a genuine attempt to settle an existing dispute, whether made in writing or orally, from being put before a court as evidence of admissions against the interest of the party which made them. There are a number of established exceptions to the rule.

Witness of fact: a person who, usually on oath or solemn affirmation, gives evidence before a tribunal on a question of fact.

Further reading

Most of the items below can be obtained via RICS Books (www.ricsbooks.com). Please note that some publications reference earlier editions of *Surveyors acting as expert witnesses* or *Surveyors acting as advocates*.

Agricultural Arbitrations and Independent Expert Determinations (2nd edition), RICS guidance note, 1998

Baker, E. and Lavers, A., *Case in Point: Expert Witness*, RICS Books, 2005

Barry, P., *The Expert Witness* (training pack), College of Estate Management, 2006

Bond, C., Burn S., Harper P., and Solon M., *The Expert Witness in Court – A Practical Guide*, Shaw & Sons, 1999

Boundaries: Guide to Procedure For Boundary Identification, Demarcation and Disputes in England and Wales (1st edition is out of print; a 2nd edition is under preparation)

Burns, S. (in association with Bond Solon Training), *Successful Use of Expert Witnesses in Civil Disputes*, Tottel Publishing (Crayford, Shaw's), 2003

Cato, D., *The Expert in Litigation and Arbitration,* LLP Professional Publishing, 1999

Civil Procedure Rules, together with associated Practice Directions, Pre-Action Protocols and Forms, available at: www.justice.gov.uk/civil/procrules_fin/index.htm – and the *Protocol for the Instruction of Experts to give Evidence in Civil Claims* (issued by the Civil Justice Council (CJC), June 2005, approved by the Master of the Rolls), available at: www.justice.gov.uk/civil/procrules_fin/contents/form_section_images/practice_directions/pd35_pdf_eps/ pd35_prot.pdf

Clarke, P. H., *The Surveyor in Court*, Estates Gazette, 1985 (out of print but available from the RICS Library)

Dilapidations (5th edition), RICS guidance note, 2008

Direct Professional Access to Barristers (2nd edition), RICS guidance note, 2003 (current edition under review)

Farr, M., *Surveyor's Expert Witness Handbook: Valuation*, EG Books, 2005

Hodgkinson, T., and James, M., *Expert Evidence: Law & Practice* (2nd edition), Thompson Sweet & Maxwell, 2007

Morris, A., *The Surveyor as Expert Witness: building and development play*, EG Books, 2005

Pamplin, C. (Dr), *The Little Book on Expert Witness Fees*, JS Publications, 2007

Pamplin, C. (Dr), *The Little Book on Expert Witness Practice*, JS Publications, 2007

Rating Appeals (2nd edition), RICS guidance note, 2001 (current edition under review)

Rating Consultancy Code of Practice (2nd edition), RICS practice statement, 2005 (current edition under review)

Surveyors acting as advocates, RICS practice statement and guidance note, 2008

Surveyors Acting as Arbiter or as Independent Expert in Commercial Property Rent Reviews (Scottish edition), RICS guidance note, 2002

Surveyors Acting as Arbitrators and as Independent Experts in Commercial Property Rent Reviews (8th edition), RICS guidance note, 2002

The *Civil Evidence Act* 1995, available at: www.opsi.gov.uk/ACTS/acts1995/Ukpga_19950038_en_1.htm

The *Civil Evidence (Scotland) Act* 1988, available at: www.opsi.gov.uk/acts/acts1988/Ukpga_19880032_en_1.htm#tcon

The Laws of Scotland, Stair Memorial Encyclopaedia, Butterworths

Watson, J., *Nothing but the truth – expert evidence in principle and practice for surveyors, valuers and others* (2nd edition), Estates Gazette Ltd, 1975

For the various court guides, see www.hmcourts-service.gov.uk

The RICS Dispute Resolution Faculty and RICS Library may be able to provide further information relevant to expert witness practice.

[Further reading is then followed by a list of acknowledgments of those who contributed to the publication.]

Appendix 3B: RICS PS and GN: Surveyors acting as advocates

The text of the 1st edition RICS practice statement and 2nd edition guidance note: *Surveyors acting as advocates* is reproduced below. This edition comes into effect on 1 January 2009.

Surveyors acting as advocates: RICS practice statement (1st edition) and guidance note (2nd edition)

Acknowledgments

An extract from *The Surveyor in Court* is reproduced in this document with the permission of P. H. Clarke FRICS.

Crown copyright material is reproduced with the permission of the Controller of HMSO and the Queen's Printer for Scotland.

Contents

Copyright notice

Reproduction (other than as specified above) or republishing in any format requires express written permission from RICS. A request for such permission, or any other enquiry related to copyright, may be addressed to:

RICS Publishing and Content Services
Surveyor Court
Westwood Way
Coventry
CV4 8JE
United Kingdom

Surveyors acting as advocates: RICS practice statements

This is a practice statement (PS). There may be disciplinary consequences for RICS members for a failure to comply with a PS.

RICS members should also note that when an allegation of professional negligence is made against them, the court is likely to take account of any relevant PS published by RICS in deciding whether or not they acted with reasonable competence. Failure to comply with practice statements may, accordingly, lead to a finding of negligence against an RICS member.

In the opinion of RICS, if RICS members conform to the requirements of this PS they should have at least a partial defence to an allegation of negligence by virtue of having followed those practices.

Where RICS members depart from the practice required by this PS, they should do so only for good reason and the client must be informed in writing of the fact of and the reasons for the departure. In the event of litigation, the court may require you to explain why you decided to act as you did. Also, an RICS member who has not followed this PS and whose actions are called into question in an RICS disciplinary case, may be asked to justify the steps he or she took.

Investigation of alleged breaches of a practice statement

In the interest of maintaining the highest professional standards, breaches of any aspect of a practice statement that are reported to RICS will be reviewed, and may be investigated, by RICS Regulation, normally when the underlying dispute has been resolved. Reports of this nature should be made in writing and can be made confidentially to:

RICS Regulation
PO Box 2291
Coventry
CV4 8ZJ
United Kingdom
T: + 44 (0)20 7695 1670
E: regulation@rics.org

Any RICS member adjudged to merit referral by RICS investigative staff may be referred for disciplinary action. If the relevant disciplinary body considers it justified, an RICS member may be publicly reprimanded, fined and/or expelled from RICS, depending on the severity of the breach.

Comments on this publication

Although RICS cannot undertake to respond personally to each such communication, if you have any comments or feedback on any aspect of this publication, please feel free to write to:

RICS Dispute Resolution Faculty
12 Great George Street
London
SW1P 3AD
United Kingdom
E: dr.faculty@rics.org

Surveyors acting as advocates: practice statement: Preamble

Whilst in general this text is gender neutral, on occasions where masculine terms only are used (such as in legislation quotes) these should be taken as also referring to the feminine (e.g. 'she', 'her'), and to 'they' or 'it' (in the case of a corporate body), as the context so requires.

References to the singular also include the plural and vice versa where the context so requires. Unless otherwise specified, references to 'member', 'you', 'surveyor' or 'surveyor-advocate' are to members of RICS of any class of membership, save for Honorary Members. References to 'PS' denote 'practice statement'.

Where you are acting as an Assessor, Valuation Officer, Listing Officer, District Valuer or Commissioner of Valuation (or as an authorised representative thereof) in local taxation matters and are acting in pursuit of a statutory duty, you will not usually be operating in a client/adviser framework and will generally not have a direct client.

There are variations in terminology, legislation and case law references pertinent to advocacy practice across the different legal jurisdictions within the UK. Not all of these are exhaustively referenced below but where it is felt appropriate some are highlighted.

For the purposes of this PS, the generic expression 'tribunal' means any body whose function it is to determine disputes. This therefore includes:
- **courts and tribunals (including Lands Tribunals and Agricultural Land Tribunals; Leasehold Valuation Tribunals; Residential Property Tribunals; Valuation Tribunals);**
- **arbitrators/arbiters or arbitral panels/tribunals;**
- **adjudicators (including those operating under the *Housing Grants Construction and Regeneration Act* 1996);**
- **committees (including Rent Assessment Committees, Valuation Appeal Committees);**
- **inspectors, commissioners and reporters (e.g. in planning proceedings, including Inquiries, Hearings, Examinations in Public – independent panels; Independent Examination and proceedings of the Infrastructure Planning Commission, and Planning and Water Appeals Commissions); and**
- **independent experts.**

Note: It is expected that once provisions of the *Tribunals, Courts and Enforcement Act* 2007 are implemented, some of the tribunals listed above will take on a different designation, but at the time of publication this is not in place.

Principal message

When acting as a surveyor-advocate you owe duties to your client. However, you also owe a duty to the tribunal to act properly and fairly and to assist in the maintenance of the integrity of the tribunal's process. You must not engage in discreditable behaviour, or behaviour prejudicial to the tribunal's process.

PS 1 Application of practice statement

1.1   The start date of application of this PS is 1 January 2009. This PS applies where you agree (whether in writing or orally) to act as a surveyor-advocate before any tribunal in the United Kingdom; it does not apply where you are acting as an advocate by virtue of legal qualifications, and of rights of audience gained through an authorised or duly recognised body (such as the General Council of the Bar, Law Society, Faculty of Advocates, etc.). You must have regard at all times to the applicable law, rules, directions, orders or procedures relevant to a particular tribunal, and comply with these in those circumstances when they apply.

1.2   This PS does not apply to the provision of professional advice prior to the commencement of any formal proceedings before any tribunal, nor does it apply to those surveyors who may assist an advocate. It does, however, apply to all instructions to act as a surveyor-advocate whenever given, and in particular governs the preparation of any documents containing submissions to the tribunal.

1.3   Where you act as a surveyor-advocate and consider that there are special circumstances which render it inappropriate or impractical for the assignment to be undertaken wholly in accordance with the PS, the fact of, and reasons for, the departure must be given in writing to your client; alternatively you may wish to decline instructions or withdraw from a case. Any surveyor who does depart from the PS may be required to justify to RICS the reasons for the departure. RICS is entitled to take disciplinary measures if it is not satisfied with the reasons given and/or the manner in which the departure has been notified or evidenced. In the event of litigation, a court may require you to explain why you decided to act as you did.

PS 2 Principal duties

2.1   As a surveyor-advocate you must:
    (a)   take personal responsibility for the conduct and presentation of your client's case, and act in the best interests of your client;
    (b)   advance the case you are presenting by all fair and proper means;

(c)   act promptly, diligently and competently in all respects when acting as an advocate;

(d)   act with independence in the interests of the tribunal's process, assist the tribunal in the maintenance of the integrity of its process and comply with any applicable rules, directions, orders or procedures of the tribunal;

(e)   not conduct yourself in a manner which is discreditable, or prejudicial to the integrity of the tribunal's process;

(f)   not allow your integrity or professional standards to be compromised;

(g)   not deceive or mislead the tribunal or any opposing party;

(h)   have adequate and appropriate professional indemnity insurance cover.

PS 3 Acting as a surveyor-advocate, and instructions

3.1   You may act only in matters where you have:

(a)   the experience, knowledge and expertise appropriate to the case; and

(b)   the resources to carry out the assignment to the required timescale and to the appropriate standard.

3.2   (a)   You must not act (or where you have already accepted instructions, you must cease to act):

(i)   in any matter where to act (or to continue to act) would involve you in a breach of the law or where your ability to act (for the client) properly is compromised;

(ii)   in a matter in which there is a risk of a breach of confidential information entrusted to you (or to a partner or fellow employee) by another client, or where the knowledge you possess of one client's affairs might give an undue advantage to a new client. It is permissible to act (or to continue to act) in these circumstances if the original or previous client's consent to act is given, or the original or previous client's permission is given to the use of pre-existing information and knowledge;

(iii) in a matter where a fellow employee or partner has an interest of which you are (or become) aware and it impairs your ability to act properly.

(b) **Conflicts of interest**

(i) Where a conflict of interest exists between you, or your firm, and any of the parties to the proceedings, or where a risk that such a conflict may arise exists, you must raise this with your prospective client as soon as it becomes apparent and you must advise your client in writing if you consider that you should, given all the circumstances of the case, decline the instructions. Similarly, where already instructed, you must advise the client in writing if you consider that you should, given all the circumstances of the case, terminate the instructions. You may act (or continue to act if already instructed) if the client has given informed consent in writing. 'Informed consent' requires:

- that the client has given permission in the knowledge that you or your firm have a potential or actual conflict of interest;
- that all relevant issues and risks have been clearly drawn to the attention of the client; and
- that you have a reasonable belief that these issues have been understood by the client.

(ii) Where a conflict of interest exists, or a risk that such exists, between two or more (potential) clients in relation to a matter, you or your firm may act (or continue to act if already instructed) if the client has given informed consent in writing. 'Informed consent' requires:

- that the client has given permission in the knowledge that you or your firm acts, or may act, for another client in competition;
- that all relevant issues and risks have been clearly drawn to the attention of the client; and

- that you have a reasonable belief that these issues have been understood by the client.

3.3 Providing advocacy services for an organisation by which you are employed is permissible.

3.4 Prior to accepting instructions you must:
(a) advise your prospective client in writing that this PS applies and make a written offer to supply a copy of the PS (where a copy of the PS is later supplied, the copyright notice on page 1 of this document must be adhered to).
(b) notify your prospective client in writing that your firm operates a Complaints Handling Procedure (CHP) (if applicable) which can be provided on request.

3.5 You must confirm to your prospective client in writing and in good time whether you accept instructions. Your acceptance should cover your terms of engagement (including the basis upon which your fees will be charged), and any specific mandates given as to important or contentious matters. You must then ensure that all such documents, together with communications from your client, are kept by you as a proper record of your instructions. Any change or supplement to the terms that may be made from time to time should be added to your records.

3.6 You and your client may enter into an agreement that makes the fee for your services conditional upon the outcome of the case before the tribunal provided you have advised your client in writing of the nature, effect and operation of the agreement, and any risks to the client that might be associated with it. If you are to act in a case (but not at the same time) in a dual role as surveyor-advocate and expert witness (see further PS 3.9), you must also follow the requirements of *Surveyors acting as expert witnesses*: practice statement 10.1 (declaration of fee basis) for your expert witness role.

3.7 You must only cease to act on reasonable notice, and where you are satisfied that:
(a) instructions have been withdrawn or terminated; or

      (b)   your professional conduct is being impugned; or

      (c)   there is some other good reason for so doing.

3.8   You must not:

      (a)   cease to act without having first explained to your client your reasons for doing so, or having taken all reasonable steps to do so, unless to do so would breach the law;

      (b)   pass an instruction to another surveyor-advocate or other professional without the client's consent;

      (c)   terminate an instruction accepted (and for which a fixed hearing date has been secured), nor break any other professional engagement in order to attend a social engagement, unless the client, and where required the tribunal, consents.

3.9   A dual role: surveyor-advocate and expert witness

You must only act in a dual role as surveyor-advocate and as expert witness where:

      (a)   neither the rules nor the customs of the particular tribunal prohibit you from so acting; and

      (b)   other relevant factors make it appropriate (e.g. the disproportionality of retaining two persons in separate roles).

3.10   Where however you intend, or are invited, to act in a dual role as surveyor-advocate and as expert witness you must:

      (a)   consider both whether it is permissible to do so and also whether it is appropriate; and

      (b)   promptly communicate to your client the results of such considerations, setting out in writing the likely advantages and disadvantages, as you see them, of acting in a dual role in the particular circumstances of the case, so as to enable the client to decide whether you should indeed act in such a dual role. In such communication you must detail:

            (i)   the possible impact on your impartiality as expert witness, and any possible impact in terms of the perception of that impartiality by others; and any possible impact on your advocacy submissions;

            (ii)   whether or not you will be able to fulfill both roles properly at all times; and

(iii) whether or not it would be disproportionate in all the circumstances, or otherwise in the client's best interests, for a separate person to be retained to undertake one of the roles.

3.11 Having complied with PS 3.10 above, you may only act in both roles if the client instructs you so to act.

3.12 Where you confirm instructions to act in such a dual role, you must clearly distinguish between those two roles at all times, whether in oral hearings or in written presentations.

PS 4 Other duties

4.1 If at any time you consider that it would be in the best interests of your client to be represented by a lawyer-advocate or other representative (adopting an advocacy role), you must immediately advise the client of this. You must also advise your client without delay where you consider instructions unacceptable or insufficient, or if you realise you may not be able to fulfil the terms of the engagement and your duties.

4.2 You must not attempt to advise any client on, or advocate, matters beyond your professional competence.

4.3 Whether or not the relationship between surveyor-advocate and client continues, you must keep confidential all information about your client's affairs of which you learn whilst acting as a surveyor-advocate, save as to that which you are required to disclose by law; that which you are permitted to divulge by your client; and that which must be shared with colleagues in your organisation for the proper pursuit of the client's instructions. You must not use such information to the detriment of your client, or to the advantage of yourself or another party.

4.4 You must keep the client informed of progress and of any cost implications in the matter, unless otherwise agreed.

PS 5 Conduct as to statements of case, and submissions

5.1 You must not prepare a statement of case, submissions or other similar documents, unless properly arguable.

5.2 You must not allege fraud or any other dishonest or dishonourable conduct unless you have clear instructions to do so and there exists credible evidence to support such an allegation.

5.3 You must not make any statements calculated solely to malign a person.

PS 6 Conduct as to evidence

6.1 You must not mis-state facts to advance a client's case or for any other reason. If a client admits to you that he or she has misled the tribunal, you must cease to act further unless the client agrees to reveal the truth to the tribunal.

6.2 You must take all reasonable steps to ensure that all documents required by a tribunal to be disclosed are properly so disclosed.

6.3 When dealing with a witness, you:
- (a) must not rehearse or coach a witness;
- (b) must not encourage a witness to give untruthful or partially truthful evidence;
- (c) must not, except with the consent of the representative for the opposing side or of the tribunal, communicate (directly or indirectly) with a witness in connection with the case during the course of the witness's evidence;
- (d) must not ask questions calculated solely to malign a witness;
- (e) must not make assertions that impugn a witness whom you have had the chance to cross-examine unless in such cross-examination you have afforded the witness an opportunity to answer the allegation;
- (f) must put your case to an opponent's witness if you intend to challenge his or her evidence and give that witness an opportunity to answer.

PS 7 Conduct in relation to the tribunal

7.1 You have a duty to assist the tribunal, and not to make statements to it that you know to be untrue.

7.2   You must not give any expert (opinion) evidence to the tribunal whilst in your capacity as a surveyor-advocate, unless permitted by the tribunal to do so.

7.3   You must draw the tribunal's attention to all relevant legal decisions and legislative provisions of which you are aware, whether supportive of your client's case or not. In the event that an advocate on the other side omits a legal decision or provision, or otherwise makes an erroneous reference to such, you must draw the tribunal's attention to this.

7.4   You must advise the tribunal of any procedural irregularity or error which may occur, and not hold back any such matter to be raised on appeal.

Surveyors acting as advocates: RICS guidance notes

This is a guidance note (GN). It provides advice to members of RICS on aspects of the profession. Where procedures are recommended for specific professional tasks, these are intended to embody 'best practice', that is, procedures which in the opinion of RICS meet a high standard of professional competence.

RICS members are not required to follow the advice and recommendations contained in the GN. They should however note the following points.

When an allegation of professional negligence is made against an RICS member, the court is likely to take account of the contents of any relevant GN published by RICS in deciding whether or not the member had acted with reasonable competence.

In the opinion of RICS, if RICS members conform to the practices recommended in this GN they should have at least a partial defence to an allegation of negligence by virtue of having followed those practices. However, RICS members have the responsibility of deciding when it is inappropriate to follow the guidance.

On the other hand, it does not follow that RICS members will be adjudged negligent if they have not followed the practices recommended in this GN. It is for each surveyor to decide on the appropriate procedure to follow in any professional task.

However, where RICS members depart from the good practice recommended in this GN, they should do so only for good reason. In the event of litigation, a court may require an RICS member to explain why he or she decided not to adopt the recommended practice. Also, an RICS member who has not followed this GN, and whose actions are called into question in a RICS disciplinary case, may be asked to justify the steps he or she took and this may be taken into account.

In addition, guidance notes are relevant to professional competence in that every surveyor should be up to date and should have informed him or herself of guidance notes within a reasonable time of their promulgation.

Surveyors acting as advocates: guidance note: Preamble

Whilst in general this text is gender neutral, on occasions where masculine terms only are used (such as in legislation quotes) these should be taken as also referring to the feminine (e.g. 'she', 'her'), and to 'they' or 'it' (in the case of a corporate body), as the context so requires.

References to the singular also include the plural and vice versa where the context so requires. Unless otherwise specified, references to 'member', 'you', 'surveyor' or 'surveyor-advocate' are to members of RICS of any class of membership, save for Honorary Members. References to 'PS' denote 'practice statement', and those to 'GN' denote 'guidance note'.

Where you are acting as an Assessor, Valuation Officer, Listing Officer, District Valuer or Commissioner of Valuation (or as an authorised representative thereof) in local taxation matters and are acting in pursuit of a statutory duty, you will not usually be operating in a client/adviser framework and will generally not have a direct client.

There are variations in terminology, legislation and case law references pertinent to advocacy practice across the different legal jurisdictions within the UK. Not all of these are exhaustively referenced below but where it is felt appropriate some are highlighted.

GN 1 Application of guidance note and introduction

1.1   (a)   The start date of application of this GN is 1 January 2009. This GN applies where you agree (whether orally or in writing) to act as a surveyor-advocate before any *tribunal* (see the *Preamble* in the PS) in the United Kingdom. It is recommended that you have regard at all times to the applicable law and rules, orders, directions, practices and procedures relevant to a particular tribunal. It is recommended that the GN be considered in conjunction with the foregoing PS.

   (b)   The PS and GN do not apply if you are acting as an advocate by virtue of legal qualifications, and of rights of audience gained through authorised or duly recognised bodies; in those latter cases you will have regard to rules of conduct and guidance formulated by such bodies (see PS 1.1).

1.2   Supplementary guidance may be produced from time to time relating to the appropriate conduct before certain tribunals and it is recommended that you therefore satisfy yourself as to the existence of such supplementary guidance and, where appropriate, familiarise yourself with its contents.

1.3   If acting as a surveyor-advocate you may, in the same or a related matter, also act in one or more of the following roles at different times:
   (a)   negotiator;
   (b)   case manager;
   (c)   expert witness;
   (d)   adviser;
   (e)   witness of fact.

1.4   It is recommended that you be aware at all times which role is being adopted and differentiate between them as necessary. It is advisable that you understand the fundamental importance of keeping the role of expert witness separate from that of the role of surveyor-advocate, negotiator, case manager, adviser or witness of fact. The weight, if any, that may be attached to evidence given by an expert witness has, as its cornerstone, the impartiality and independence of the opinions given. This is in direct contrast to the role of, for instance, the surveyor-advocate, who seeks to do the best for his or her client subject to limitations with respect to his or her duties to the tribunal. **It is possible that some negotiators may not find it possible to act as an expert witness as their impartiality may be damaged, or may be perceived to be damaged, by the prior or continuing role of negotiator. It is recommended that you be alert to this.**

GN 2 General duties and roles

2.1   A surveyor-advocate owes the duties set out in the accompanying PS. Failure to comply with your duties may render you and/or your client susceptible to sanctions (whether by way of costs penalties or other means) or orders by the tribunal.

2.2   A surveyor-advocate can appear before certain tribunals in an advocacy capacity. Before some tribunals permission is required to do so. It is recommended that you satisfy yourself that you may appear before a tribunal as surveyor-advocate before accepting instructions.

2.3   (a)   It is recommended that you also be satisfied that you have the appropriate experience, knowledge, expertise and resources, prior to undertaking the role of surveyor-advocate. This includes adequate knowledge of the law and practice, including all relevant time limits, applicable in the particular tribunal. The fact that you are not a lawyer will not usually excuse a failure to comply with procedural requirements (see, for example, *North British Trust Hotels v (1) Lothian Assessor and (2) Dumfries and Galloway Assessor*, LTS/VA/ 2003/35–36, at page 8). Relevant knowledge can be gained in a number of ways, including through CPD activities, on-the-job mentoring and secondments. In cases involving particularly complex points of law, evidence or procedure, it is recommended that you consider whether you would be properly placed to act as surveyor-advocate.

   (b)   You would be expected to be familiar with the procedural rules for the particular tribunal and for the particular type of case. Further guidance on these may be obtainable from the tribunal concerned. You should note that whilst in England and Wales courts are bound by the *Civil Procedure Rules* (CPR) (courts in Scotland have other rules), statutory tribunals (e.g. Leasehold Valuation Tribunals) have their own rules, often with less strict requirements concerning evidence and procedure. Arbitrators/arbiters are entitled to devise their own procedures and evidential rules, in the absence of agreement between the parties. Other forms of tribunal (including independent experts) will apply their own rules, or they may be governed by the appointing document or agreement by the parties.

2.4 (a) A surveyor-advocate's role is distinct from that of an expert witness. The PS expects you to ensure at all times that the submissions you make on behalf of any client as surveyor-advocate are seen as submissions, and cannot be construed by the tribunal as expert witness opinion; as PS 7.2 indicates, *only* with the permission of a tribunal might you give expert evidence whilst acting as a surveyor-advocate.

(b) It is recommended that you always remain alert to any risk that a tribunal might misconstrue elements of a submission as expert witness opinion. Particular care should be taken in this regard where the tribunal (or one or more members of it) is professionally qualified in – and/or has technical expertise in – the same field as yourself.

(c) It is advisable in your submissions that you avoid use of terms and expressions that, in the context they are used, connote any form of personal belief in any facts, expert evidence or arguments put forward. It is impossible to prescribe in advance an exhaustive list of such terms but the following may be indicative and are to be avoided:

- 'in my experience of such matters the only conclusion to be drawn is ...';
- 'in my opinion, your argument is ...';
- 'the arguments put forward support a rent of £50 psf, *which in my view is exactly the right answer*'.

An advocate is advocating and arguing an outcome for his or her client, and so his or her own opinion on any issue is irrelevant. Care is therefore to be taken not to interpose your own judgments and opinions as a surveyor-advocate between your client and the tribunal.

2.5 When taking on the role of surveyor-advocate, it is recommended that you are aware that communications to and from your client *may* subsequently have to be disclosed to the other party. It is therefore critically important:

(a) that you are aware of the rules regarding 'disclosure' (other terms may be used outside of England and Wales) and privilege (see GN 5.8);

(b) that you are careful about what is said in written communications between you and your client; and

(c) that you explain these considerations to your client.

2.6 As surveyor-advocate, it is recommended that, in the best interests of the client, you bear in mind at all times the possibility of effecting a compromise settlement and that you notify your client of your opinion of the merits of doing so, keeping the client updated where your opinion changes. Such opinion may reflect your view of the strengths of each party's case and may not necessarily coincide with any professional opinion expressed to the client at an earlier stage or in another role you may undertake in the same or a related matter (e.g. the role of expert witness). The PS mandates you not to attempt to advise on matters outside your remit or competence.

2.7 In an effort to effect an acceptable compromise, you may be in frequent communication with the other party (usually on a 'without prejudice' basis) throughout the case: the need to keep certain communications separate from open (i.e. those not 'without prejudice') procedural discussions with the opposing side, which may continue throughout the case, ought not to be forgotten. The former (non-procedural discussions with the opposing side) may be protected by privilege, whereas the latter will not be privileged and may be brought to the attention of the tribunal.

2.8 If the matter in dispute is agreed between the parties, you will need to be aware of the circumstances in which it may be appropriate to refer the agreement to the tribunal for a formal record (e.g. an agreed award in arbitration). You will also need to be aware of the circumstances in which the tribunal concerned is entitled to make such an award.

2.9 It is recommended that you ensure that a full and proper record is kept of all actions in the case and that files are well ordered and noted, as these may be required for examination later as part of any appeal process or for detailed assessment of costs.

2.10 Some tribunals give reasons for their decision unless the parties agree otherwise, whereas others do not give reasons, or may do so only if requested to do so by either or both parties. It is recommended that the client be advised of the implications, and in particular of the risk that dispensing with reasons might inhibit or preclude any subsequent appeal.

2.11 It is recommended that you be aware as to whether the proceedings before the tribunal are private or public and advise your client, and any witnesses for whom you are responsible, accordingly.

2.12 In complex or lengthy cases you may wish to consider the advisability of arranging with the tribunal and the other party for a full record to be made of the proceedings, whether by employing stenographers or by recordings.

GN 3 A 'dual role': surveyor-advocate and expert witness

3.1 The PS makes it clear that you should only act in a dual role, as surveyor-advocate and as expert witness, where:
   (a) neither the rules nor the customs of the particular tribunal prohibit you from so acting; and
   (b) other relevant factors make it appropriate (e.g. the disproportionality of retaining two persons in separate roles).

Typically some surveyors will adopt a dual role before bodies such as:
   (i) Valuation Tribunals, Valuation Appeals Committees; Leasehold Valuation Tribunals;
   (ii) Agricultural Land Tribunals;

(iii)   Planning Inspectors, Reporters, Commissioners;

(iv)   arbiters/arbitrators or arbitral panels;

(v)   independent experts;

(vi)   Rent Assessment Committees;

(vii)   adjudicators.

The Lands Tribunal for Scotland, for example, will usually exercise its power to allow a surveyor who is also giving evidence as an expert witness to act as representative in cases where the employment of two professionals would be disproportionate.

3.2   Where instructions are contemplated which may lead to you undertaking a dual role of expert witness and surveyor-advocate, you are obliged by *Surveyors acting as advocates*: RICS practice statement 3.10–3.11 to ensure that the two roles of surveyor-advocate and expert witness are clearly explained to, and approved by, the client, before being undertaken (see also *Surveyors acting as expert witnesses* PS 9, GN 18 and GN 20, which are reproduced in Appendix C of this publication).

3.3   (a)   The principal advantages and disadvantages of a dual role may be summarised as follows:

        (i)   A dual role may avoid or limit expense and delay, and therefore be a proportionate response to the circumstances of a case and the needs of the client.

        (ii)   The weight to be attached to the evidence given by you as an expert witness, and to the submissions you make as surveyor-advocate, may be adversely affected if the dual role of surveyor-advocate and expert witness is undertaken.

    (b)   It is always imperative to understand the distinction between the two roles and that it is impossible for both roles to be carried out at the same time. The PS obliges you to distinguish at each stage which role you are undertaking. On occasions where surveyors undertake the dual role and fall below the necessary standards required of each role, the effect can be adverse, leading to the case being much weakened and often to criticism of the surveyor by the tribunal (which may subsequently come to the attention of the client). For example, if you give expert evidence unsupported by proper reasons or omit material facts, the tribunal may form the view that it is in effect little more than advocacy of the (client's) case, and thus give it little or no weight. Advocacy that mixes expert (opinion) evidence in its submissions is not allowed (see PS 7.2). A tribunal will do its best to assess the merits of each party's case: the weight of the opinion evidence presented and the nature and power of the advocacy submissions are important factors in the formation of any decisions by the tribunal.

See further *Surveyors acting as expert witnesses* PS 9, GN 18 and GN 20, which are reproduced in Appendix C of this publication.

3.4   PS 3.12 insists on you clarifying which capacity you are undertaking throughout a matter. The separation of facts from opinion (of the surveyor as expert witness) and from argument/submissions as surveyor-advocate, will also be vital in this regard. The use of language also plays a role in this differentiation (see GN 3.5 below).

3.5   It is particularly important in document-only proceedings that any dual role is clearly distinguished to the relevant tribunal. One way of so doing would be to introduce different paragraph headings 'Opinion' and 'Submission' (the former covering expert witness evidence and the latter advocacy) or to present two separate documents. Alternatively (or in conjunction with the foregoing), the use of different coloured paper could feature.

It is further recommended that consistent, iterative use of language would also be of assistance:
- 'I think that ...' or;
- 'I believe that ...' or;
- 'It is my opinion that ...';

to introduce your expert opinion

and
- 'I suggest that (on the facts presented and the opinion evidence of Ms Y) ...'; or
- 'I submit that (there can be no other explanation of) ...';

to introduce submissions/arguments as a surveyor-advocate. You are also reminded of the recommendation of GN 2.4(c).

For example (the text below contains instances that are purely fictional exemplars):

'OPINION

For the following reasons, in my opinion, the amount of adjustment for factor A is between x and y and much closer to y ... '.

Then in counter-submissions:

'SUBMISSION

For the following reasons, I suggest that my opinion [introduced earlier/elsewhere in my capacity as expert witness] of the adjustment for factor A should be preferred ... item C is inadmissible on grounds that ... Mr D has wrongly interpreted the rent review provisions because ... etc. ... It is therefore our contention that the value should be ... '.

As a general observation, many surveyors often loosely use the terms 'representations' and 'submissions' in general parlance as interchangeable terms, to refer to either expert opinion evidence or advocacy (or both) when using either term. It is recommended that wherever possible and appropriate in context, the use of the term 'representations' to denote expert witness (opinion) evidence be avoided; rather, 'expert witness report' or 'expert evidence' are preferable, and the term 'submission' is better used to denote an advocacy submission.

GN 4 Acting as a surveyor-advocate, and instructions

4.1 (a) PS 3.4(a) requires you to make a written offer to supply a copy of the practice statement (PS) to a prospective client. For this purpose a stand-alone version of the PS is available to members to download from www.rics.org

     (b) PS 3.4(b) requires you to notify your client in writing that your firm operates a Complaints

Handling Procedure (CHP) (if it is an RICS-regulated firm). If your firm is not an RICS-regulated firm, it is recommended nonetheless that you notify your client in writing of the existence and terms of any applicable complaints handling procedures.

(c) PS 3.5 provides that instructions must be obtained in writing. The *Sample Terms of Engagement* set out in Appendix A is a set of exemplar terms provided for the use of surveyors, which may be adapted as required. Care should be taken to ensure that any instructions received or acknowledged do not contain information, which, if disclosed, would prove prejudicial to the client's case, save as to information required for the proper application of this GN and accompanying PS.

4.2 Certain tribunals will require production of a formal appointment document signed by the surveyor-advocate's client before allowing a surveyor-advocate to address them.

4.3 Often instructions from the client provide for a surveyor to act initially as a negotiator attempting to settle the dispute with the opposing party. This is likely to require different skills and expertise from that of advocacy, reflecting the different objectives and responsibilities of each role. The role of negotiator, for example, includes no responsibility to, and should not include any involvement with, any tribunal.

4.4 PS 3.2(b) refers to conflicts of interest. A conflict of interest may arise out of a previous or current involvement with, for example, any party, dispute, or property, such that it would cause you to be unable – or seen by a reasonable disinterested observer to be unable – to fulfill your responsibilities to the tribunal and/or to your client. A conflict of interest could be of any kind, including: a pecuniary interest; a personal connection; an obligation (e.g. as a member or officer of some other organisation); links to a business in competition with one of the parties to the dispute, etc. It is not possible to prescribe in advance a list of all such circumstances. For a helpful discussion concerning conflicts of interest, members may wish to read *Save & Prosper Pensions Ltd v Homebase* [2001] L&TR 11.

4.5 (a) Before accepting instructions it is recommended that you discuss the following with your client, and record the outcome of your discussions in writing:
  (i) the identity of the surveyor-advocate;
  (ii) a summary of possible methods of potentially settling the dispute which might, for example, include mediation, and the advisability of adopting a proportionate approach to resolution of the case;
  (iii) a description of the preferred or recommended dispute-resolving tribunal, and its general procedures (including whether the dispute will proceed by way of written submissions or an oral hearing).

(b) To the extent that you are able to do so prior to acceptance of instructions, but otherwise as soon as possible after accepting instructions, it is also recommended that you:
  (i) give a forecast of the likely timetable and cost for the case;
  (ii) give an outline of the merits of the case, including:
    • the overall prospects,
    • possible outcomes,
    • the costs consequences associated with those outcomes (to include a summary of the assessment procedures that the tribunal may impose in the event that your client is unsuccessful, and of the liability to the other party that your client may have if unsuccessful),
    • advice on the methods that may be used to safeguard your client against liability for costs.
    See also the particular obligations of PS 3.6;
  (iii) state whether or not your remit includes negotiation to settle, as well as to act as a surveyor-advocate, or to act in any other role or roles (such as expert witness or case manager);
  (iv) outline the inspections, enquiries and meetings with the other party that may be required with a view to settling the dispute;
  (v) outline the reports which will be required during progress of the case and whether the client requires any such report to be

addressed to the client's lawyer to establish privilege where possible;

(vi) outline the appeal processes which may apply, including the ability or otherwise to appear as surveyor-advocate in any such circumstance.

4.6 Surveyor-advocates and their clients will sometimes wish to enter into an arrangement that makes the fee payable to the surveyor-advocate dependent in some way upon the outcome of the case (i.e. a 'conditional fee' arrangement – see the definition in Appendix B). PS 3.6 sets out points that must be observed in relation to such arrangements. You are advised to note the following matters by way of additional guidance and explanation.

(a) You should be aware of the longstanding rule that outlaws conditional fee arrangements for certain types of cases undertaken before some tribunals in England, Wales and Northern Ireland (but not Scotland). (Although the case law pertaining to this issue is drawn, for the purposes of this document, from decisions of the courts in England and Wales, it is believed these would be persuasive to tribunals in Northern Ireland.)

Your concern should be to ensure that:

(i) the rule does not apply to you; and

(ii) the rule does not apply to the proceedings in which you are engaged as surveyor-advocate or the tribunal before which you will be acting.

In practice, there is very little guidance in the decided case law on these two subjects; this part of the guidance note is therefore conservative and cautionary.

(b) As to GN 4.6(a)(i) above, historically, the rule has only been used so as to penalise lawyers. However, the rule has its roots in the perceived need to protect the integrity of public justice, and in particular to avoid *advocates* putting themselves in a position where their own interest may conflict with their duties to the court. The public policy behind the rule would therefore appear to apply as readily to surveyors as it does to lawyers, although there is no recorded instance of a case in which a surveyor-advocate or a client has been penalised by the rule. In practice, it is unlikely (but not inconceivable) that the rule would now be extended to include surveyor-advocates.

(c) As to GN 4.6(a)(ii), it is difficult to provide a conclusive list of the types of proceedings to which the rule applies. Disputes between parties that require resolution by tribunals (e.g. litigation, arbitration, adjudication, independent expert determination, and proceedings before the land(s) tribunals) are more likely to fall within the ambit of the rule than other proceedings involving the consideration of questions of an administrative or public nature (e.g. determination of planning permission, rating and fair rents). It should however be stressed that there is only one recorded instance in which the rule has been applied outside the sphere of litigation (in that case, to arbitration).

(d) In practice, the impact of the rule can be avoided altogether by lawyers supplying advocacy or litigation services, provided they enter into a detailed and complex agreement with their client that complies with rules made under the *Courts and Legal Services Act* 1990 (as amended by the *Access to Justice Act* 1999). These rules apply only to those with rights to conduct litigation, and those who have rights of audience, by virtue of various categories set out in the 1990 Act. Most surveyor-advocates who are entitled to appear in tribunals derive their rights from practices preceding the 1990 Act, and are not affected by its specific rules regarding conditional fee agreements. Nevertheless, they remain subject to the wider rule referred to in GN 4.6(b) above.

(e) Where the rule does apply, the effect is to render the conditional fee arrangement unenforceable. The result will be not merely that the successful party will be unable to recover the conditional fee from the other party, but also that the surveyor-advocate will be unable to recover the conditional fee from his or her client. Accordingly, where you, as surveyor-advocate, are thinking of entering into a conditional fee arrangement for a case in England, Wales and Northern Ireland (but not Scotland) a critical consideration will be whether, in the event of a challenge to a conditional fee arrangement, the tribunal you will appear before will regard the proceedings as of the type to which the rule would apply (using the criteria referred to in GN 4.6(c) above). (Although the case law pertaining to this issue is drawn, for the purposes of this document, from decisions of the courts in England and Wales, it is believed these would be persuasive to the Northern Irish courts, and that the position referenced is applicable to tribunals in Northern Ireland.) If the proceedings are not likely to be so regarded, then you are likely to be within the law when entering into the arrangement. It is strongly recommended that you advise your client of the risk of unenforceability as set out in this paragraph 4.6, and decide whether you yourself wish to proceed in those circumstances.

4.7 PS 3.7 refers to grounds for ceasing to act. Examples of reasons to cease to act under PS 3.7(c) might be:
  (a) where a client refuses to authorise you to make a disclosure to the tribunal, which your duty as a surveyor-advocate requires you to make;
  (b) where there is a breakdown in confidence between you and the client; or
  (c) where you are unable to obtain proper instructions or the client goes into bankruptcy.

PS 3.7 makes reference to the need to give 'reasonable notice' to one's client. What amounts to 'reasonable' will be influenced by the particular circumstances. For example, it would generally be unreasonable to cease acting immediately before a hearing where it would be extremely difficult or impossible for the client to find alternative representation. Alternatively, there may be circumstances where it would be reasonable to give no notice.

4.8 Where you act as an advocate you will owe duties to your client and to the tribunal in a similar manner as a lawyer-advocate would do so. There is now no (lawyer) advocate's immunity from civil proceedings in England and Wales – *Arthur J. S. Hall & Co. v Simons (A. P.)* [2002] 1 AC 615. The leading Scottish case on advocates' immunity is *Wright v Paton Farrell* [2006] SC 404 (IH), in which the court, although concerned with criminal proceedings, indicated that *Hall* would be highly influential in relation to the question of an advocate's immunity from suit for the negligent conduct of civil proceedings. Although there is no direct authority on the point, it is likely to be the case, similarly, that you will have no immunity as a **surveyor**-advocate either. You will therefore need to be careful to ensure that it is always clear when you are acting in the role of surveyor-advocate rather than another role (such as expert witness).

4.9   As regards PS 2.1(g) and PS 7.1, the advocate's task is to seek to persuade a tribunal to reach a certain conclusion based on the evidence, without misleading the tribunal. There are however three points to note about this apparently extensive limitation.

First, the surveyor-advocate is allowed to use his or her powers of persuasion to their fullest extent, consistently with the evidence before the tribunal. In this context, the following words of Sir Michael Rowe CBE QC (2nd President of the Lands Tribunal for England and Wales in 1968) are worth noting:

> 'An advocate has a duty not to mislead the tribunal in any way ... in discussing fact he must not twist any evidence, though he can put the most favourable construction on it ...'.

Secondly, the surveyor-advocate is of course entitled to present an argument that may not coincide with his or her own views as an expert, provided that it is reasonably arguable on the basis of the evidence in front of the tribunal.

Thirdly, the surveyor-advocate may suspect or even believe that the evidence given by his or her witness is factually incorrect, but provided the surveyor-advocate does not *know* that it is, he or she will not be misleading the tribunal by submitting that it should reach a certain conclusion based upon that evidence.

An extended example – drawn from a rent review arbitration involving surveyor-advocates – should serve to illustrate these distinctions.

(a)   The surveyor-advocate is not entitled to say 'there is no authority on this point' if he or she knows that there is, or is unaware that there is but has not taken the trouble to research the point.

(b) Conversely, the surveyor-advocate is entitled to say 'there is authority on this point, but it is distinguishable', if that point is reasonably arguable, even if his or her own view is that he or she will lose.

(c) The surveyor-advocate is not entitled to say 'there is no evidence that the property suffers from aeroplane noise' if in fact there is such evidence.

(d) Conversely, the surveyor-advocate is entitled to say 'there is no evidence that the property suffers from aeroplane noise' if in fact there is no such evidence before the tribunal, even if the surveyor-advocate knows from his or her own experience that the property does in fact suffer from aeroplane noise.

(e) By contrast, the surveyor-advocate is not entitled to say 'the property does not suffer from aeroplane noise' (even if there is no evidence before the tribunal that it does) if the surveyor-advocate knows from his or her own experience that it does in fact suffer from such noise.

(f) Conversely, the surveyor-advocate is entitled to say 'the evidence that the property suffers from aeroplane noise should be dismissed' if there are reasonable arguments to support a dismissal, even if the surveyor-advocate does not personally subscribe to them.

(g) Importantly, if the surveyor-advocate is aware of damaging evidence, but which the other side has overlooked, he or she is under no obligation to draw the attention of the tribunal to it. The surveyor-advocate's duty to the tribunal does not extend to drawing the tribunal's attention to evidence favourable to the other side, thereby breaching the duty to his or her own client in so supplementing any deficiencies of the opponent's evidence.

Other instances of conduct by a surveyor-advocate that would fall foul of the practice statement's stricture not to mislead the tribunal would be:

- to fabricate or alter evidence; or
- to try to persuade a witness to change his or her evidence.

4.10   As regards the application of the duty to cite relevant legal decisions (PS 7.3), it is recommended that, when citing a legal decision, you state the proposition of law that the particular decision demonstrates, and clearly identify, for the benefit of the tribunal, the parts of the judgment that support such a proposition. If citing more than one decision in support of a given proposition, it is advisable to consider stating to the tribunal the reason for doing so. You may leave yourself open to the displeasure of a tribunal if you cite, without good cause, multiple legal decisions in support of the same basic proposition. If citing legal decisions from another jurisdiction, it is advisable to outline what such a decision adds to authority in the jurisdiction within which you act. See also GN 8.2.

GN 5 Case preparation and preliminaries

5.1   In addition to the role of surveyor-advocate, you may have responsibility for the management, administration, timetabling and general conduct of the case (on behalf of the client), and in these circumstances it is recommended that you attend to procedural matters as the case proceeds. In these respects you will be acting as case manager. It is recommended that you are conversant with the procedural rules relating to the tribunal in question and the type of case involved. Further guidance may be gained from the relevant tribunal.

5.2   In those instances where the tribunal is appointed by, or on the application of, either party, responsibility for applying for, or making, such appointments, or objecting thereto, can rest with the surveyor as part of a role as case manager. You may also have to reach agreement with the tribunal and the other party as to the fees charged by the tribunal.

5.3   In some cases it may be unclear initially as to which party is the claimant and which party is the respondent. In such cases it is recommended that you seek to clarify and agree which is which with the other party as soon as practicable, and make representations and seek a ruling on this point from the tribunal if necessary.

5.4   As case manager, the surveyor will usually have responsibility for seeking or agreeing timetables for the proper progress of the case, any amendments thereto and any adjournments during the course of the case. You will need to be satisfied so far as reasonably possible that such timetables, amendments and adjournments are consistent with the best presentation of the client's case.

5.5   Many cases will involve the tribunal issuing directions or procedural instructions, usually after discussion with the parties' representatives at a preliminary meeting or in correspondence. If acting as surveyor-advocate, and also as a case manager, you will need to contribute to these discussions or to such correspondence; PS 2.1(d) requires you to ensure that all directions and procedural instructions of the tribunal are complied with, whether or not it is in the interests of the client.

5.6   In certain cases, you will be required to agree with the tribunal and the other party the date, time and venue for any hearing, and will be responsible for ensuring that, as far as is reasonable, these are acceptable to your client's witnesses and to your client.

5.7   Identifying and dealing with the issues
(a)   The purpose of the reference to the tribunal is to have your client's dispute determined as expeditiously, fairly and economically as possible. To that end, it will be vital to approach the identification of the issues, and to formulate the best way of dealing with them, as quickly and as carefully as possible.
(b)   One of the best ways of formulating the issues is for the parties to agree (or the tribunal to order) that statements of their case should be supplied to each other. It is usual for these statements to be sequential, with the claimant filing points of claim, to which the respondent/defendant will respond with a Defence (or 'Points of Defence', which may introduce a counter-claim). The claimant may then file a Reply (or 'Points of Reply'). These documents are important, and it is obviously critical that they should be succinct, clear and complete. Where the facts cannot easily be condensed, it may be appropriate for a schedule to be appended to the

statement setting out the claimant's detailed case in table format, with room for the respondent/defendant to add his or her own comments. As surveyor-advocate, you will be responsible for:

(i) the production of such statements on behalf of your client;

(ii) considering whether there should be any response;

(iii) responding to any requests for further information; and

(iv) liaising with the tribunal, with the client, and with any witnesses whose evidence is required to support the statements made.

In each case, it is recommended that you consider whether you are able and qualified to act in this way without legal advice. If you are not sure, it is strongly recommended that you take legal advice from the client's solicitor, and/or lawyer advocate as appropriate.

(c) In an effort to narrow down the issues in dispute, the tribunal may direct that parties or their experts meet to narrow the issues, to produce schedules of agreed facts, items in dispute and items to be disregarded, by specified dates before any hearing or before the deadline for representation. If you as surveyor-advocate are also adopting the role of case manager, you will be responsible for ensuring that such meetings take place and for ensuring the production of such schedules by the dates prescribed.

(d) Once you have identified the issues, you will need to consider whether it is necessary to request the tribunal to deal with any of those issues as preliminary issues, and if so:

(i) how any such request should be made; and

(ii) whether a right of appeal is required or allowed.

Similarly, you may need to respond to any such requests from the other party.

(e) Some of the issues may raise or involve points of law. It is recommended that you be alert to identify them, be aware of the manner in which the tribunal can be required to deal with them, and make recommendations to your client as to how they should be tackled. If you are not competent to provide such advice yourself, it may be necessary for you to recommend that the client seek legal advice and/or instruct a lawyer to argue the points of law (whether in writing or in the course of an oral hearing before a tribunal). It is recommended that your terms of engagement allow for such advice to be sought whether or not the client deems it necessary.

5.8 Disclosure and privilege

(a) Courts and other tribunals have power in most circumstances to require the parties to a dispute to reveal to each other all the documents that are relevant to the matters in dispute. This process is called 'disclosure' (other terms may be used outside of England and Wales), and at its most formal takes place in two stages:

(i) the listing of all documents within the disclosing party's possession or control that are relevant to the issues (this process does not always exist outside of England and Wales, for example, in Scotland); and

(ii) the production when requested of the listed documents.

(b) There are limits to disclosure.

(i) Not all tribunals routinely order disclosure to take place.

(ii) Even if disclosure is ordered, the order may be confined to specific classes of documents – say those relating to a particularly contentious issue of fact.

(iii) Documents that are privileged (see (c) below) need not be disclosed (technically, they ought to be listed as existing documents, but there is no requirement to produce them).

Some tribunals in Scotland that are not courts of law are likely to adopt an approach closer to that of the courts, which only require documents to be produced upon request and identification of specific categories/documents.

(c) Documents need not be revealed to the other side, even where an order for disclosure is made, if they attract 'privilege'. There are a number of classes of privilege, and it is recommended that the surveyor-advocate be conversant with (and able to explain to the client) the most important three: 'legal professional privilege', 'litigation privilege' (see *Appendix B: Definitions*) and 'without prejudice privilege'. In Scotland, privilege will not normally attach to documents where these are prepared by an individual who is not a professional legal adviser and, in general terms, it is advisable to err on the side of caution, preparing documents on the basis that they will not be privileged; where it is intended to claim privilege in relation to a particular document, you should ensure it is marked as 'private and confidential – privileged legal communication' and that its circulation is kept to a bare minimum.

(d) It will be particularly important for the surveyor-advocate to safeguard from disclosure correspondence that is intended to be kept confidential. First, as a general rule, communications between a surveyor-advocate and a client will not be privileged from disclosure (i.e. they will not attract legal professional privilege). However, where the communications are produced for the purposes of, or in contemplation of, proceedings, they may be privileged (because they will attract litigation privilege). Secondly, simply marking correspondence 'without prejudice' will have no protective effect unless created for the genuine purpose of settling the dispute.

(e) PS 6.2 imposes a duty upon surveyor-advocates to take reasonable steps to obtain and disclose the necessary documents required rather than simply make enquiries about such documents. It is therefore recommended that surveyor-advocates be aware what rules of disclosure might apply in a particular case, and how the rules relating to privilege operate.

5.9 PS 7.3 requires you to draw the tribunal's attention to all relevant legal decisions and legislative provisions of which you are aware, whether these are supportive of your client's case or not. This is a fundamental requirement for the surveyor-advocate. When you discover a point that appears to be contrary to your case, it is better to confront it at an early stage, and explain to the tribunal how you intend to deal with it, rather than wait for it to be raised, and then attempt to grapple with it.

5.10 You will need to decide whether to rely on any expert witnesses or witnesses of fact, and if so, in what respects. Most tribunals require details of witnesses in advance and seek to limit the number of expert witnesses on each side. You will, as soon as practicable, need to establish and/or be aware of such requirements. You will need to be aware of the circumstances in which witnesses can be compelled to appear (e.g. by use of witness summons), and also the circumstances in which:

(a) only experts' written reports may be allowed; and

(b) an expert may be appointed by the tribunal.

5.11 In many cases the tribunal will direct that the parties provide it with an agreed bundle of documents by a date in advance of any hearing and/or ahead of written representations. The surveyor-advocate in conjunction with the other party will usually be responsible for producing any such agreed bundles, which should be as helpful as possible in identifying the issues in dispute, by the date prescribed. It is recommended that you be familiar with the tribunal's rules or directions for the preparation of such bundles including what type of documents are to be included and how they should be laid out.

5.12 After receiving any witness statements from the other party, it is usually advisable for you to consult with your witnesses as to which points made by the other side ought to be challenged.

GN 6 Evidence and documents

6.1 It is advisable to make yourself aware of all evidence to be adduced from the witnesses on whose evidence you are relying for the presentation of your case. Where evidence is written you may wish to discuss it prior to it being finalised with a view to expanding or clarifying the witness statement. However, it is recommended that you do not – beyond such clarification – seek to influence the contents of a witness's statement, or to rehearse or coach a witness. You must not encourage the witness to give evidence which is not the truth, the whole truth and nothing but the truth. Witness familiarisation and preparation (e.g. regarding arrangements in the tribunal, tribunal layout, roles of different participants, basic generic requirements for giving evidence, such as listening carefully, speaking clearly, etc.) is permissible, but great care needs to be exercised in not doing or saying anything that could be taken as suggesting what a witness should say in giving evidence. Although a criminal case, and explicitly dealing with issues of witness coaching in the context of barristers' responsibilities, the case of *R v Momodou* [2005] EWCA Crim 177 is instructive reading.

6.2   It is recommended that you be aware of the rules of evidence, the legislation relating thereto and the tribunals before which such rules apply. In particular, you may need to be aware of, for example (in England and Wales), the *Civil Evidence Act* 1995 and its effect upon hearsay evidence (see also *Appendix D: Hearsay evidence*). The application of these rules can limit witnesses, their evidence, their attendance and their liability to cross-examination.

6.3   You are responsible for checking the admissibility of the evidence that your witnesses wish to adduce, and, if necessary, challenging the admissibility of the other party's evidence. It is also important for you to establish whether all expert witness reports (of experts for each party or that of any tribunal-appointed expert) comply with the requirements of the expert witness's primary professional body and of the tribunal to whom the evidence will be given.

6.4   The tribunal may encourage or direct the parties to agree evidence in order to avoid or reduce the time and cost of the dispute resolution procedure, whether or not the procedure involves a hearing. In any event you are well advised to ensure (insofar as you reasonably can) that the case is conducted in a proportionate manner. It is recommended (though you may in any event be required so to do) that you liaise with the other side as to what evidence is agreed, when it may become part of any schedule of agreed facts or any agreed bundle, or what can be submitted without strict proof. If something is agreed between the parties as accurate, or is to be treated as accurate, then it is no longer capable of challenge. However, in cases where the CPR apply, agreement between expert witnesses will not bind the parties, unless the parties also agree that they are prepared to be so bound. Nevertheless, if agreement between expert witnesses prejudices or destroys one party's case then that may be the end of the case. The purpose of any agreement between the parties is to agree what cannot be challenged, or cannot be challenged by evidence which is available. It is pointless to fight a case purely because the client cannot face the inevitable consequences of the material which they have. Challenge is legitimate only in circumstances where agreement on facts or opinion cannot be reached.

6.5 You may need the prior agreement of the tribunal and/or the other party if any of your witnesses intend to rely on photocopies of documents rather than originals. You will need to be aware of any original documents that are not available, and why not, and be satisfied with the reason for any non-availability.

6.6 Many tribunals require expert witness reports or witness statements to be produced to them and exchanged with the other side by a set date, most usually before any hearing. It is recommended that you liaise with your party's witnesses, the other party and the tribunal regarding the dates for such exchange and you should ensure that expert witnesses' reports or statements are exchanged as agreed.

6.7 In an effort to narrow the issues in dispute, the tribunal may direct that the experts should meet. If you are acting in the sole role of surveyor-advocate, you are advised to avoid involvement in the arrangement of such meetings, and to avoid being present or seeking to influence the agenda or discussion except where directed by the tribunal. However, where a meeting of experts takes place and, where you are acting as a surveyor-advocate and also an expert witness, you must at that meeting act as expert witness and **not** as surveyor-advocate, and take care with respect to any 'without prejudice' negotiations.

6.8 Whilst PS 6.3(c) makes it clear that it is generally impermissible to communicate with a witness once he or she has begun to give evidence, it is very occasionally permissible to communicate with an expert witness while that expert is giving evidence (with the consent of the tribunal) for purposes of clarification – in no circumstances in order to influence the evidence being given.

GN 7 Hearings

7.1 If a hearing is to take place, the guidance contained in GN 8–13 may apply. Whilst these sections encompass situations where witnesses are anticipated to be involved, it is the case that there will be instances where no witnesses are involved, and therefore the guidance should be read accordingly. Where a dispute involves a number of issues, consideration may usefully be given at an early stage to hearing issues, or groups of issues, separately, and having separate decisions.

However, in certain circumstances, mindful of commercial considerations, and in an effort to save costs and/or expedite matters, tribunals may seek to deal with certain cases by written procedures rather than oral hearing. It is recommended that you be alert to the best overall procedure from the client's point of view and seek to arrange its adoption by agreement with the other party and/or with the tribunal.

7.2 Even where the bulk of a case is to be by oral hearing, many tribunals will require an advocate to provide them, and the other party, with an outline of the arguments from their opening statement in advance of the hearing.

GN 8 Opening the case

8.1 Prior to any hearing, the parties to the proceedings will have been designated as claimant (applicant) or respondent (defendant). It is usual for the claimant to open the case. In planning appeal hearings and inquiries the local planning authority (equivalent to the defendant) usually opens first. As surveyor-advocate you will usually include in the opening statement an outline of the case and how it will be supported by the evidence you intend to adduce. You may include in the opening statement an explanation of your response to any counter-claim by the other party and the evidence which will be given to support that response. In Scotland, practice on opening statements is likely to vary according to tribunal; some very brief identification of the issues may be welcomed and the advocate should be prepared for the tribunal to raise questions designed to establish the extent of agreement on the facts and/or to clarify the issues. It would be very unusual in Scottish practice to be provided with an opening summary of the case.

8.2   It is recommended that you raise all legal points except where these are clear on the face of the existing statement of case. By the beginning of the hearing, advocates for both parties should have exchanged a list of authorities if they intend to canvas any point of law. It is not acceptable for a new point to be raised for the first time in the claimant's reply without the opposing party being given the chance to respond further. Where a new legal authority is raised or notified for the first time in the claimant's closing submission, the tribunal must allow the opposite party an opportunity to respond. Where you intend to refer to a legal authority, it is recommended that you familiarise yourself with the status accorded to a particular law report series and refer the tribunal to the entire case, pinpointing as appropriate the relevant passages. It is advisable not to abstract only part of the report.

8.3   The surveyor-advocate for the respondent makes his or her opening statement after the claimant. By this time the case should normally have been outlined fully to the tribunal, so the respondent's surveyor-advocate is recommended to avoid repetition. However, it may be unnecessary for the respondent's surveyor-advocate to open his or her case at all; it can be the closing submission which is more important so that the surveyor-advocate may comment in full on the position as at the close of the evidence.

8.4   It is by no means unusual for a case to be heard where the evidence is not in dispute so that the hearing is confined mainly or wholly to legal argument only. In such cases, you are recommended to have a thorough understanding of the legal issues; if you do not, it is recommended that you as surveyor-advocate do not act and instead a lawyer should act as advocate.

GN 9 Examination-in-chief

9.1 Examination-in-chief is the process by which each surveyor-advocate takes his or her witness through their evidence.

9.2 In general an advocate is ill-advised to ask leading ('closed') questions of his or her own witness on any except procedural and undisputed points; there may be situations (e.g. before planning inspectors) where leading questions are prohibited. However, with the leave of the tribunal, leading questions might be allowed in examination-in-chief if the witness is uncooperative or 'hostile'. Accordingly, you need to be aware of the nature of a leading question (i.e. a question asked of a witness in a manner that suggests the answer sought by the questioner). Where possible (except where leading is permissible), questions should be in the 'open' form (Who? Where? When? What? Why? How? How much?). In Scottish practice it is not usual to ask permission to treat a witness as 'hostile'. If it is necessary to move to leading, or closed, questions to force a witness to be responsive, this can be done without permission. The essential difficulty is that evidence in response to leading questions may have less weight than evidence in response to an entirely open question.

9.3 Where a witness statement, witness's report or proof of evidence has been provided to the tribunal and other party before the hearing, examination-in-chief of its contents is usually confined to checking with the witness that their evidence remains unchanged. However, it is not unusual for supplemental matters to be added, but notice should have been given to the other side if the matters are of primary importance, and the consent of the tribunal is usually required.

9.4 It is recommended that you ensure that any expert witness that is called deals with the case put forward by the other side.

9.5 Many tribunals require evidence to be given on oath or affirmation and you are recommended to alert less experienced witnesses to this requirement, and explain to them the importance of telling the truth, and the sanctions for untruthful testimony.

9.6   Where the tribunal is dealing with the case in writing rather than at a hearing, evidence-in-chief is in the form of a witness's report or witness statement, possibly (where allowed) with the addition of separate written submissions (in the form of advocacy). PS 3.12 makes clear that these two elements should be clearly distinguished.

GN 10 Cross-examination

10.1   Cross-examination is the questioning of the other party's witnesses by the opposing surveyor-advocate, during which leading questions may be, and generally are, asked.

10.2   Questions in cross-examination can be addressed not only to the evidence-in-chief given by that witness, but also to any evidence relevant to the case within the knowledge or expertise of that witness. Any notes taken into the witness box by any witness may be disclosed and form the subject of cross-examination.

10.3   Interrupting the cross-examination of the opposing surveyor-advocate is to be avoided except where there is a clear objection to the question being put. In this case, it is recommended that the tribunal be requested to adjudicate immediately on the legitimacy of the objection. Typically, you will, during cross-examination, question the other party's witness on those points where their evidence disagrees with your own witness. It is important that all contested points are covered in cross-examination, otherwise the tribunal may think that the points omitted are not in dispute. It is essential to put each point in your client's case fairly to every opposing witness who might reasonably be expected to be able to comment on it. The level of detail involved in this exercise will vary from case to case and common sense must be a guide. This is nonetheless an important point to consider.

10.4   Where the tribunal is dealing with the case in writing there is no opportunity for cross-examination unless an oral hearing also takes place (e.g. where granted after a request).

GN 11 Re-examination

11.1 Re-examination is the further questioning by each surveyor-advocate of his or her own witness, on matters first arising out of responses to cross-examination. It is recommended that no new matter be adduced at this stage; in some sectors no new matters may be introduced, save by permission of the tribunal. The same rules as to leading questions apply as in examination-in-chief (see GN 9.2). It is recommended that amplification and clarification of evidence already given in cross-examination, if necessary, should take place. This should also help to re-establish any credibility lost in hostile cross-examination, but re-examination may also enable an advocate to make a point because of new material which has been introduced by clumsy cross-examination.

11.2 Once a witness has completed giving evidence, the witness is obliged to remain at the hearing unless the tribunal, after consulting the other party, allows the witness to leave. In more complex disputes, problems might occur if witnesses from either side are excused from the hearing too soon and it is recommended to be alert to this.

11.3 Occasionally witnesses are recalled to give further evidence, typically arising out of evidence from the other parties by way of rebuttal. You are recommended to avoid having to recall a witness due to poor preparation of the case.

GN 12 Questions by the tribunal

12.1 Whilst the tribunal may, without prompting, ask its own questions of witnesses during examination-in-chief, cross-examination, and any re-examination, it is usual for each party's surveyor-advocate to enquire whether the tribunal has any questions before each witness stands down.

12.2 Surveyor-advocates for each party may ask further questions on points arising out of each witness's answers to any questioning by the tribunal.

GN 13 Summing up

13.1 When all the evidence has been heard, the surveyor-advocate for the respondent/defendant will sum up first. This is done by giving a résumé of the case and the evidence that they have called, and seeking to contrast that with the case and evidence from the other party and to persuade the tribunal that their evidence should be preferred. In the case of matters dealt with in writing, rather than orally, summing up takes the form of (advocacy) submissions. This is the point at which it is recommended that any final legal submissions be made. NB in some circumstances, with the leave of – or at the discretion of – the tribunal, the advocate for the claimant will sum up first (e.g. where an arbitration is about a counter-claim). In Scottish practice it is common for the claimant's advocate to sum up first.

13.2 The hearing will conclude with the surveyor-advocate for the claimant summing up in similar fashion.

13.3 It is likely to be useful for the tribunal if each surveyor-advocate presents his or her summing up, either at the end or beginning of this stage, in writing; the hearing may be adjourned for this purpose.

GN 14 Costs

14.1 (a) Where the tribunal has the power to deal with costs, it is recommended that you are aware of how to protect your client's interests. In planning appeals the parties are expected to meet their own costs, but for planning inquiries, hearings and some forms of written representations, costs may be awarded where one party incurs unnecessary expense as a result of the unreasonable behaviour of another.

(b) You will need to advise the client of when and in what terms formal offers to settle should be made. Such offers may include Calderbank offers (see *Appendix B: Definitions*) and it is recommended that you are aware of when to request the tribunal to make an interim decision reserving costs for a later determination.

14.2 It is recommended that you are aware of the correct time or times to make both an offer 'without prejudice' save as to costs (referred to as a Calderbank offer) and submissions on costs. Usually any submission on costs will not be made until the tribunal has made its decision, but in those cases where the decision is made at the end of the hearing, submissions on costs are often made immediately. Where, however, a party has made an offer or offers to settle, it may ask for submissions and a decision on costs to be deferred until the outcome of the decision on the substantive issues is known and/or has been properly assessed.

14.3 If the issues are complex, you may request an oral hearing to deal with costs; alternatively you may consider that written submissions will suffice. It is possible to make Calderbank offers purely in respect of the assessments of costs.

14.4 It is recommended that you are aware of whether the tribunal has the power to award simple or compound interest on any sum awarded, and it is advisable to claim if appropriate. You may need to take advice regarding the assessment of reasonable costs other than your own costs, such as the parties' legal fees.

14.5 It is advisable that you be aware of the fact that some tribunals, in determining costs or expenses, may treat advocacy work conducted by you as work done by a lay representative.

GN 15 Re-opening of the case

15.1 Occasionally, new evidence relevant to the case becomes apparent after the hearing, or after written *submissions* (other terms may be used in different forums) and their counters have been lodged. In such situations you are recommended to consider whether to ask the tribunal to re-open the proceedings. In planning appeals, the proceedings can be re-opened only on the direction of the Secretary of State; and that discretion is exercised only rarely.

15.2 In general, the tribunal will re-open the case only if it considers that the new evidence is so fundamental to the issues in dispute that its exclusion will prejudice a fair resolution. In the event that such a situation exists, you will need to act without delay and may need to seek legal advice.

GN 16 Inspections

16.1 The tribunal may wish to carry out an inspection of any relevant property or facility and any comparables referred to in evidence. It is recommended that you clarify whether the tribunal wishes to be accompanied during these inspections and, if so, you will need to confirm in what capacity you will accompany the tribunal and will also need to liaise with the other party to ensure that arrangements are made. Site inspections are invariably made in planning appeals.

16.2 Often the tribunal may prefer and find it more convenient, with the agreement of both parties, to make inspections unaccompanied. Inspections should be conducted in the presence of both parties or neither party, or their representatives, unless either party indicates in advance that they have no wish to be present and no objection to the inspection taking place in the presence of the other party.

16.3 You will need to clarify whether further submissions will be invited during any inspection or whether the inspection is simply to assist the tribunal in weighing up the evidence already adduced. Inspections are not normally appropriate occasions for re-opening the case. In planning appeals, no representations are permissible during a site inspection.

GN 17 The tribunal's decision

17.1 In certain cases the decision of the tribunal will not be made available to the parties until the fees and expenses of the tribunal have been paid. You are advised to be aware of such circumstances and ensure that timely arrangements for such prior payments are made.

17.2 It is recommended that you study the decision and check for slips or clerical errors in a timely manner. If there are any, the tribunal may be called upon to correct them.

17.3 You may consider that there might be more serious errors or problems with the decision constituting grounds for an appeal, challenge, or application for it to be set aside. You should be clear as to whether you are able to make this judgment, and also whether such a matter will be considered by a tribunal where you do not have a right of audience. If you do not feel able to consider whether an appeal could be launched, or if you have no right of audience then the matter should be passed expeditiously to a lawyer utilising (where appropriate) 'Licensed Access' (formerly known as 'Direct Professional Access' in England and Wales; see *Appendix B: Definitions*), or under similar provisions in other jurisdictions. Equally, you may need to advise the client on the enforceability of the decision. If you do not have the competence to advise in this respect, it is recommended that you inform the client expeditiously and suggest that the matter is referred to the client's solicitor or to an advocate utilising (where appropriate) Licensed Access.

17.4 The procedure for challenging, appealing or applying to set aside decisions from some tribunals is subject to strict time limits to which the surveyor-advocate should be alert. In particular it is recommended that you be aware of whether any time limit runs from the date the decision is made or signed rather than from the date on which the parties receive the decision. Funds may need to be organised to facilitate the release of the decision within the appropriate timescale. This may include your reserving the right for the client to pay all of the costs without prejudice to the final decision.

17.5 Following the making of the decision on costs, you should be aware of the potential requirement for the assessment of costs as well as the prospect of appealing against the decision in respect of liability for costs. You will need to decide whether the process of assessment of costs is one that you can undertake, or whether it would better to be handed over to a solicitor, lawyer-advocate, or costs draftsperson.

Appendix A: Sample Terms of Engagement

Note: This appendix forms a part of *Surveyors acting as advocates*: RICS guidance note, and is for the use of surveyors appointed to provide advocacy services to a tribunal where a surveyor is permitted to appear. The sample terms are not intended to be mandatory or prescriptive, and may be adapted as required. It is recognised that a variety of circumstances will prevail in the range of assignments surveyors may undertake, and that clauses may not be appropriate in every circumstance.

Terms of Engagement

1 Recital of appointment

1.1 The Client has appointed the Surveyor-Advocate named below (see 1.4) to provide the following advocacy services:

[*state the nature and extent of the services which are to be provided*]

Such services shall be subject to these Terms of Engagement.

1.2 The appointment is one which is subject to *Surveyors acting as advocates*: RICS practice statement, a copy of which is available on request.

1.3 The Client is:

1.4 The Surveyor-Advocate is:

1.5 The Tribunal is:

[*state name of tribunal in relation to which advocacy services are to be provided*]

2 Definitions

Unless otherwise agreed by the parties:

2.1 'Client' means the person(s), organisation(s), or department(s) to whom the Surveyor-Advocate has been asked to provide the above-stated services.

2.2 'Surveyor-Advocate' means the person named at 1.4, and appointed to provide advocacy services as described in 1.1 of these Terms of Engagement.

2.3 'Assignment' means the matter referred to the Surveyor-Advocate by the Client, in respect of which the stated services are required, and to which these Terms of Engagement apply.

2.4 'Fees' means (in the absence of written agreement to the contrary) the reasonable charges of the Surveyor-Advocate based on the Surveyor-Advocate's agreed hourly/daily rate. Time spent travelling and waiting may be charged in full. [*Set out hourly/daily rates*]. Value Added Tax (VAT) will be charged in addition where applicable.

2.5 'Disbursements' means the cost, reasonably incurred, of all other professional advice or opinion, photography, reproduction of drawings, diagrams, etc., printing and duplicating, and all out-of-pocket expenses, including travel, refreshments and hotel accommodation. Value Added Tax will be charged in addition (where applicable).

3 The Client

3.1 The Client agrees:

    (a) to provide timely, full and clear instructions in writing supported by good quality copies of documents within his or her possession; or to arrange or ensure the provision of all these things;

    (b) to treat expeditiously every reasonable request by the Surveyor-Advocate for authority, information and documents;

    (c) where possible, at the Surveyor-Advocate's request, to arrange access to the property/facility relevant to the Assignment in order that the Surveyor-Advocate can inspect such and make relevant enquiries;

    (d) subject to reasonable prior consultation, that the Surveyor-Advocate may obtain such legal or other professional advice as is deemed reasonably necessary by the Surveyor-Advocate for the Surveyor-Advocate to provide the services set out at 1.1 above; and

    (e) that circumstances may arise where the Surveyor-Advocate's duty to the tribunal could require him or her to act in a manner that may not be perceived to be in the best interests of the client.

Under such circumstances, if the Surveyor-Advocate is obliged to withdraw, he or she will be entitled to charge for work undertaken to the date of withdrawal on a fair and reasonable basis.

4 The Surveyor-Advocate

4.1   The Surveyor-Advocate shall:
(a)   undertake only those tasks in respect of which he or she considers he or she has adequate experience, knowledge, expertise and resources;
(b)   use reasonable skill and care in the performance of his or her instructions and duties; and
(c)   comply with all relevant rules, codes, guidelines and protocols, including those of RICS.

5 Fees and Disbursements

5.1   The Surveyor-Advocate may present invoices at such stipulated intervals as he or she considers reasonable during the Assignment and payment of each invoice is due on presentation.

5.2   For the avoidance of doubt, the Surveyor-Advocate shall be entitled to charge fair and reasonable Fees and Disbursements where, due to settlement of the dispute or to any other reason not being the fault of the Surveyor-Advocate:
(a)   the Surveyor-Advocate's time has been necessarily reserved for a specific hearing, meeting, appointment or other relevant engagement but the reservation of time is not required because the engagement has been cancelled or postponed and/or the instructions have been terminated due to settlement of the dispute, or for any other reason that is not the fault of the Surveyor-Advocate, regardless of the period of notice given by the Client; and/or
(b)   such Fees and Disbursements have been incurred by the Surveyor-Advocate prior to receiving notice from the Client of any update and/or variation to the instructions for the Assignment.

5.3   The Client shall pay to the Surveyor-Advocate interest under the *Late Payment of Commercial Debts (Interest) Act* 1998 on all unpaid invoices, or will pay to the Surveyor-Advocate, at the Surveyor-Advocate's sole discretion, interest at [...]% per month (or part thereof) on all invoices which remain unpaid after 30 days from the date of issue of the invoice to the Client calculated from the expiry of such 30-day period. The Client shall also pay the full amount of administrative, legal and other costs incurred in obtaining settlement of unpaid invoices.

6 Disputes over Fees and Disbursements

6.1   In the event of a dispute as to the amount of the Surveyor-Advocate's Fees and Disbursements, such sum as is not disputed shall be paid forthwith pending resolution of the dispute, irrespective of any set off or counter-claim that may be alleged.

6.2   Any dispute relating to the amount of the Surveyor-Advocate's Fees and Disbursements shall, in the first instance, be referred to [*state mechanism or process e.g.* the Surveyor-Advocate's firm's Complaints Handling Procedure].

6.3   Where any dispute over Fees or Disbursements cannot be resolved by [*state mechanism or process*], such dispute shall be referred to [*e.g.* a mediator chosen by agreement of both parties]. Where agreement cannot be reached on the identity of [*e.g.* a mediator], the services of [*e.g.* the RICS Dispute Resolution Service] shall be used to appoint [*e.g.* a mediator].

In the event that any dispute cannot be resolved by [*state mechanism e.g.* mediation], the courts of [*state jurisdiction e.g.* England and Wales] shall have exclusive jurisdiction in relation to the dispute and its resolution.

(*Note: clause 6.3 is applicable solely in the context of a firm not 'Regulated by RICS'.*)

6.4   The law of [*state law e.g.* England and Wales] shall govern these Terms of Engagement.

Appendix B: Definitions

This appendix is a part of both the practice statement (PS), and the guidance note (GN). The following are short definitions of key terms in the PS and/or GN. In certain circumstances other terms may be used. Users are also advised to refer to a legal dictionary (or legal textbooks), and/or to the relevant rules, directions and procedures of the tribunal in question.

Surveyor-advocate: a person who presents to the tribunal a client's properly arguable case as best as he or she may on the evidence and facts available; a spokesperson for a client who, subject to any restrictions imposed by the surveyor's duty to the tribunal, must do for his or her client all that the client might properly do for him or herself if he or she could. Sometimes also referred to as party representative (although this term is occasionally loosely also used to refer to the surveyor as a negotiator). The advocacy role is markedly different from the role of an expert witness or negotiator.

Applicant: a person who makes an application during the course of ongoing civil proceedings (see also 'claimant' and 'referring party', also known in Scotland as the 'pursuer').

Award: the conclusions reached on the main issues in dispute by an arbitral tribunal. This term is also occasionally misused to describe a 'decision' made by an adjudicator.

Calderbank offer: a firm offer to settle one or more disputes or part of it/them, written without prejudice save as to costs, so that the offer may be brought to the tribunal's attention only on the question of costs and after a ruling on the matter which is the subject of the offer has been made. Providing the offer is in terms enabling like to be compared with like (enabling the claim or claims to be satisfied), it may act to protect the person making the offer on costs subsequent to the date the offer ought reasonably to have been accepted if the offeree achieves no more than that offer by proceeding with the case. The procedure is available, for example, where in non-court proceedings (such as arbitration) there are no provisions for a 'payment in'. So called because the first time such an offer was used was in *Calderbank v Calderbank* [1975] 3 All ER 333. The equivalent in Scotland is known as a 'Minute of Tender'.

Case manager: a person who, acting on behalf of a party, is responsible for the general conduct, management and administration of the case, marshalling and coordinating that party's team (if any) and liaising as appropriate with the tribunal and opposing party.

Claimant: a person who brings an action. Sometimes also referred to as an 'applicant' or 'referring party'. Known in Scotland as the 'pursuer'.

Conditional fee: this term refers to any arrangement where remuneration – however fixed or calculated – is to be made conditional upon the outcome of proceedings. Other labels in common use are 'incentive-fee', 'speculative fee', 'success-fee', 'success-related fee', 'performance fee', 'no-win, no-fee', and 'contingency fee'.

Costs: a term used to describe the legal costs and other expenses incurred by each party in preparing and advancing their case before the tribunal. These may extend (in cases of arbitration but not litigation) to include the fees of the tribunal itself. Rules governing costs and costs allocation are usually governed by the rules and powers of a particular tribunal or by statute (to take but one example, see sections 60–65 of the *Arbitration Act* 1996). Some tribunals may decide not to make an order on costs.

Counter-representation: this is a reply/response to a 'representation'.

CPR: The *Civil Procedure Rules* (known as CPR) (available at www.justice.gov.uk/civil/procrules_fin/index.htm) is the set of rules governing the procedure of the Supreme Court and County Court in England and Wales. These procedural rules are supplemented by Protocols, Pre-Action Protocols, Practice Directions and court guides. In summary, the objectives of the CPR are to make access to justice cheaper, quicker and fairer. Some of the CPR apply to action taken before proceedings are issued and so the scope of the CPR should be considered in respect of any matter likely to be litigious.

Decision: refers to the conclusion reached by an adjudicator (or other relevant tribunal).

Direct Professional Access (DPA): see **Licensed Access**.

Direction: a requirement laid down by a tribunal.

Disclosure: the production and inspection of documents in accordance with applicable rules and/or directions of a tribunal. Different rules apply in the Scottish courts where documents can be recovered from another party (known as the 'haver') using 'commission and diligence'.

Evidence: this may be evidence of fact, expert (opinion) evidence or hearsay evidence. The weight to be attached to evidence by a tribunal will depend on various factors, the importance of which may vary from case to case.

Expert witness: a witness called by a tribunal to give expert opinion evidence by virtue of experience, knowledge and expertise of a particular area beyond that expected of a layperson. The overriding duty of the expert witness is to provide independent, impartial and unbiased evidence to the tribunal – covering all relevant matters, whether or not they favour the client – to assist the tribunal in reaching its determination. Different to a witness of fact (see below).

Hearsay evidence: evidence by way of the oral statements of a person other than the witness who is testifying and/or by way of statements in documents, offered to prove the truth of what is stated. See also the *Civil Evidence (Scotland) Act* 1988 and the *Civil Evidence Act* 1995. In arbitral proceedings, subject to any agreement between the parties or prior direction given by the arbitrator, hearsay will be admissible, subject to notice being given to the other party.

Leading question: a question asked of a witness in a manner that suggests the answer sought by the questioner.

Legal professional privilege (sometimes called '**legal advice privilege**'): legal professional privilege attaches to, and protects:
- communications (whether written or oral) made confidentially;
- passing between a lawyer (acting in his or her professional legal capacity) and his or her client;
- solely for the purpose of giving or obtaining legal advice.

Licensed Access: RICS members are currently permitted by the General Council of the Bar of England and Wales to instruct a barrister direct, without the services of a solicitor for certain purposes. The surveyor should be experienced in the field to which the referral relates. The regime in England and Wales was formerly known as *Direct Professional Access* (DPA). The RICS guidance note *Direct Professional Access to Barristers* is currently under review. RICS members are also able to instruct counsel direct under the terms of the Scottish *Direct Access Rules* and, in Northern Ireland, under *Direct Professional Access*. The relevant Bar Councils (of England and Wales; and Northern Ireland) or the Faculty of Advocates in Scotland, can be consulted for further advice.

Litigation privilege: where litigation is in reasonable contemplation or in progress, this protects:
- written or oral communications made confidentially;
- between either a client and a lawyer, OR either of them and a third party;
- where the dominant purpose is for use in the proceedings;
- either for the purpose of giving or getting advice in relation to such proceedings, or for obtaining evidence to be used in such proceedings.

The privilege applies to proceedings in the High Court, County Court, employment tribunals and, where it is subject to English procedural law, arbitration. With regard to other tribunals, the position is less clear.

Negotiator: Person who negotiates a deal (of property or asset) or solution. Also, in dispute resolution, a person who seeks to negotiate the resolution of the dispute as best he or she may. A negotiator has no involvement in this role with a tribunal. A negotiator's role is markedly different to that of an advocate, expert witness, case manager or witness of fact.

Referring party: in Scottish court proceedings, a person who brings an action.

Representation(s) (see also **counter-representation**): this term may be any of the following, depending on the circumstances and context:
- a statement of case;
- an assertion of fact(s);
- expert opinion evidence; and
- an advocacy submission.

Representations may be made orally or in writing.

Respondent: a person against whom proceedings are brought, or who is party to a dispute referred to a tribunal for determination. In an appeal, the party resisting the appeal is referred to as the respondent. Sometimes also referred to as a defendant, or 'defender' in Scotland.

Scott Schedule: a document setting out in tabular form the items in dispute and containing (or allowing to be added) the contentions or agreement of each party. Named after a former Official Referee.

Statement of case: **usually** a formal written statement served by one party on the other, containing the allegations of fact that the party proposes to prove at trial (but not the evidence) and stating the remedy (if any) that the party claims in the action.

Submission(s): the presentations by way of advocacy of a matter in dispute to the judgment of a tribunal. The term is occasionally used loosely in the surveying community to refer to evidence of fact or expert opinion evidence, or to a mix of such expert opinion evidence and advocacy; such usage is often misplaced.

Tribunal: see definition in *Preamble* to the PS.

'Without prejudice': the without prejudice rule will generally prevent statements made in a genuine attempt to settle an existing dispute, whether made in writing or orally, from being put before a court as evidence of admissions against the interest of the party which made them. There are a number of established exceptions to the rule.

Witness of fact: a person who, usually on oath or solemn affirmation, gives evidence before a tribunal on a question of fact.

Witness statement: A witness statement is one that a person may put forward as evidence to a tribunal during the course of proceedings. It is a statement of facts within the personal knowledge and belief of the person making the witness statement. The person must also specify the source of the information or belief laid out in the statement. A witness statement might ideally (amongst other formal requirements) specify the title of the proceedings, the person making the statement, their address and occupation (and if not employed, a description of the person), and the party to the proceedings on whose behalf the statement was made.

Witness summons ('witness citation' in Scotland): an order by a court or other tribunal, requiring a third party to either:

- appear before a tribunal on a particular day and give evidence; and/or
- produce certain documents that are required as evidence.

Failure to comply with a witness summons constitutes contempt of court and will usually result in a fine or even imprisonment. In other tribunal proceedings penalties may also follow for breach.

Appendix C: Extracts – Surveyors acting as expert witnesses

This appendix forms part of *Surveyors acting as advocates*: guidance note. PS 9, GN 18 and GN 20 below are reproduced from *Surveyors acting as expert witnesses*: RICS practice statement and guidance note.

[This appendix then replicates the text as stated. See Appendix 3A of this book for the relevant text.]

Appendix D: Hearsay evidence

This appendix forms a part of *Surveyors acting as advocates*: RICS guidance note.

The *Civil Evidence Act* 1995 and the *Civil Evidence (Scotland) Act* 1988 contain provisions that alter the previous hearsay rules (that hearsay evidence was not admissible). The Acts abolish the rule against hearsay evidence in civil proceedings, set out guidance as to hearsay evidence and require a party who wishes to adduce hearsay evidence to serve notice on the other party.

The Acts therefore provide that in civil proceedings evidence otherwise admissible shall not be excluded solely on the grounds that it is hearsay. 'Civil proceedings' means civil proceedings before any courts and tribunals where the strict rules of evidence apply, whether as a matter of law or by agreement of the parties (in Scotland, this also includes any hearing by the Sheriff under the *Children (Scotland) Act* 1995).

It would appear therefore that the provisions of the Acts would apply to an arbitration where the arbitrator has ruled that the strict rules of evidence shall apply or the parties have agreed that this shall be the position.

A party wishing to rely on hearsay evidence must first serve notice on the other party, giving particulars of this evidence. Failure to comply with this requirement will not affect the admissibility of the evidence. However, it may be taken into account by the tribunal in the exercise of its powers in connection with the proceedings and costs, and by the tribunal as a matter adversely affecting the weight to be given to the hearsay evidence.

The change in the hearsay rule by the Acts is a change of emphasis from admissibility to weight.

Generally, a tribunal would have regard to any circumstances from which any inference can be drawn as to the reliability of the hearsay evidence.

Further reading

Most of the items below can be obtained via RICS Books (www.ricsbooks.com). Please note that some publications reference earlier editions of *Surveyors acting as expert witnesses* or *Surveyors acting as advocates*.

Agricultural Arbitrations and Independent Expert Determinations (2nd edition), RICS guidance note, 1998

Blank, G., and Selby, H., *Winning Advocacy* (2nd edition), Oxford University Press, 2004

Boon, A., *Advocacy* (2nd edition), Cavendish Publishing Limited, 1999

Civil Procedure Rules, together with associated Practice Directions, Pre-Action Protocols and Forms, available at: www.justice.gov.uk/civil/procrules_fin/index.htm – and the *Protocol for the Instruction of Experts to give Evidence in Civil Claims* (issued by the Civil Justice Council (CJC), June 2005, approved by the Master of the Rolls), available at: www.justice.gov.uk/civil/procrules_fin/contents/form_section_ images/practice_directions/pd35_pdf_eps/ pd35_prot.pdf

Clarke, P. H., *The Surveyor in Court*, Estates Gazette, 1985 (out of print but available from the RICS Library)

Dilapidations (5th edition) RICS guidance note, 2008

Direct Professional Access to Barristers, RICS guidance note, 2003 (current edition under review)

du Cann, R., *The Art of the Advocate*, Penguin, 1993

Evans, K., *The Golden Rules of Advocacy*, Blackstone Press, 1993

Morley, I., *The Devil's Advocate*, Sweet & Maxwell, 2005

Napley, D., *The Techniques of Persuasion* (4th edition), Sweet & Maxwell, 1991

Rating Appeals (2nd edition), RICS guidance note, 2001 (current edition under review)

Rating Consultancy Code of Practice (2nd edition), RICS practice statement, 2005 (current edition under review)

Ross, D., *Advocacy*, Cambridge University Press, 2007

Surveyors Acting as Arbiter or as Independent Expert in Commercial Property Rent Reviews (Scottish edition), RICS guidance note, 2002

Surveyors Acting as Arbitrators and as Independent Experts in Commercial Property Rent Review (8th edition), RICS guidance note, 2002

Surveyors acting as expert witnesses (3rd edition), RICS practice statement and guidance note, 2008

The *Civil Evidence Act* 1995, available at: www.opsi.gov.uk/ACTS/acts1995/Ukpga_19950038_en_1.htm

The *Civil Evidence (Scotland) Act* 1988, available at: www.opsi.gov.uk/acts/acts1988/Ukpga_19880032_en_1.htm#tcon

Wellman, F., *The Art of Cross-Examination*, Standard Publications, 2007

The RICS Dispute Resolution Faculty and RICS Library may be able to provide further information relevant to advocacy practice.

[Further reading is then followed by a list of acknowledgments of those who contributed to the publication.]

References

1 British Property Federation/Investment Property Databank, *Annual Lease Review 2007*

2 Beale, H., *Chitty on Contracts* (29th edition), Sweet & Maxwell, 2007 (ISBN 978 0 42184 260 1)

3 Rooney, A., and Cridge, J., *Business Tenancy Renewals: A Surveyor's Handbook*, RICS Books, 2006 (ISBN 978 1 84219 241 2)

4 Dowding, N., and Reynolds, K., *Dilapidations the Modern Law and Practice* (3rd edition), Sweet & Maxwell, 2004 (ISBN 0 42188 260 3)

5 *Code of Practice for Commercial Leases in England and Wales (2007)*, Commercial Leases Working Group (2007)

6 *Monitoring the 2002 Code of Practice for Commercial Leases: An Interim Report*, University of Reading (2004)

7 McGhee, J. (ed.), *Snell's Equity* (31st edition), Sweet & Maxwell, 2007 (ISBN 978 0 42198 006)

8 Reynolds, K., and Fetherstonhaugh, G., *Handbook of Rent Review* (looseleaf), Sweet & Maxwell, 1981 (ISBN 978 0 42127 980 3)

9 Dale, G., Dowding, N., Duncan, B., Fetherstonhaugh, G. and Makepeace, P., *Manual for Rent Review Arbitrators*, RICS training manual, June 2008

Index

Index